Guide to the
Homes of Famous Pennsylvanians
Houses, Museums, and Landmarks

Guide to the
Homes of Famous Pennsylvanians

Houses, Museums, and Landmarks

Arthur P. Miller Jr.
and Marjorie L. Miller

STACKPOLE
BOOKS

Published in 2003 by
STACKPOLE BOOKS
5067 Ritter Road
Mechanicsburg, PA 17055
www.stackpolebooks.com

Printed in the United States of America

10 9 8 7 6 5 4 3 2 1

First Edition

Cover design by Caroline Stover

Front cover:

Top row, left to right: the reconstructed house of William Penn at Pennsbury Manor, photo by the authors; Benjamin Franklin by David Rent Etter, courtesy of Independence National Historical Park; Clayton, home of Henry Clay Frick, courtesy of Frick Art and Historical Center, Pittsburgh.

Middle row, left to right: Marian Anderson, courtesy of Marian Anderson Historic Site; Joseph Priestley House, photo by Kyle R. Weaver; Andrew Carnegie, courtesy of the Library of Congress.

Bottom row, left to right: N. C. Wyeth House, photo by Jim Graham, courtesy of Brandywine River Museum; Andy Warhol, courtesy of Andy Warhol Museum; Pearl S. Buck, courtesy of Pearl S. Buck International.

Back cover:

Top to bottom: Milton Hershey, courtesy of Hershey Community Archives, Hershey, Pennsylvania; the house at Daniel Boone Homestead, photo by Kyle R. Weaver; Fonthill, home of Henry Mercer, courtesy of Mercer Museum of the Bucks County Historical Society; James Stewart, courtesy of Jimmy Stewart Museum.

Library of Congress Cataloging-in-Publication Data

Miller, Arthur P., Jr.
    Guide to the homes of famous Pennsylvanians : houses, museums, and landmarks / Arthur P. Miller and Marjorie L. Miller.—1st ed.
        p.   cm.
    Includes index.
    ISBN 0-8117-2628-2 (pbk.)
    1. Pennsylvania—Biography.   2. Pennsylvania—Guidebooks.   I. Miller, Marjorie L. (Marjorie Lyman), 1929–   II. Title.
CT257 .M55   2003
920.0748—dc21

2002014131

Contents

Preface

Pennsylvania is a seedbed that has produced many famous men and women. Although only one U.S. president—James Buchanan—grew up as a native of Pennsylvania (Dwight D. Eisenhower retired to Pennsylvania after his presidency), many other men and women from the state have excelled in industry, science, art, religion, music, the military, government, and athletics. Others came later to the state and here gained their fame.

By visiting the homes and sites associated with these notable individuals, you can get a firsthand feeling for the people who lived and worked there. You can read about an age without electricity, running water, or central heat, but you can't appreciate it until you've spent a day without them. You can see pictures of grand Victorian homes, but you can't imagine the ambience and craftsmanship until you experience them. To see someone's surroundings is to better understand his or her life story. The person's biography no longer remains just words on tattered pages, but comes alive in a burst of reality.

The thirty-six individuals profiled on the following pages reflect the full sweep of four centuries of Pennsylvania's heritage. They are the ones who stand out in our history books. Some fought as colonists against the French, the Indians, and finally, their own British mentors. Others led the way toward the industrialization of the commonwealth or invented the machines that laid the groundwork for such progress. Some established our patterns of finance and governance. Still others dramatized what they saw around them in the art, music, or literature they created.

Of course, choosing thirty-six individuals to represent major achievements of the state was no easy task. You might even say that we have described here Benjamin Franklin and thirty-five others, because Franklin was perhaps the closest thing to a Renaissance man that Pennsylvania has produced. He made notable achievements not only in government, but also in science, business, invention, and literature, even in music with his invention of the armonica, a musical instrument played by running a finger across the wet tops of glass bowls. It was his biographer, Carl Van Doren, who called this man of many talents "a harmonious multitude."

There is, moreover, no guarantee that some who do not appear here would not preempt some who do. But as befits a guidebook, we have chosen those men and women whose legacies are permanently preserved today by sites that played significant roles in their lives—childhood homes, principal residences, or homes in retirement—or museums that interpret their careers.

In these pages you will meet a galaxy of persons whose lives have added immeasurably to their chosen fields and to Pennsylvania's heritage. Take a walk, for example, through the reconstructed Pennsbury Manor along the Delaware River, the country estate so lovingly built by William Penn, then enjoyed by him and his family for scarcely two years before he was called back to England. View the sturdy brick Wheatland, in Lancaster, little changed from the day in 1856 when Democratic Party leaders dismounted from their horse-drawn carriages and climbed the front steps to offer James Buchanan the nomination for president of the United States. Stroll through Dwight D. Eisenhower's retirement home in Gettysburg—the only house he and his wife, Mamie, ever owned—where everything is still set in place just as the Eisenhowers left it. See the museum that actor Jimmy Stewart modestly allowed Indiana, Pennsylvania, to organize so that his hometown would have an attraction to draw visitors. Visit the white clapboard farmhouse northeast of Pittsburgh where Rachel Carson, the crusading environmentalist, grew up surrounded by the fields, forest, and the Allegheny River that provided the background and inspiration for her life's work.

So read on. As Thomas Carlyle once wrote, "Biography is by nature the most universally profitable, universally pleasant of all things; especially biography of distinguished individuals."

Acknowledgments

It was a privilege to walk in the footsteps of Pennsylvania's best-known sons and daughters as we traveled the four thousand miles it took to research this book. Visiting these sites firsthand often confirmed what we knew about our subject but at other times surprised us with a revelation we had not expected.

At Bartram's Garden in Philadelphia, for example, the staff pointed out a specimen of the rare Franklin tree *(Franklinia alatamaha)*, a descendant of a species that John and William Bartram had saved from extinction and named for John's friend Benjamin Franklin.

At Lackawaxen, the home of Zane Grey, we were surprised to come upon a floor-model dental drill, the actual drill that Grey used when he practiced as a dentist in New York City before he turned to writing novels to earn his living.

To gather such interesting facts, we relied on the many knowledgeable and enthusiastic experts we found at these sites. If we have succeeded in casting new light on the talented Pennsylvanians you find in these pages, we have these people to thank: Douglas Miller and Lara Murphy, Pennsbury Manor; Andrew Zellers-Frederick, Historic Rittenhouse Town; James Lewars and Michael Emery, Conrad Weiser Homestead; Debra Olsen, Historic Bartram's Garden; Philip Sheridan, Independence National Historical Park; Andrea Bashore, Joseph Priestley House; James Lewars and Rick Stratton, Daniel Boone Homestead; Bennett Hill, Historic Waynesborough; Elizabeth Laurent, Girard College; Andrew Marconi, Lisa Moulder, and Lori Dillard-Rech, American Flag House and Betsy Ross Memorial; Joanne Hanley, Brian Reedy, and Kitty Seifert, Friendship Hill National Historic Site; Suzanne Lamborn, Robert Fulton Birthplace; Linda Boice, Mill Grove Audubon Wildlife Sanctuary; Sam Slaymaker and Carol Goetz, James Buchanan's Wheatland; Ronald Sheehan, Asa Packer Mansion; Steve Sitarski and Helen McKenna, Edgar Allan Poe National Historical Site; Brigitte Day, National Shrine of St. John Neumann; Dean Root and Kathryn Miller Haines, Stephen C. Foster Memorial.

Also, Robert Gangewere and Betsy Momich, Carnegie Museums of Pittsburgh; Gregory Langel, Frick Art and Historical Center; Rod Sturtz and LeVerne Love, West Overton Village; Edward Reis, George Westinghouse Museum; Karen Benson and David April, Fonthill Museum and Mercer Museum; Charles Yeske, Moravian Pottery and Tile Works; Pamela Whitenack, Amy Taber, and Denise Hernandez, Hershey Museum; Sister M. Ruth Catherine Spain, St. Katharine Drexel Shrine; Charles Croston and Lynn Dennis, Grey Towers National Historical Landmark; Paula Valentine, Zane Grey Museum; James Duff and Halsey Spruance, Brandywine River Museum; Carol Hegeman, Eisenhower National Historical Site; Heather Walton, Pearl S. Buck House; Blanche Burton-Lyles and Phyllis Sims, Marian Anderson Historical Society; Mary Beth Trout, Rachel Carson Homestead; Lynn Durgin and Linda Milanesi, James A. Michener Art Museum; Elizabeth Salome, Jimmy Stewart Museum; Mary Popola, Mario Lanza Institute and Museum; and Thomas Sokolowski, Colleen Criste, and Matthew Wrbican, Andy Warhol Museum.

The researchers at the Library of Congress Prints and Photographs Division helped us find some of the rare images that bring these Pennsylvanians to life. Our editor at Stackpole, Kyle Weaver, steered us through the editorial rapids from the beginning idea to final product with a gentle hand and helpful guidance.

Map to the Sites

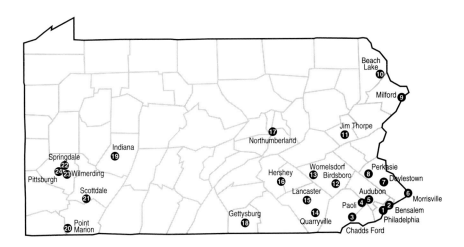

❶ PHILADELPHIA
Historic Rittenhouse Town (William Rittenhouse)
Historic Bartram's Garden (John and William Bartram)
Franklin Court (Benjamin Franklin)
Second Bank of the United States (Charles Willson Peale)
Founder's Hall, Girard College (Stephen Girard)
American Flag House and Betsy Ross Memorial (Betsy Ross)
Edgar Allan Poe National Historic Site
National Shrine of St. John Neumann
Marian Anderson Residence Museum and Birthplace Museum
Mario Lanza Museum

❷ BENSALEM
St. Katharine Drexel Shrine

❸ CHADDS FORD
Brandywine River Museum and N. C. Wyeth House and Studio (Wyeth Family)

❹ PAOLI
Historic Waynesborough (Anthony Wayne)

❺ AUDUBON
Mill Grove Audubon Wildlife Sanctuary (John James Audubon)

❻ MORRISVILLE
Pennsbury Manor (William Penn)

7 DOYLESTOWN
Fonthill Museum (Henry Mercer)
Moravian Pottery and Tile Works (Henry Mercer)
Mercer Museum (Henry Mercer)
James A. Michener Art Museum

8 PERKASIE
Pearl S. Buck House

9 MILFORD
Grey Towers National Historic Landmark (Gifford Pinchot)

10 BEACH LAKE
Zane Grey Museum

11 JIM THORPE
Asa Packer Mansion

12 BIRDSBORO
Daniel Boone Homestead

13 WOMELSDORF
Conrad Weiser Homestead

14 QUARRYVILLE
Robert Fulton Birthplace

15 LANCASTER
James Buchanan's Wheatland

16 HERSHEY
Hershey Museum and Milton Hershey School (Milton S. Hershey)

17 NORTHUMBERLAND
Joseph Priestley House

18 GETTYSBURG
Eisenhower National Historic Site

19 INDIANA
Jimmy Stewart Museum

20 POINT MARION
Friendship Hill National Historic Site (Albert Gallatin)

21 SCOTTDALE
West Overton Museums (Henry Clay Frick)

22 SPRINGDALE
Rachel Carson Homestead

23 WILMERDING
George Westinghouse Museum

24 PITTSBURGH
Stephen Foster Memorial and Foster Hall Collection
Carnegie Museums of Pittsburgh (Andrew Carnegie)
Frick Art and Historical Center (Henry Clay Frick)
Andy Warhol Museum

William Penn

(1644-1718)

The man who gave his family's name to a new colony in America, Pennsylvania, produced a framework for governing that was far ahead of the political and social standards of his time, guaranteeing religious freedom, ethnic tolerance, and an elected government to all who lived in his colony. This included Native Americans and earlier settlers, such as the Swedes and the Dutch, as well as new immigrants. He wanted them to "understand their liberty as men and Christians . . . ," he said. "We put the power in the people." The ideals of William Penn that thus took root in Pennsylvania foreshadowed in many ways the democratic and representative government that exists in the United States today.

William Penn was born in London, the son of a British admiral. An idealist, he early formed a belief that individuals had the right to worship as they pleased. As a student, he was expelled from Oxford University for refusing to attend services of the established Church of England. After two years of travel and study in Europe, he was sent by his father to Ireland to manage the family estates. While there, he was inspired by a leader of the Society of Friends, derisively known as Quakers, and he soon became a member of this pacifist sect. In the next years, he became the leading defender in England of religious tolerance and was imprisoned six times for expressing his views, which were considered blasphemous.

Penn's attention soon turned to the new lands being colonized in America. When, in 1677, a group of Quakers and others settled in West Jersey, the colonists brought with them the document Concessions and Agreements, a liberal charter of liberties that reflected the beliefs of William Penn. Later, in 1681, he transferred these ideas to the wilderness on the west side of the Delaware River when he received a charter for a new colony from King Charles II. The charter was given as repayment for an earlier debt the king owed his late father, Adm. William Penn. Penn had suggested the name Sylvania, meaning "woods," for the new colony; the king attached Penn's father's name to it, thus making it Pennsylvania.

Penn's Frame of Government for the colony called for a democratic assembly and council under the proprietor's direction and for guarantees

A fanciful portrait of William Penn by Henry Inman. INDEPENDENCE NATIONAL HISTORICAL PARK

of fundamental individual liberties. It provided for the security of individual property, virtually unlimited free enterprise, a free press, trial by jury, and religious tolerance. It was also the first constitution to provide for peaceful change through amendments.

He arrived for his first visit to America aboard the ship *Welcome* in 1682. Over the next two years, the new proprietor superintended the design of the town of Philadelphia. On tours of the area, Penn saw that Philadelphia was surrounded by what would become the richest agricultural hinterland of any colonial city. It lay in a circle of splendid farm country that reached in every direction, drawing New Jersey as well as Pennsylvania and Delaware into its orbit. As new settlers later poured into the region and cleared the forests, they not only produced commodities for Philadelphia merchants to export, but also created a market for Philadelphia imports.

Penn achieved peaceable relations with the local Indians—Susquehannock, Shawnee, and Lenape. They admired Penn's courage because he ventured among them without guards or personal weapons. Legend has it that he was a superior sprinter in those days and could outrun the Indian braves, winning their respect. He took the trouble to learn their dialects but conducted negotiations with an interpreter. From the beginning, he acquired Indian lands through peaceful, voluntary exchange. His peace policies continued for some seventy years, although relations with the Native Americans became more strained under his sons. Nevertheless, Pennsylvania offered a sharp contrast to the harsh treatment of the Indians by other colonies.

He also set about building for himself a mansion, named Pennsbury Manor, twenty-six miles up the Delaware River, but had not completed it before he had to return to England in 1684 to defend the boundaries of Pennsylvania against claims by Lord Baltimore, the proprietor of Maryland. His pregnant wife, Gulielma, had stayed behind in England with their children, hoping to join her husband when their new home in Pennsylvania was completed.

Penn remained in England for the next fifteen years, which were troubled times as the country changed kings twice. Charles II died and was succeeded by his brother, James II, a Catholic. Then James, a benefactor of Penn's, was overthrown in 1688 by William III and Mary II, and Penn immediately came under suspicion. During these days, Penn sometimes had to hide from the authorities. By the time he had finally cleared his name, his beloved wife had died in 1694 after a lingering illness.

In December 1699, Penn returned to his "fine greene countrie towne" of Philadelphia and his growing colony of Pennsylvania, bringing with him his new wife, Hannah Callowhill, a devout Quaker woman twenty-seven years younger than himself. But after his long absence, he found that the colonists now challenged his authority and often refused to pay their rent and taxes. In fact, Penn never earned enough from the colonies to offset the costs of administration, which he paid out of his own pocket. Toward the end of his life, he complained that Pennsylvania had been a net loss, costing him some £30,000.

In response to protests from the colonists, in 1701, Penn negotiated a new frame of government, adopting the Charter of Privileges. This constitution, which lasted for three-quarters of a century, confirmed the democratic form of government, guaranteed again the individual rights of the inhabitants, and for the first time gave the assembly the power to initiate bills. However, the governor retained his right to veto an action if he thought it necessary.

When an unfriendly Parliament in England proposed to annex all proprietary colonies, Penn went back to England, this time never to return. He was able to retain his proprietorship, but his last years were full of trouble and disappointment. His debts mounted so high that he even had to spend time in debtors' prison. After he suffered a stroke in 1712, his capable wife, Hannah, and his colonial secretary, James Logan, ably supervised his business interests until his death in 1718 at age seventy-four. After Hannah's death in 1726, the proprietorship passed into the hands of Penn's surviving sons, John, Thomas, and Richard. Pennsylvania remained a proprietary colony of the Penn family until it gained its statehood during the Revolutionary War in America.

William Penn was the first great hero of American liberty. Whereas most colonists stole land from the Native Americans, Penn traveled unarmed among them and negotiated peaceful purchases. He gave Pennsylvania a written constitution that limited the power of government, provided a humane penal code, and guaranteed many fundamental liberties. As a result, this new society showed how individuals of different races and religions can live together peacefully.

Pennsbury Manor

If you had buckles on your shoes, you would feel like you actually were stepping onto the original plantation that William Penn built for himself and his family north of Philadelphia along the Delaware River. With its

Visiting Pennsbury Manor

400 Pennsbury Manor Rd., Morrisville, PA 19067

PHONE: 215-946-0400

E-MAIL: willpenn17@aol.com

WEBSITE: www.pennsburymanor.org

ADMINISTRATION: Owned and operated by Pennsylvania Historic and Museum Commission.

HOURS: Open year-round Tuesday–Saturday, 9–5; Sunday, 12–5; closed Monday.

ADMISSION FEES: $5 for adults; $4.50 for seniors; $3 for children ages 6–12; $13 for families.

TOURS: Guided tours only; call for availability and to confirm times:
Tuesday–Friday, 10:00, 11:30, 1:30, and 3:30;
Saturday, 11:00, 12:30, 2:00, and 3:30;
Sunday, 12:30, 1:30, 2:30, and 3:30.
Winter schedule: Tuesday–Saturday, 11:00 and 2:00; Sunday, 2:00 only.

TIME NEEDED: $1^1/_2$ to 2 hours.

SPECIAL EVENTS: Manor Fair in September; Holly Nights in December; Charter Day in March. All Sundays April–November, interpreters re-create seventeenth-century manor life. Summer camps for school-age children.

SPECIAL CONSIDERATIONS: Handicapped-accessible; wheelchairs available. Call 215-946-0400 or 215-443-3481 for TDD or special assistance.

PARKING: Free on-site parking.

SALES OUTLETS: Gift shop offers historical books and materials, souvenirs, and craft items. A guidebook, *Pennsbury Manor: Pennsylvania Trail of History Guide,* is on sale at the gift shop or from Stackpole Books, 800-732-3669.

DIRECTIONS: From Pennsylvania Turnpike, take Exit 29 to Route 13N. Turn right on Green Lane at first traffic light. Turn left on Radcliffe Street. Continue 4.6 miles and turn right on Pennsbury Manor Road. (Note: Road changes name twice: Radcliffe becomes Main Street, which becomes Bordentown Road.)

handsome Georgian-style mansion looking out over the river, numerous outbuildings, kitchen, formal gardens, orchards, and grazing lots for cattle and horses, the estate is typical of that of an English gentleman of three centuries ago.

After Penn's death, Pennsbury's buildings collapsed through neglect, and the estate degenerated into ruins. Penn's descendants sold the land, but between 1933 and 1942, the Pennsylvania Historical and Museum Commission repurchased forty-three of the original eight thousand acres

The reconstructed manor house at Pennsbury Manor. PHOTO BY THE AUTHORS

and reconstructed the plantation, including the manor house, outbuildings, and landscaped gardens and orchards. Today the historic site again resembles Penn's original estate. Several pieces of furniture and tableware that were owned by William Penn are on display. Outbuildings include a joiner's shop, icehouse, worker's cottage, smokehouse, woodshed, barn, bake and brew house, blacksmith shop, and a "necessary" (outhouse). Animals roaming the barnyard and pastures include Red Devon cattle, Arabian horses, sheep, chickens, geese, guinea hens, and peacocks. Visitors can view a replica of the barge that Penn used for his frequent trips downriver to Philadelphia.

Tours, exhibits, workshops, and special programs offer visitors and school groups a realistic glimpse into seventeenth-century plantation life. Living history, animal husbandry, garden and crop activities, and colonial crafts are demonstrated. Tours start at the visitors center, with a video orientation to the site, exhibits of artifacts, and a museum shop.

William Rittenhouse

(1644-1708)

The man who would establish the first paper mill in America emigrated from his homeland in present-day Germany by way of Holland in 1688, partly for economic reasons, partly for religious. In the Old World, he had been born Wilhelm Rittenhausen. In the New World, he anglicized his name to William Rittenhouse. He was one of the earliest settlers in the colony, arriving just seven years after the first Germans set foot on Pennsylvania soil.

In America, he had been told, there was no paper mill in any of the then-British colonies. He therefore saw the possibility of achieving a monopoly in paper production in this potentially large colonial market. Paper was an important product in the colonies—and precious. Documents like deeds, titles, and contracts were printed on paper. Newspapers and pamphlets depended on it. So did soldiers, who used paper to make cartridges and gun wadding.

In addition to this economic incentive, he and his fellow Mennonites were attracted by William Penn's policy of religious tolerance in this new colony of Pennsylvania. Rittenhouse, his wife, and their three children migrated to New York, where they stayed for two years. In 1690, they settled in Germantown near Philadelphia, a town founded by thirteen families who were also Mennonite in religious belief and mostly weavers by trade. Soon after his arrival, he was chosen to be the first Mennonite minister in America. As a devoted church leader, it was Rittenhouse who donated the land in Germantown where the first Mennonite church was constructed.

The forty-six-year-old Rittenhouse had the know-how to manufacture paper, but he needed money in order to build a mill. He formed a company with three partners, one of whom was William Bradford, at that time the colony's only printer. The company acquired a twenty-acre plot of land on a branch of Wissahickon Creek, later known as Paper Mill Run, and there he built a paper mill in 1690, the first in North America. William brought his son Nicholas (Claus) into the business with him.

The association with Bradford was mutually beneficial. Bradford provided part of the capital needed to finance the construction and operation of the mill. In return, Rittenhouse guaranteed to sell Bradford the paper he needed for his printing business—thus producing a steady buyer for the mill's production. Within two years, circulars publicizing Pennsylvania to new immigrants were calling attention to the mill in Germantown that made fine white paper from castoff rags.

A few key pieces of equipment, as well as a free-flowing stream, were required for a mill to make paper. The mill's waterwheel powered a stamping machine that pounded the rags to a pulp. The tiny shreds of rags were then mixed with water to form a slurry. A vat man dipped a wire screen called a mould into the slurry, coating the screen with the liquid pulp. He lifted out a layer of fibers that would become the sheet of paper, laying the sheet between pieces of absorbent felt. A pile of sheets separated by felt was squeezed by a press to extract the water. Then each sheet was coated with a sizing of animal glue and hung over ropes to dry.

When held up to the light, "laid" papers showed the distinctive marks of the laid wires of the mould. Many early papermakers took advantage of this phenomenon to add watermarks to their products, marks produced by lacing figures twisted in wire onto the surfaces of their moulds. The finished sheets when held up to the light showed not only the laid lines, but also the impressions of the watermarks. The Rittenhouses used moulds with several different watermarks. The earliest seems to have been in use by 1692 and consisted of a shield enclosing a fleur-de-lis design with the monogram NR, for Nicholas Rittenhouse.

But in 1700, raging spring floodwaters swept away the entire mill, along with its inventories of paper, machinery, and tools. William and Nicholas Rittenhouse managed to rebuild their mill, buoyed in part by an appeal from proprietor William Penn to give the papermakers "relief and encouragement in their needful and commendable employment." Bradford, who by now had moved his printing plant to New York, declined to put any new money into the rebuilding and in 1704 sold his share to the Rittenhouses, who were then free to sell their paper to whomever they desired. By 1706, the other two partners had also sold their shares of the business, and the two Rittenhouses, father and son, became the sole proprietors. After the death of the elder Rittenhouse in 1708, Nicholas Rittenhouse, who had also become a Mennonite minister, carried on the business. Although there are no records of his wife, Gertrude, William Rittenhouse had two sons, Nicholas and Gerhard, and a daughter, Elizabeth.

Until 1710, the Rittenhouse operation was the only paper mill in America, but soon others were built. Papermaking continued in the Rittenhouse family for several generations, but in the early 1800s, it faded in the face of competition from larger, more mechanized and efficient paper mills that used wood pulp instead of rags to make paper.

The Rittenhouse name later gained even greater recognition due to the accomplishments of William's great-grandson David Rittenhouse (1732–96). Born in the company village on Paper Mill Run in Germantown and self-taught, David became a leading American astronomer and maker of clocks and mathematical instruments. He is noted for the mechanical models he built to demonstrate the relative motions of the planets, and for designing and constructing high-quality telescopes and surveyors' instruments. In the rebellion against England, he threw in his lot early with the patriot cause and turned his talents to casting cannons and making ammunition as an active member of the Committee of Safety and the Board of War. He was also Pennsylvania's state treasurer.

Historic Rittenhouse Town

Once you leave the busy streets leading through Philadelphia's Fairmount Park, you will discover the remnants of this early industrial village that once contained forty buildings, including several paper mills, homes of the owner and workers, a firehouse, bakehouse, church, and school. Seven structures remain from Rittenhouse Town, but none that date back to

The home of William Rittenhouse's son, Nicholas, built around 1707, stands in Historic Rittenhouse Town. PHOTO BY THE AUTHORS

Visiting Historic Rittenhouse Town

206 Lincoln Dr., Philadelphia, PA 19144

PHONE: 215-438-5711
E-MAIL: HistRitTwn@aol.com
WEBSITE: www.rittenhousetown.org
ADMINISTRATION: Historic RittenhouseTown, Inc., administers this National Historic Landmark owned by the Fairmount Park Commission.
HOURS: Weekdays for groups by advance reservations; weekends May–October, 12–4.
ADMISSION FEES: $4 for adults; $2 for seniors and children. Fees vary for special events and group programs.
TOURS: May–September, weekends 12–4 and by appointment.
TIME NEEDED: 1 to 2 hours.
SPECIAL EVENTS: Easter egg hunt; 5K run in September; *Spirits of the Past* lantern tours in October; Monoshone Creek Watershed Appreciation Day in November; holiday tours. Papermaking workshops.
SPECIAL CONSIDERATIONS: Most buildings are handicapped-accessible, although terrain is hilly with loose gravel.
PARKING: On-site parking.
SALES OUTLETS: Gift shop offers maps and books on the Rittenhouse family and papermaking, gifts, and craft items.
DIRECTIONS: Entrance is on Wissahickon Avenue between Lincoln Drive and Walnut Lane in Fairmount Park. From Schuylkill Expressway, take Exit 32, Germantown/Wissahickon Avenue/Ridge Avenue, and follow signs for Lincoln Drive. Take Lincoln Drive 1.5 miles to first traffic light, and turn right on Rittenhouse Street. Follow one block, and turn left on Wissahickon Avenue. Entrance is up the hill on left.

William, the founder. One of the oldest is a house built in 1707 by William's son Nicholas. It is medieval in design, with a sixteen-foot fireplace reported to be one of the largest in colonial Pennsylvania. In this house, years later, David Rittenhouse, William's great-grandson, was born. Both the first mill and its replacement, built in 1702, have disappeared, although the foundations have been located.

Near the entrance to Rittenhouse Town is the home of the third-generation Abraham Rittenhouse. This larger house serves as the visitors center, where displays tell the story of early papermaking and the life of the founder and his family. Hand papermaking workshops and demonstrations for groups are held throughout the year in a papermaking studio located in the village barn.

Conrad Weiser

(1696-1760)

A central thread was woven into the fabric of Conrad Weiser's life in 1712, when his father, a recent immigrant to this country from Germany, sent the young teenager off to live as an "adopted son" with friendly Mohawk Indians of upstate New York in order to learn to interpret dialogues between the Indians and the settlers.

During a long snowbound winter, Conrad lived with his Indian family in its longhouse, went hunting with his Native American brothers, and learned to speak the dialects of the Iroquois tribes of the Five Nations—the Mohawk, Oneida, Onondaga, Cayuga, and Seneca—a league of Indians of similar cultures that had for years controlled a large area of the East between the Delaware River and the Ohio River, and from the Great Lakes to the Chesapeake Bay. By the time he returned to his family in the spring, Conrad had developed into a competent interpreter who could help his fellow settlers negotiate land and water rights with the nearby Indians.

Born in 1696, Weiser took up farming as a young man and married Anna Eve Feg, a German-born settler like himself. In 1729, Weiser and his wife and their four young children moved from Schoharie, near Albany in upstate New York, to the fertile Tulpehocken Valley of Pennsylvania, now part of Berks County. It was the region to which his father-in-law had moved earlier in response to an appeal from the Penn family, which was looking for new settlers for its province. After living temporarily in a log house, the ambitious Weiser built a sturdy, square stone house. Here he turned his hand to farming and operating a tannery.

It was probably inevitable that this frontier farmer who knew the Indian languages and cultures so well would prove invaluable to the Pennsylvania colony in its continuing negotiations with nearby Indian tribes—and so he was. Soon after arriving in the area, he met Shickellamy, an Oneida Indian who had been sent by the Council of the Five Nations to oversee the Indians in this part of Pennsylvania. Shickellamy made his home at the forks of the Susquehanna, the present-day site of Sunbury.

The man in the center of this painting is probably Conrad Weiser. The event in the painting by Anna Arndt, after an original by J. V. Haidt, is the 1742 meeting in Shamokin of Moravian leader Count Nicholas Ludwig von Zinzendorf (left) and the representatives of the Iroquois Confederacy, whose chief spokesman was Shickellamy. UNITY ARCHIVES, HERRNHUT, GERMANY

In 1731, Shickellamy and a group of Indians, on their way to meet with James Logan, the provincial secretary and advisor to the Penn family, stopped by Weiser's home and requested that he accompany them to Philadelphia as an interpreter. Weiser agreed, little realizing that this venture would start him on a career as a vital intermediary between the Pennsylvania settlers and the Native Americans. This career would eventually turn him into a frontier statesman, a public figure who would be called the "cornerstone of the colony's successful Indian policy."

In 1736, Weiser again accompanied a delegation of Indians led by Shickellamy to Philadelphia for a conference. The three sons of William Penn, now the proprietors of the province of Pennsylvania, were continuing their late father's policy of buying land from the Indians rather than simply occupying it as other colonies had done. But James Logan decided that he preferred to purchase land not from individual chiefs in separate negotiations, but from the Council of the Six Nations (now enlarged by the addition of the Tuscaroras), which controlled all the Pennsylvania Native Americans. In an agreement facilitated by Weiser that year, the Penns confirmed the right of the Iroquois to speak on behalf of all the colony's Indians. For its part, the council, in return for a few guns, hats, tobacco pipes, and other items, dropped its claims to lands of the lower Susquehanna Valley, thus opening up this region of Pennsylvania to settlers. After the conference, both sides expressed pleasure with Weiser as their interpreter. The Indians paid him the compliment of calling him "one-half . . . Indian and one-half Englishman."

It seemed that whenever an Indian problem arose, the authorities now called on Conrad Weiser for some backwoods diplomacy. Three times in eight years, he trekked many miles overland to Onondaga, the headquarters of the Six Nations and the site of present-day Syracuse. In 1737, he nearly died of exposure when he tried to find his way through deep midwinter snows. After staggering into Onondaga and later recovering his health, he succeeded in his mission. Weiser persuaded the Iroquois not to "unsheath their hatchet" against the combative Catawba and Cherokee of the South, a conflict that would have caught the Pennsylvania and Virginia colonies in the cross fire.

In the next few years, Weiser's life took a surprising twist. Despite the fact that he had prospered as a farmer, owned eight hundred acres of land, possessed horses and cattle, and established a tannery, he turned his back on both his farm and his family, and isolated himself in a religious community at the nearby Ephrata Cloister. Here he lived like a monk, subsisting on a few simple foods eaten only once a day, sleeping on a narrow wooden bench, shunning luxuries of any kind, and spending hours in prayer. But after two years, he became disenchanted with the inflexible leadership of Conrad Beissel, his religious mentor. He returned to his family and the world.

Hostilities were now looming between the French traders and trappers, whose king laid claim to the Ohio River system, and the English traders and settlers who were moving westward across the Appalachian Mountains from the eastern seaboard. The Pennsylvania authorities and Conrad Weiser worked hard to maintain the "Chain of Friendship" they had forged with the Iroquois. When warfare broke out between France and England in 1754 in western Pennsylvania, the Six Nations refused to join the French as did a number of other tribes, remaining neutral. In addition, the Six Nations ceded a huge tract of land in western Pennsylvania to the colony. This treaty, negotiated at Albany, New York, opened up the region for trade and settlement as far as the Ohio River.

But the war unleashed raids by hostile Indians, who murdered pioneer families and set fire to their cabins and fields across Pennsylvania. Weiser was soon called into military service as a lieutenant colonel of the 1st Battalion of the Pennsylvania Regiment and was given responsibility for the defense of eastern Pennsylvania. He superintended the construction of several forts and helped negotiate a number of treaties at Easton to protect both the white settlers and the friendly Indians.

In 1758, as the war turned in favor of the British, Weiser helped organize a wagon train of food and supplies for the British and American forces under Gen. John Forbes and Col. Henry Bouquet. This army marched across Pennsylvania and captured the French Fort Duquesne, thus effectively evicting the French from western Pennsylvania and assuring the British control of the Ohio River. Weiser was then summoned to help negotiate the Easton treaty of 1758, which ended Indian hostilities in eastern Pennsylvania, an effort that brought to a close Conrad Weiser's career as interpreter.

During the last years of his life, this energetic man devoted his efforts to improving Berks County and its county seat, the town of Reading, a county and town he had been instrumental in establishing. He had long been active in political affairs, serving as a local justice of the peace and running unsuccessfully for the Pennsylvania legislature three times. By the time he died at his farm in 1760, he had served unstintingly as a farmer, devout churchman, ambassador, interpreter, soldier, and judge.

"The confidence that both the Indians as well as the government had in him had been a vast addition to his importance," said a top Philadelphia official who had worked closely with Weiser. "I think it will be long before we find another equal to him."

Conrad Weiser Homestead

Step into the small stone house where Conrad Weiser and his family lived for thirty years, and you feel what life must have been like in the eighteenth century at the edge of the Pennsylvania frontier. This talented pioneer built his home with thick limestone walls in a square shape, with one large room and a loft. The structure was enlarged by later owners into a rectangle with the addition of a second room.

The Conrad Weiser Homestead, built in the early eighteenth century, was restored in the 1920s. PHOTOS BY KYLE R. WEAVER

Visiting Conrad Weiser Homestead

28 Weiser Rd., Womelsdorf, PA 19567

PHONE: 610-589-2934

WEBSITE: www.state.pa.us

ADMINISTRATION: Administered by the Pennsylvania Historical and Museum Commission, with support from the Friends of the Conrad Weiser Homestead.

HOURS: Open March–December, Wednesday–Saturday, 9–5; Sunday, 12–5; closed Mondays, Tuesdays, and most holidays. Modified schedule January and February.

ADMISSION FEES: $2.50 for adults; $2 for seniors; $1 for youth; $6 for families.

TOURS: Wednesday–Saturday, 9–5; Sunday, 12–5.

TIME NEEDED: At least 1 hour.

SPECIAL EVENTS: Lectures, living-history and encampment days, summer concerts, book sales, and candlelight tours.

SPECIAL CONSIDERATIONS: Handicapped-accessible; no stairs; call in advance to discuss special needs.

PARKING: Free parking near house and visitors center.

SALES OUTLETS: Visitors center bookstore offers historical books, maps, and craft items. A guidebook, *Conrad Weiser Homestead: Pennsylvania Trail of History Guide,* is on sale at the bookstore or from Stackpole Books, 800-732-3669.

DIRECTIONS: Entrance located just off U.S. Route 422 east of Womelsdorf in Berks County.

The main room is dominated by a large, open fireplace, complete with a bake oven, that supplied heat for cooking and warmed the house in cold weather. A spinning wheel, cradle, table, and other pieces of furniture, although not original to the Weiser family, are authentic to the period. A hidden doorway at one end of the room leads to the loft, where children and guests probably slept.

A second room contains a desk similar to the one Weiser used to write his many reports of negotiations and proposals, as well as exhibits that describe his career. Outside, other restored buildings include a springhouse and a log house similar to the one Weiser built when he first arrived in the Tulpehocken Valley.

The family graveyard lies nearby. Weiser's tombstone is inscribed in German, marking the final resting place of "the late and high esteemed magistrate." A striking statue of Shickellamy recalls the times he and Weiser struck out from this farm on long treks, westward to the Shamokin

Indian settlement at the forks of the Susquehanna River or to Onondaga in New York, or eastward to Philadelphia. One can also envision the groups of Indians from the Iroquois homeland in New York who set up their tents and fire pits around the Weiser homestead, camping here for a time before they resumed their journey to negotiations in Philadelphia.

The visitors center is housed in a Pennsylvania Dutch farmhouse built in the 1830s. Here you can view a video, exhibits that describe Weiser's life, and personal items such as a monogrammed silver spoon that probably belonged to the frontier negotiator.

More than a century after his death, the citizens of Berks County honored Weiser by surrounding the historic homestead with an elaborate, formal park that includes gardens, statues, walking paths, pond, and gazebo. The park was designed by Olmsted Brothers, the celebrated landscape architecture firm operated by the sons of Frederick Law Olmsted.

John and William Bartram

To the two Bartrams, father and son, belongs the distinction of being the first to describe and document the rich diversity of plant life that grew in the newly colonized land of America. Each of the Bartrams, impelled by an unquenchable curiosity, explored the world of plants with the same intensity shown by the mountain men and land explorers of the same era as they pushed westward on the newly settled continent.

Their natural curiosity was fueled by the strong desire of a few wealthy estate owners in England to add exotic plant species to their showplace gardens. It was the patronage of these English gentlemen that enabled both father and son to follow their passion and wander the country to build a catalog of native flora.

Between them, John and William ranged across eastern America from Canada to the Gulf of Mexico, from the Atlantic seaboard to the Mississippi River and Great Lakes. They sent or brought back their treasures, both plants and seeds, to the family farm in Philadelphia and there established America's oldest living botanical garden.

John Bartram
(1699–1777)

Few would have predicted that John Bartram, an unschooled farmer on the banks of the Schuylkill River, would become what the renowned Swedish botanist Carolus Linnaeus called "the greatest natural botanist in the world."

By his early thirties, John Bartram was a successful farmer. He had built his own stone house and with his wife, Ann, was raising a family that would eventually number six sons and three daughters. But he had long been fascinated with botany, especially herbs that could cure disease, and wanted to learn more. He taught himself Latin so he could comprehend botanical names. In his eager search for knowledge, he was helped by neighbors who possessed libraries and by a fellow Philadelphian, Benjamin Franklin, who along with Bartram founded the American Philosophical Society and who helped raise the money that enabled Bartram to undertake one of his plant-finding expeditions.

Through his Philadelphia friends, Bartram learned that a wealthy English wool merchant and amateur scientist named Peter Collinson was eager to find exotic American plants for his garden. Thus began an arrangement that was to continue for forty years: Bartram would send seeds and plants to Collinson and other aristocratic "subscribers," in return for a retainer that financed his continuing field expeditions. Strangely enough, although Collinson spread Bartram's fame throughout England and to other countries and brought about a change in the style of English gardens, he and his field agent never met.

But Bartram did not give up farming, which was his livelihood. He pursued his botanical ventures in late fall and early spring, when he could get away from the farm. In 1738, he journeyed on horseback through the colony of Virginia, covering eleven hundred miles in five weeks, resting only one day. In 1742, he ventured to the Pennsylvania and New York frontier with Conrad Weiser as Weiser negotiated with the Onondaga Indians. Bartram collected many valuable specimens, and later Collinson published his journal of the trip as a book.

In 1753, he took his teenage son, William, nicknamed Billy, along with him on a plant-collecting trip to the Catskill Mountains, initiating the lad as a botanical investigator. In 1761, he traveled across Pennsylvania to Pittsburgh with Col. Henry Bouquet, the military hero who had recently led British and American troops to capture Fort Duquesne, a campaign that drove the French and their Indian allies from western Pennsylvania.

Bartram explored and collected along the Ohio River and in South Carolina. At age sixty-six, he made his last major trip. Accompanied once more by William, he traveled up Florida's St. John's River to its source. Among the plants they identified was a white-blooming shrub William later named the Franklin tree, genus *Franklinia,* after his father's old friend. The *Franklinia* tree later vanished from the wild. Only seeds collected by William have saved the species from extinction.

Back home in Philadelphia, he was among the first botanists in America to produce hybrid plants. Bartram's admirers acknowledged that he knew far more about America's flora than he ever published. In 1765, thanks to lobbying in England by his faithful patron Peter Collinson, John Bartram was appointed royal botanist to King George III. By the time he died at his Philadelphia farm in 1777 at age seventy-eight, the one-time farm boy was known and respected by Europe's most prominent naturalists. He is buried in the Darby Meeting House burial ground in nearby Darby, where he was born.

William Bartram
(1739–1823)

Although William Bartram grew up at his family's Philadelphia farm home and accompanied his father on two of his plant explorations, it was only after a number of years that William recognized his own overriding interest in nature.

After a solid education at the Philadelphia Academy, he apprenticed with a local merchant, then opened a store on his uncle's plantation in North Carolina. He did, however, go with his father on the 1765 exploration of the St. John's River, where he used his exceptional artistic talent to paint images of many of the plants the expedition found. But when the expedition ended, young Bartram remained in Florida to start an indigo plantation, only to abandon this "unpleasant, unhealthy" site a year later and return to Philadelphia.

At age thirty-three, William seemed to be adrift in life, jobless, wifeless, and rootless, a situation that annoyed his father. Then an English patron, Dr. John Fothergill, who admired William's detailed images of plants and flowers, set William squarely in his father's footsteps. Fothergill sponsored William on another plant-collecting expedition to Florida, that great hothouse of exotic flora.

The expedition turned into a four-year odyssey, far longer than any his father had undertaken. The epic journey took him along the coasts of South Carolina, Georgia, and northern Florida, where he returned to many of the sites he had visited in 1765. William also traveled inland, across present-day Georgia, Alabama, and Louisiana, eventually reaching the Mississippi River.

William Bartram, 1808, by Charles Willson Peale. INDEPENDENCE NATIONAL HISTORICAL PARK

Plunging into the backcountry on horseback for months at a time, the happy wanderer would surface in a port town long enough to ship his discoveries to England, and then plunge again into the green unknown. On the Gulf Coast, he contracted a near-fatal illness that left his eyesight permanently impaired. He later said he had ridden six thousand miles on one horse.

In his far-ranging expedition, William gained not only firsthand knowledge of the native vegetation, but also an understanding of the southeastern Indian societies, observing their dances, attending their councils, and sharing their mysterious ceremonial "black drink" brewed from yaupon holly.

When he finally arrived back in Savannah early in 1776, the drums of the Revolutionary War were throbbing. By the time he reached Philadelphia, the war had severed all ties with England and dashed all prospects of further patronage from Dr. Fothergill. His father died eight months after his return, leaving the house and botanical garden to William's younger and more business-minded brother, John Jr.

Not quite thirty-eight, William spent the remaining years of his life close to home, painting and writing, helping tend the botanical garden, and studying nature. He spent fourteen years reworking the journals of his epic exploration, which he finally published at the urging of his friends. His *Travels* was the first serious work on American natural history to be published in post-Revolutionary America. When it finally appeared in 1791, his account won critical acclaim but had only limited sales in the United States. Editions were soon published in French and German, however, as well as English, and Bartram found an admiring audience among Romantic writers such as William Wordsworth and Samuel Taylor Coleridge, who made use of his vivid descriptions and imagery in their poetry.

Yet even when opportunities to gain some glory fell into his lap, the humble Quaker resolutely shunned the spotlight. In 1782, William was elected professor of botany at the University of Pennsylvania, but he declined. President Thomas Jefferson invited him to serve as the naturalist on the 1806 Red River expedition, but again Bartram begged off.

Honors found him anyway. The American Philosophical Society made him a member, like his father, in 1786. A procession of scientific colleagues came to his garden, and he served as a mentor for an early American ornithologist, Alexander Wilson. William Bartram died at age eighty-four, while walking quietly in his garden on a summer day in 1823.

Historic Bartram's Garden

Remarkably, the botanical garden that John Bartram first planted two and a half centuries ago continues to bloom. It is now an oasis of green in the midst of the urban sprawl of West Philadelphia. When you enter its gates, you exchange the busy city streets for the tranquillity of a forty-five-acre sanctuary.

Visitors may tour the famed garden, native plant collection, restored eighteenth-century kitchen garden, wildflower garden, water garden, trail along the Schuylkill River, and a freshwater tidal wetland, as well as attend occasional plant sales, lectures, workshops, festivals, performances, and children's programs. The garden annually hosts more than seven thousand Philadelphia-area students through its popular educational programs that combine lessons in science, nature, and history.

Visiting Historic Bartram's Garden

54th St. and Lindbergh Blvd., Philadelphia, PA 19143

PHONE: 215-729-5281

E-MAIL: explore@bartramsgarden.org

WEBSITE: www.bartramsgarden.org

ADMINISTRATION: John Bartram Association, in cooperation with Philadelphia's Fairmount Park Commission.

HOURS: Historic Garden open Monday–Sunday, 10–5; Bartram House open for tours March–December, Tuesday–Sunday, 12–4.

ADMISSION FEES: $3 for adult guided tour of house.

TOURS: House and garden tours available year-round for groups of 10 or more by reservation.

TIME NEEDED: 1 to 2 hours.

SPECIAL EVENTS: Plant sale and living-history festival in May; fall harvest festival in October; holiday greens sale in early December. Educational programs for children and adults throughout the year.

SPECIAL CONSIDERATIONS: Persons in wheelchairs should have assistance.

PARKING: Free parking.

SALES OUTLETS: Museum shop offers books, nature items, and gifts.

DIRECTIONS: From Schuylkill Expressway (I-76) south, take exit 41, Gray's Ferry Avenue. Turn left at exit ramp light. Turn right at next light on Gray's Ferry Avenue. Follow along Schuylkill River, and take first left onto Paschall Avenue. Turn left at next light onto 49th Street (name changes to Gray's Avenue and Lindbergh Boulevard). Just past 54th Street sign and railroad bridge, turn left into Bartram's Garden.

John Bartram's eighteenth-century house is situated within America's oldest botanical gardens. JOHN BARTRAM ASSOCIATION, HISTORIC BARTRAM'S GARDENS

John Bartram's barn has been converted to a classroom facility for these young visitors.

The city of Philadelphia acquired Bartram's Gardens in 1891. Bartram descendants formed the John Bartram Association in 1893 to help the city preserve the site and the Bartram legacy. The nonprofit association operates the garden today in cooperation with the city's Fairmount Park Commission.

Benjamin Franklin, 1767, by David Rent Etter, after the original by David Martin. INDEPENDENCE NATIONAL HISTORICAL PARK

Benjamin Franklin

(1706-90)

To Benjamin Franklin goes the distinction of being the only one of the nation's founding fathers to endorse all four major documents that established the United States of America—the Declaration of Independence (1776), the treaty with France (1778), the peace treaty with England (1783), and the U.S. Constitution (1787).

The life of this self-made and mostly self-taught man is a vivid example of how a person in a democratic country can rise from humble beginnings to the peak of intellectual and political influence. In Franklin's case, he rose from apprentice printer in his hometown of Boston to become a citizen of the world.

He was born in 1706, the fifteenth child of Josiah Franklin, to Josiah's second wife, Abiah. After only two years of schooling, Franklin was pulled out of the classroom by his father and put to work at age eleven in the family's candlemaking shop. Young Benjamin wanted to be a sailor, but one of his brothers had died at sea, so his parents forbade it. Even at this early age, Franklin displayed a trait that would characterize his entire life—rebellion against the conventional order of things. When Franklin objected to candlemaking, his father apprenticed him to his older brother, James, who had just opened a print shop. Franklin adapted readily to the printing business, perhaps because books and reading were the boy's great passion. He read at night, before he went to work in the morning, and on Sunday mornings, when he would often skip church services.

Franklin worked nine years for his brother, who began publishing a newspaper, the *New England Courant,* in 1721. When James was sent to jail by the colonial authorities for printing "radical ideas," Franklin, at age sixteen, published the newspaper on his own. In gratitude, James released him from his indenture as an apprentice, and Franklin soon departed for New York to make a life for himself.

When he learned of prospects for a printing job in Philadelphia, the young man walked across New Jersey and floated down the Delaware River in a large rowboat to reach his destination. He got the job in Philadelphia, left briefly for another printing opportunity in London, and then returned to Philadelphia in 1728 to open his own print shop. As a businessman, Franklin was thrifty, shrewd, and hardworking. He established a newspaper, the *Pennsylvania Gazette,* which was the first newspaper to carry a cartoon and the first to illustrate a news story with a map. As the editor, he wrote the popular "Poor Richard's Almanac," a collection of pithy sayings. Franklin got a contract as the official printer for Pennsylvania and within a few years dominated the printing trade in Philadelphia. He bought some of the paper he needed from William Rittenhouse.

In 1730, Deborah Read Rogers became his common-law wife, after her first husband had deserted her. Together he and Deborah had two children: a son who died in childhood and a daughter, Sally, who grew to adulthood. He also had two illegitimate children, a daughter and a son, William, who later became the Loyalist governor of New Jersey and remained opposed to his father's independence policies.

By 1748, Franklin had completed twenty years as a successful printer and had accumulated a comfortable income. Furthermore, he had financed several printers in other colonies and was receiving one-third of the profits from these enterprises. Now he decided to make a big change in his life. Selling his business to his partner, he determined to use his new leisure time "to read, study and make experiments . . . and produce something for the common benefits of mankind."

Turning his attention to science, this Renaissance man became fascinated with electricity. His experiments with electrical charges and with the natural phenomenon of lightning established Franklin's fame as a scientist and earned him respect both in the colonies and in Europe. During these days, his agile brain also devised the Pennsylvania fireplace, which later gained fame as the Franklin stove. He invented bifocal eyeglasses, an improved type of clock, the lightning rod, and the armonica, a musical instrument played by holding the fingers against rotating glass bowls that touch water and produce a sound like musical glasses.

He also put his clever mind to work on community improvements. He initiated projects for establishing a city police force and for the paving, cleaning, and lighting of city streets. In 1731, he was largely instrumental in establishing a circulating library in Philadelphia, the first in America. In 1743, he founded the American Philosophical Society for scholars, and in 1751, a city hospital and the Academy for the Education of Youth, which later became the University of Pennsylvania. He was clerk of the Pennsylvania Assembly and deputy postmaster at Philadelphia from 1737 to 1753.

When in 1753 he was appointed deputy postmaster general of all the colonies, Franklin's life took on a new dimension. Traveling throughout the colonies, he promoted improved service and the consolidation of mail deliveries to save money. Furthermore, he believed that cooperation among the colonies should be extended to other endeavors, such as a unified defense against Indian attacks, defense against coastal pirates, and joint plans for new settlements west of the Appalachian Mountains.

The stage for Franklin's actions widened yet again in 1759, when he was sent by Pennsylvania to London to smooth out the colony's differences with the sons of William Penn, now the proprietors of the colony. The younger Penns, who lived in England, cared little for the religious freedom that had motivated their father and were interested only in the income they could extract from the colony.

Although unsuccessful at gaining concessions from the Penns, Franklin was soon caught up in a larger problem, the Stamp Act. This act, passed by Parliament in 1765, imposed duties for the first time on commerce within the American colonies. Franklin, as a colonial agent, argued against the tax in Parliament, and a month later it was repealed. But Parliament did not rule out imposing other, similar internal taxes on the colonists and did nothing to give the Americans the privilege they sought of being represented in Parliament, a right held by other Englishmen.

Tensions increased in America, inflamed by the inflexible attitude of King George III. In 1775, after presenting a petition to the king from the First Continental Congress and having it turned down, Franklin boarded a ship to return to Philadelphia. While he was crossing the ocean, American militiamen at Lexington and Concord exchanged gunfire with British troops, and the violent rebellion began that Franklin had so long worked to avert. No sooner had he landed than he was elected a delegate to the Second Continental Congress. He helped to write the Articles of Confederation, which guided the colonies during the wartime years.

A year later, in the midst of the Revolutionary War, following the adoption of the Declaration of Independence, Franklin was sent as one of three envoys to France. His goal was the vital mission of persuading France to support the Americans by declaring war on England. Months later, after the American army had defeated the British at the Battle of Saratoga, French King Louis XVI in 1778 agreed to a military alliance. The influx of French money and supplies, later to be supplemented by troops and the French fleet, helped turn the tide of war in favor of the rebelling Americans. Even John Adams, no admirer of Franklin, said that the Pennsylvanian's friendships with influential Frenchmen had clinched the treaty.

The American defeat of the British at the Battle of Yorktown brought the victory of independence from England, and Franklin was appointed one of the diplomats to negotiate the peace treaties. After the official signing in 1783 of the treaties between America and England and America and France, Franklin wrote: "May we never see another war! For in my opinion there never was a good war or a bad peace."

An elderly Franklin was a guiding presence at the Constitutional Convention of 1787. It was he who suggested the compromise that created the two houses of Congress—one, the House of Representatives, determined by "property representatives," the other, the Senate, by "equality of votes." Finally, at the end, he counseled each of the delegates to "doubt a little of his own infallibility" and to "put his name to the instrument." Franklin wept, it was reported, as he affixed his signature to the new Constitution.

Benjamin Franklin died April 17, 1790, at age eighty-four and lies buried at Christ Episcopal Church Burial Ground in Philadelphia. It was estimated that half the population of Philadelphia attended his funeral.

Franklin Court

As you walk the sidewalk on Market Street between Third and Fourth Streets in Philadelphia's historic district, you pass five brick row houses, three of which were originally built by Benjamin Franklin. A carriageway

An architectural outline of Franklin's house at Franklin Court. PHOTO BY THE AUTHORS

Visiting Franklin Court

Market Street, between Third and Fourth Streets, Philadelphia, PA

PHONE: 215-597-8974

WEBSITE: www.nps.gov/inde

ADMINISTRATION: National Park Service.

HOURS: Open daily, 10–5, except some national holidays.

ADMISSION FEES: Free admission.

TOURS: Self-guided, but rangers are available on site for further information.

TIME NEEDED: 2 hours to visit Franklin Court; 1 or 2 days to visit all the sites at Independence National Historical Park.

SPECIAL EVENTS: Public reading of Declaration of Independence at Independence Square on July 8. Exhibits and events scheduled throughout the year.

SPECIAL CONSIDERATIONS: Franklin Court and most sites at Independence National Historical Park are handicapped-accessible. Call 215-597-8974 or 215-597-1785 for the hearing impaired.

PARKING: Underground parking garage at visitors center, Sixth Street between Market and Arch Streets; another parking garage on Second Street between Chestnut and Walnut Streets.

SALES OUTLETS: Museum shops in Franklin Court, Independence Park visitors center, and Pemberton House.

DIRECTIONS: Franklin Court is located in the block between Market and Chestnut Streets and between Third and Fourth Streets in Philadelphia. Independence National Historical Park visitors center is located at Sixth and Market Streets. Southbound on I-95, take Exit 17 and go straight to Second Street; turn left and go two blocks to parking garage. Northbound on I-95, take Exit 22, I-676/Independence Hall. Follow the signs for Sixth Street. Take Sixth Street to Chestnut Street, and turn left. Follow Chestnut Street to Second Street, and turn right into parking garage.

leads beneath the center house to an inner courtyard, where stood the only house Franklin ever owned, now symbolized by a "ghost framework" that outlines its dimensions. Visitors peer through viewing windows to see the original foundation.

There's a lot to see within the replica row houses as well: In a working print shop, a living-history printer demonstrates how Franklin and his fellow printers laboriously turned out newspapers, handbills, posters, and government proclamations. There is a bindery to fashion books and a replica of the office of the *General Advertiser* or *Aurora,* a daily newspaper published at this site by Franklin's grandson, Benjamin Franklin Bache.

An active U.S. Post Office offers a unique stamp cancellation and a postal history museum. An exhibit showing the stripped-down interior of one building discloses how architects can "read" a historic building. It is a unique way to learn the story of a neighborhood from the artifacts archeologists have unearthed. A nearby gift shop carries items related to colonial America.

Beneath the courtyard and the ghost framework is a contemporary underground museum that reflects the ingenuity of the man it honors. Featured are Franklin family portraits; some of his inventions, such as a Franklin stove, a long arm to reach books high on a shelf, and an armonica; a film and a diorama; and exhibits on Franklin's contributions to printing, politics, and science.

Two blocks away, at the Christ Church Burial Ground at Fifth and Arch Streets, is the burial place of Benjamin Franklin and other early notables.

Joseph Priestley

(1733-1804)

Joseph Priestley, who gained fame as the discoverer of oxygen and other contributions to chemistry, was even better known in his own time as a clergyman, outspoken theologian, and independent thinker.

This man of multiple talents was difficult to define. He was a minister who broke with the established Church of England and helped form the first Unitarian church in America. He was a talented educator and linguist who taught history and languages to private-school students. He was a venturesome scientist who identified oxygen and isolated eight other gases. He was also a controversial public figure who incited such strong political passions that an angry mob once burned his house to the ground and destroyed his scientific papers. Although he spent the last ten years of his life in Pennsylvania, he remained a staunch Englishman who felt at liberty to strenuously agree with or criticize the policies of his adopted country.

Priestley was born in 1733, the son of a cloth dresser, in Yorkshire in the British midlands. His mother later died in childbirth when he was six, and he was adopted and raised by his father's eldest sister. Since he tended to stammer, he often sought comfort and refuge in books. A precocious child, he mastered Latin and elements of Greek at an early age and later studied Hebrew with a Congregational minister. He taught himself French, Italian, and Dutch, as well as rudiments of several other languages.

After three years at Daventry Academy, known for its liberal, nonconformist teachings, he embarked on a career as a minister in 1755 with strong ideas of his own. He was not ordained, however, until 1762. For religion to survive in an enlightened age, he believed, it was essential to distinguish those elements of Christianity that were consistent with reason and logic from those statements of faith and doctrine that he believed were vestiges of earlier and less progressive times. He encouraged his contemporaries to scrutinize the history of Christianity and the scriptures. He was known as a "dissenter," one who did not conform to the Church of England, which at that time was the only authorized church in the country.

Priestley, who had little knowledge of science, began in his early thirties to learn more about the subject. To supplement his income as a minister, he opened a school and, among other subjects, shared his knowledge of science, in which he had begun to experiment. By 1752, the young Priestley had discussed his scientific ideas with Benjamin Franklin, who at that time was on an assignment in London. On the recommendation of Franklin and others, he was made a fellow of the Royal Society in 1766. The following year, he published his first notable report on his scientific inquiries, *The History and Present State of Electricity, with Original Experiments,* a book that summarized the knowledge of electricity to that point and was widely read.

Later, he accepted a better-paying position as a tutor of languages at Warrington Academy, a private school where, on his own, he continued to experiment with electricity and gases and published several books. He also found time to court and marry Mary Wilkinson in 1762, and they later had three sons and one daughter.

In 1767, Priestley returned to the ministry, this time at Leeds, near where he had grown up. He would fulfill preaching tasks at church and then dive into his scientific experiments at home. He saw no contradiction in these two endeavors. "The humblest growing things to the greatest works of man are merely manifestations of the all-embracing power of God," he said.

It was partly to have more time to pursue his fascination with chemistry that in 1773 he again left the ministry. For the next seven years, he served as historian, traveling companion, tutor, and confidant in the household of the powerful and liberal Sir William Petty, second earl of Shelburne. The earl encouraged his protégé's experiments, which involved combining different substances to produce various gases. The leisure that this position gave Priestley allowed him to make his most notable contributions to science. It was in 1774 that Priestley first isolated eight gases and identified oxygen, a "flammable air" he called "dephlogisticated air." The gas was given its

Joseph Priestley, c. 1801, by Rembrandt Peale. ARCHIVES AND SPECIAL COLLECTIONS, DICKINSON COLLEGE, CARLISLE, PENNSYLVANIA

accepted name "oxygene" by Antoine Lavoisier, a French scientist, who was investigating its properties at the same time. In these days of fruitful intellectual activity, Priestley also formulated and described the basic process involved in photosynthesis in plants.

He had great powers of concentration. Much of his writing was done in the evening, "in the parlour before the fire," with his wife and children conversing around him. He could chat and write at the same time without losing his concentration.

In 1780, Priestley again returned to the ministry, at a church in Birmingham, England. While there, his outspoken views on the separation of church and state and his defense of the French Revolution, which had violently overthrown the French monarchy, earned him a reputation among many people as a subversive. In 1791, a mob, whipped to a frenzy to "defend church and king," set fire to his home and laboratory, his meetinghouse, and the homes of other dissenters. They destroyed most of Priestley's scientific papers, and drove the "traitor" and his family out of town and eventually out of his native England.

After the British declared war on France in 1793, public anger against friends of the French Revolution intensified. Priestley faced threats to his life. His three sons, realizing that career opportunities might be closed to them in England because of their father's reputation, emigrated to America that year. The next year, at age sixty-one, Priestley and his wife followed, joining other English immigrants to Pennsylvania. Here they attempted to organize a community on a large tract of land between the two main branches of the Susquehanna River, using the small town of Northumberland as their headquarters.

What Priestley hoped would develop into a colony of freethinkers did not evolve, nor did his dream of founding a college in Northumberland. He did, however, build a handsome home in a typically American style, a home that contained a well-equipped laboratory, where he continued his scientific experiments. His library, adjacent to the laboratory, contained no less than sixteen hundred books, one of the largest libraries in the country at that time. During his final ten years, this transplanted scientist-theologian succeeded in identifying carbon monoxide, the last gas he would isolate, and published more than twenty scientific papers.

He also wrote more than a dozen religious works, including his six-volume *History of the Christian Church*. He conducted Sunday services in his home and helped found the first Unitarian church in the United States, located in Philadelphia. He delighted in bringing together persons of very different beliefs and outlooks, demonstrating that people of different convictions could live together in harmony despite their differences.

Strong in his own religious, scientific, and political convictions, he wrote numerous articles of opinion and corresponded with U.S. leaders such as Presidents George Washington, John Adams, and Thomas Jefferson. He never intended to become a U.S. citizen, a fact that, with his pro-French and revolutionary politics, brought him under suspicion as a foreigner under the Alien and Sedition Acts.

His son Henry, who had settled on a nearby farm, died in 1795. His wife, Mary, died in 1796, never seeing the completion of their new house. Joseph Priestley died at home in 1804 and was buried in Northumberland. John Adams

Joseph Priestley House was completed in 1798. Above is Priestley's library as exhibited at the historic site today. PHOTOS BY KYLE R. WEAVER

Visiting Joseph Priestley House

472 Priestley Ave., Northumberland, PA 17857

PHONE: 570-473-9474

WEBSITE: www.phmc.state.pa.us (click on Trail of History)

ADMINISTRATION: Administered by the Pennsylvania Historical and Museum Commission.

HOURS: Open Tuesday–Saturday, 9–5; Sunday, 12–5. Closed Mondays and holidays except Memorial Day, July 4, and Labor Day.

ADMISSION FEES: $3.50 for adults; $3.00 for seniors; $1.50 for children ages 6–12; group rates available.

TOURS: Guided tours hourly.

TIME NEEDED: 1 hour.

SPECIAL EVENTS: "Twelfth Day" is celebrated in January; Commonwealth Charter Day in March; Heritage Day, with chemistry demonstrations, in October; candlelight tours in December. Summer history camp for children ages 6–10.

SPECIAL CONSIDERATIONS: Visitors center is handicapped-accessible, and handicapped parking is provided. Most exhibits are on the first floor of Priestley House, and an illustrated guidebook of second-floor exhibits is available.

PARKING: On-site parking lot and on-street parking.

SALES OUTLETS: Gift shop offers biographical books, pamphlets, and videos about Joseph Priestley. A guidebook, *Joseph Priestly House: Pennsylvania Trail of History Guide,* is on sale at the gift shop or from Stackpole Books, 800-732-3669.

DIRECTIONS: Take U.S. Route 11 into Northumberland north of Sunbury, and follow signs to Joseph Priestley House, which is one block south of Route 11.

publicly mourned the loss of "this learned, indefatigable, most excellent and extraordinary man."

Joseph Priestley House

Begin your visit at the reconstructed 1800 carriage barn and visitor center. As you are guided through the spacious house that Joseph and Mary Priestley built overlooking the Susquehanna River on the raw edge of the American frontier, you can visualize this learned English gentleman, an exile from his homeland, pursuing experiments in a well-equipped laboratory and discussing his religious views with visitors over dinner.

Several pieces on exhibit in the house today were used by the scientist-theologian. They include a microscope that Priestley used to examine plant specimens and a telescope through which he peered at the night sky. You may also view his chessboard, a bracket clock, and his walking cane. He once told a friend that he regretted not having enough years left to become an expert in botany and zoology. His laboratory, which was located at one end of the house, has now been thoroughly researched by archeologists, and there are plans for its restoration and interpretation.

A small brick building at one side of the property was built in 1926 as a library and museum by a group of Penn State chemistry alumni who wanted to preserve the Priestley heritage. The Joseph Priestley House was designated a National Historic Chemical Landmark in 1994; Northumberland was the site of an early meeting that led to the formation of the American Chemical Society.

A historical walking tour of Northumberland describes the beginnings of the town as an Indian hunting and fishing ground and takes the visitor to a number of houses built before 1850, including the Priestley House and the Joseph Priestley Memorial Chapel, built in 1834.

Daniel Boone

(1734-1820)

This courageous frontiersman who led the way for American pioneers eager to make their homestead west of the Appalachian Mountains was born and bred with the independent spirit of the country's early colonial settlers.

Daniel Boone was born in November 1734, the sixth of eleven children on a farm in the backcountry of Oley Valley, near today's city of Reading. His father, Squire Boone, was a blacksmith and weaver, supplementing the family income with subsistence farming. Daniel's schooling was scanty, but the boy didn't mind—he was much more interested in exploring and wandering in the forest, where he could hunt to add to the family's food supply.

Daniel's Quaker grandfather had emigrated from England in 1717, undoubtedly seeking the religious freedom offered by the new colony of Pennsylvania. Now, ironically, it was the Boones' Quaker religion that prompted them to leave Pennsylvania for North Carolina when Daniel was sixteen. First one of Daniel's brothers, then one of his sisters "married out" of the Quaker faith, and the church disciplined the Boones. Rather than apologize and thus redeem himself in the eyes of the church, Squire Boone and his family followed other Pennsylvania settlers looking for less crowded land. They moved south through the Shenandoah Valley to the Yadkin River Valley in northwest North Carolina, just east of the Appalachians. In this way he not only avoided the church controversy, but also found cheaper land for farming.

By 1755, war was brewing between the French, who claimed the Ohio River Valley for their fur trade, and the English, who had settled along the eastern seaboard but wanted to spread westward. To push the French out of the territory, British major general Edward Braddock launched an attack against the French-held Fort Duquesne, a strongpoint that stood at the strategic river location where Pittsburgh stands today. The twenty-one-year-old Daniel Boone hired on with Braddock's troops as a wagon driver. A fellow driver was John Finley, who had returned from a trading venture with Indians in Kentucky. Finley filled Boone with visions of a land rich

Daniel Boone, 1820, by Chester Harding. MASSACHUSETTS HISTORICAL SOCIETY (NEG. 386)

beyond measure in buffalo, deer, bear, geese, and turkeys—a strong attraction for any hunter. What's more, the commissary officer for the troops was Dr. Thomas Walker, who in 1750 had been the first-known white man to find his way through the Cumberland Gap, one of the few feasible routes to transect the forbidding Appalachians. When the overconfident Braddock and his soldiers were ambushed at the Battle of Monongahela and soundly defeated by the French-led Indians, Boone and others in the supply section, well behind the troops, escaped the ensuing slaughter.

Back in North Carolina, he took up hunting, selling the hides of deer and other animals shot with his flintlock rifle. At age twenty-one, he married the seventeen-year-old Rebecca Bryan. In their fifty-seven years of married life, she bore him ten children and raised nine of them in one or another of the dirt-floored cabins in which the family lived. By the late 1760s, Boone, with his many forays of exploration, probably knew the Blue Ridge and eastern Appalachian Mountains as well as any man, but he still dreamed of Kentucky and its untapped wonders. In the winter of 1768–69, his old friend John Finley found his way to Boone's North Carolina home, and the following spring, Boone, Finley, and several others took off into the Kentucky wilderness on a two-year hunting and exploration expedition.

Finally, in 1773, Boone attempted to lead a group of settlers into the Kentucky country—a movement that had to be kept secret because the British king, through the Proclamation Act, had declared it illegal for any white man to settle west of the Appalachians. Hostile Shawnee Indians attacked the pack train filled with household goods and its herd of cattle, scattering the adventurers and killing Boone's eldest son, James, and two of his companions. Frightened and disheartened, the settlers turned back.

Two years later, with British attention diverted by the looming Revolutionary War, Boone tried again. Starting from what is now Kingsport, Tennessee, he led the settlers of the Transylvania Company through the Cumberland Gap and into Kentucky where the rivers run northward. To get the wagons through, Boone and his hardy backwoodsmen hacked out what became the famed Wilderness Road, a rough route that would later allow other land-hungry pioneers to reach the fertile Kentucky lands. But the Transylvania migration came with a heavy price: Two men were killed and one was wounded by Shawnee Indians intent on stopping the white settlers.

Finally, after traversing 250 miles in three weeks, the pioneers arrived at a site on the banks of the Kentucky River. In tribute to Daniel Boone, the road cutters named their new Kentucky settlement Boonesborough, a name it still bears today, though it is now spelled Boonesboro. It lay on the south side of the river, a level, grassy area backed by forest-covered hills. The men watched a herd of nearly three hundred buffalo milling around a salt lick, "a sight," Boone said, "that some of us never saw before, nor perhaps may never again." Here they built cabins and erected a stockade to protect the settlement that seemed to be on the edge of nowhere.

Boone and his new settlement were soon caught up in the rebellion of the American colonists against the British. The British armed many of the Indians, encouraging them to attack the frontier settlers. Indians stole two hundred of the Boonesborough horses in a year and scattered or killed many cattle, leaving the settlers feeling even more isolated and starved for food.

In 1778, Boone was captured by British-allied Shawnee, who held him captive in Ohio. Using his comprehensive knowledge of Indian ways, however, he was able to outwit his captors and escape. Making his way back to Boonesborough, he led an almost miraculous defense of the village and fort against an attack by a superior force of some 450 Indians. The attackers finally gave up trying to conquer the settlement and retreated. For this courageous defense, Boone was promoted to major in the militia. He continued to lead American militiamen on the frontier during the remainder of the Revolutionary War, losing one of his brothers and another son in the fighting. Sadly, he wrote at the time, Kentucky was now full of the "freshly widowed and orphaned."

In the following years, Daniel Boone kept his family on the move. They lived for a time in Limestone, Kentucky, today's Maysville, where he prospered as an innkeeper, surveyor, and trader in furs, hides, and ginseng. Later the family lived at Point Pleasant, where Boone served as a representative to the Virginia General Assembly, to which he had first been elected in 1780. Kentucky at that time was still part of Virginia and did not become a separate state until 1792. Although he became a large landowner, he later lost most of his property to unscrupulous land speculators and lawyers.

In 1799, he led one last westward migration of settlers down the Ohio and Mississippi Rivers to the vicinity of St. Louis, homesteading on land that at the time was claimed by Spain. Boone's bubble burst in 1803 with the Louisiana Purchase. Spain had ceded the territory to the French, who in turn sold it to the young United States. A U.S. commission ruled that Boone's land title was illegal, and he, along with scores of other property owners, was stripped of his holdings.

To the end of his days, he hunted and trapped in the empty western reaches—some say he went as far west as the Yellowstone country. He died at age eighty-five at the home of his youngest son, Nathan, near Defiance, Missouri, in a stone house that may be visited by the public today. Although originally buried in Missouri, he now rests in the Frankfort Cemetery, where a monument marks his grave in Frankfort, Kentucky.

Daniel Boone was once asked if during his daring, solitary explorations he wasn't fearful. He is said to have replied: "Sure am. . . . I wouldn't give a hoot for a man who isn't sometimes afraid. But fear's the spice that makes it interesting to go ahead."

Daniel Boone Homestead

If Daniel Boone were somehow able to revisit his old homestead, he undoubtedly would be pleased with the number of young people, including Boy Scouts, who still roam the surrounding woods as he did. Each year, hundreds of young people learn woodcraft skills on the 579 acres of land preserved at the historic site, eating their meals and bunking at Wayside Lodge, which was built on the property.

But he might not recognize the home where he was born. The one-room log house built by his father in 1730 was later renovated into a two-story stone structure, part of it built on the foundation of the original log house. The front door leads visitors into the kitchen, with its large fire-

The house at Daniel Boone Homestead began as a one-room log structure in 1730 and was renovated, possibly by the Boones, with a two-story stone-house addition around 1750. A subsequent owner replaced the Boones' log house with a two-story stone structure by 1779. PHOTO BY KYLE R. WEAVER

place, then into the parlor. A second parlor and a small bedroom occupy the interior of the original log house. Three bedrooms fill the second floor, one bedroom exhibiting a loom of the type Squire Boone would have used as a weaver. The original cellar remains, enclosing a spring that in earlier times refrigerated the family's perishable food.

A nearby barn holds a variety of farm animals, including horses, sheep, and chickens, and provides a setting for hands-on activities for school groups. Demonstrations are given occasionally at a reconstructed blacksmith shop. A stone smokehouse stands close by.

Visiting Daniel Boone Homestead

400 Daniel Boone Rd., Birdsboro, PA 19508

PHONE: 610-582-4900

WEBSITE: www.berksweb.com.state.pa.us

ADMINISTRATION: Administered by the Pennsylvania Historical and Museum Commission, with support from the Friends of Daniel Boone Homestead.

HOURS: Tuesday–Saturday, 9–5; Sunday, 12–5. Closed Mondays. Open most holidays.

ADMISSION FEES: $4 for adults; $2 for children ages 6–12; $3.50 for seniors; $10 for a family; free for children under 5.

TOURS: Guided tours of the Boone House (extra admission fee); self-guided tour of outbuildings. School programs are available, including hands-on activities of Colonial life.

TIME NEEDED: 2 hours for house tour, video, and grounds. Allow extra time for hiking or picnicking.

SPECIAL EVENTS: Charter Day in March; Heritage Day in October; Daniel Boone birthday celebration in November. Encampments, living-history events, and seminars throughout year. Group camping for organized youth groups at Wayside Lodge or in tents.

SPECIAL CONSIDERATIONS: Visitors center is handicapped-accessible, and a video tour is available of the second floor of the Boone House. Call to discuss special needs.

PARKING: Parking adjacent to visitors center.

SALES OUTLETS: Museum shop offers guidebooks, biographies, books, and videos. A guidebook, *Daniel Boone Homestead: Pennsylvania Trail of History,* is on sale at the musuem shop or from Stackpole Books, 800-732-3669.

DIRECTIONS: Take U.S. Route 422 to Daniel Boone Road, halfway between Reading and Pottstown (about 10 miles from each). Follow Daniel Boone Road 1 mile north to site.

Below the foundation of the original Boone log house is a cellar and spring. PHOTO BY CRAIG A. BENNER

Four additional eighteenth-century structures have been added to the grounds as a way of preserving these historic buildings. The Bertolet House, an early Pennsylvania Dutch log house, was brought to the historic site, along with its bakehouse, smokehouse, and a water-powered, vertical-blade sawmill built around 1810. A network of equestrian and walking trails encircles the grounds.

At the visitors center, you may view a fifteen-minute video that portrays Boone's early life, see exhibits of pioneer artifacts, purchase tickets for the guided tour of the homestead, and browse among a selection of historical books.

An additional site recognizing Daniel Boone lies farther east of the Boone homestead, near Lansdale, in Montgomery County. This restored log house was built in 1695 by Edward and Elizabeth Morgan, Boone's grandparents. They had a family of ten children, including Sarah, who married Squire Boone. The Morgan Log House is open Saturday and Sunday, 12 to 5, April through December, and is located two miles east of Exit 31 (Lansdale) of the Northeast Extension of the Pennsylvania Turnpike.

Charles Willson Peale

(1741-1827)

Known to history as the American artist who best portrayed the Revolutionary leaders of the infant United States, Charles Willson Peale was an accomplished enthusiast of many pursuits. At one time or another, he was a saddler, clock repairman, portrait painter, soldier, museum curator, taxidermist, politician, archeologist, farmer, educator, inventor, and dental technician. In his autobiography, he acknowledged that he had "strayed a thousand ways" during his lifetime, but he was quick to point out that this variety of skills had contributed to his happiness. Peale truly reflected the era in which he lived, the Age of Enlightenment, when men searched diligently for knowledge that would improve their well-being as well as that of others.

Another key to Peale's career is the help he received from others at critical times. Born in 1741 in Annapolis, Maryland, the eldest son of the headmaster of a private school, Charles Willson Peale's formal education ceased at age thirteen, after his father's untimely death. Apprenticed to a saddler, he scraped together enough money after seven years to set up a saddlery shop of his own and to marry Rachel Brewer, the daughter of a family of planters and merchants whose patronage later proved useful. After seeing a collection of portraits on a trip to Norfolk, he decided he could do just as well. He began by painting commercial signs, then a few portraits of his family. But times were hard, the Peales fell into debt, and by 1765, they had to flee from Annapolis to avoid their creditors.

To earn some money, he shipped aboard a vessel owned by his brother-in-law on a voyage to Boston—a stroke of luck, as it turned out. For in Boston, he met the young but accomplished portrait painter John Singleton Copley, who allowed Peale to work with him and learn his techniques. But earning a living from his portraits remained a problem for Peale, who realized he could never compete successfully with Copley in Boston. So he arranged for free passage on a ship back to Virginia. When the ship docked, a wealthy plantation owner came aboard and admired a miniature self-portrait Peale had painted. From this chance encounter grew a six-month commission to stay at the plantation and paint portraits of the planter and his family. When he was finally able to return to Annapolis and be reunited with Rachel, he paid off some of his debts and greeted a new baby son who had been born while he was away.

Now came another fortuitous event in Peale's career. A former student of his father's persuaded a group of Maryland leaders, including the governor, to raise money so that the promising young artist could receive further training in Europe. Thus he joined the well-known expatriate American painter Benjamin West in London. Here the eager Peale attended informal life classes, drew from casts, visited the studios of the most eminent British portraitists, and worked

Charles Willson Peale, c.1795, self-portrait.
INDEPENDENCE NATIONAL HISTORICAL PARK

in various media offered for instruction—oils, miniatures, sculpture, and engraving. His first full-length allegorical portrait was of William Pitt, the English statesman who had championed the repeal of the Stamp Act, which had been so unpopular in the American colonies. These two years of hard work in London laid the groundwork for Peale's future success, and in 1769, he returned to Annapolis, now recognized as a sophisticated and skillful portraitist.

Peale painted portraits of many notables, including a forty-year-old colonel of the Virginia militia—the only known portrait of George Washington to be painted before the American Revolution. In future years, Peale painted at least sixty portraits of Washington, and more than one thousand portraits in all.

In June 1776, on the eve of the Revolution, Peale moved his family to Philadelphia in anticipation of increased patronage from visitors and delegates to the new government that was being forged in the city. Long a member of the Sons of Liberty, who advocated full separation of America from England, he now joined the Pennsylvania militia as a "common soldier." He was soon promoted to lieutenant, then to captain. During the dark days of the Revolution, he fought at the Battle of Princeton, which followed Washington's surprise victory at Trenton. In the lulls between campaigns and during the long winter at Valley Forge, the soldier-painter pulled out his palette and painted miniatures of some of his fellow officers. These battlefield portraits and miniatures that Peale did during his army days are the only life portraits that exist of some of the country's early military and political figures.

After the war, he became active in the politics of the new nation and was elected to the Pennsylvania General Assembly, but he later abandoned public life to concentrate on his artistic career. In the next three years, he painted some of his finest portraits, many of them "conversation pieces" in which details in the background of a painting symbolized events of the subject's life.

Peale now exhibited his talents as a showman. He built the first picture gallery in America in his home—and the first to have a skylight. To celebrate the peace treaty with England, the Pennsylvania General Assembly appointed "the ingenious Captain Peale" to erect a triumphal arch in Philadelphia, which was decorated with illuminated paintings. Next he unveiled an even more ambitious project—the first scientifically organized museum of natural history open to the public. Benjamin Franklin encouraged Peale's efforts, and George Washington contributed a pair of golden pheasants to the open-air zoo that was part of the project. Other animals, some of them brought from foreign lands by sea captains, were added to the zoo or preserved as specimens. Peale displayed the stuffed animals in their native habitats by painting an appropriate background for each exhibit. He even traveled to the state of New York to unearth the skeleton of a prehistoric mastodon, whose bones he assembled and added to the museum, a feat that earned him a reputation as a paleontologist. In addition, he executed a memorable painting of his mastodon project, which was a major scientific event. Ironically, his museum brought him more financial success than his paintings ever did.

Peale was always a devoted father and thrived on a close family life. He was married three times and fathered seventeen children. His first wife, Rachel, died of tuberculosis at age forty-one, and wives Elizabeth and Hannah also predeceased him. Eleven children lived to adulthood. Four of his sons were named for famous painters, and Raphael and Rembrandt Peale both grew to be painters in their own right. Unlike many people of his day, he believed that daughters as well as sons should be educated. Women were just as capable of great accomplishments as men, he stated, provided they were not confined to "affairs which allow no time for them to devote to the arduous pursuits of science."

At age sixty-nine, this man-of-all-trades decided to become a farmer. He bought a hundred-acre farm near Germantown, where he grew vegetables and grain for market, maintained a dairy herd, and produced a prized currant wine. But soon decorative gardening caught his fancy, and he energetically created a formal garden so elaborate that flocks of people came out from Philadelphia on Sundays to see it.

Later, Peale sold the farm and moved back to the city. In a last burst of artistic energy, he spent four months in the new capital city of Washington, painting portraits of President James Monroe and other political figures. He died at age eighty-six, unable to recover from a physically exhausting trip to New York City during which he failed to woo a lady to become his fourth wife. He is buried in the churchyard of St. Peter's Episcopal Church at Third and Pine Streets, only blocks from the house at Third and Lombard Streets where he opened his first gallery.

Peale Collection, Second Bank of the United States

What Matthew Brady did a century later, when he photographed many of the leaders of the Civil War, Charles Willson Peale did in paintings for the Revolutionary War period. Were it not for Peale's paintings, we would

The Second Bank of the United States at Independence National Historical Park houses a remarkable collection of Charles Willson Peale portraits of Revolutionary War figures.
INDEPENDENCE NATIONAL HISTORICAL PARK

Visiting Second Bank of the United States

Chestnut Street between Fourth and Fifth Streets, Philadelphia, PA

PHONE: 215-597-8974

WEBSITE: www.nps.gov/inde

ADMINISTRATION: National Park Service.

HOURS: Park visitors center open daily, 8–5, except some national holidays; Second Bank open 10–3.

ADMISSION FEES: $3 for adults; free for youths under 17.

TOURS: Self-guided, but rangers are available on site for further information.

TIME NEEDED: 1 hour to visit Portrait Gallery in Second Bank; 1 or 2 days to visit all the sites at Independence National Historical Park.

SPECIAL EVENTS: Public reading of Declaration of Independence at Independence Square on July 8. Special exhibits and events throughout the year.

SPECIAL CONSIDERATIONS: Entrance to Second Bank requires climbing a flight of marble steps. Most other sites at Independence National Historical Park are handicapped-accessible. Call 215-597-8974 or 215-597-1785 (TTY) for hearing impaired.

PARKING: Underground parking on Sixth Street between Arch and Market Streets. Another parking garage is on Second Street between Chestnut and Walnut Streets.

SALES OUTLETS: Museum shops are located in Franklin Court, Independence National Historical Park visitors center, and Pemberton House.

DIRECTIONS: The Second Bank of the United States is on Chestnut Street between Fourth and Fifth Streets in Philadelphia. Independence National Historical Park Visitor Center is located at Sixth and Market Streets. Southbound on I-95, take Exit 22. Turn right on Callowhill Street, then turn left on Sixth Street; garage entrance is on left, just past Arch Street. Northbound on I-95, take Exit 22, I-676/Independence Hall. Continue straight on Callowhill Street then turn left on Sixth Street; garage entrance is on left, just past Arch Street.

have little visual record of the colonial and federal leaders who fought to gain independence for the new United States.

Many of these historic portraits are gathered together and preserved in a portrait gallery in the Second Bank of the United States at Independence National Historical Park, in an exhibit called "Faces of Independence." Browsing through the carpeted gallery, you will see portraits by Charles Willson Peale as well as by other painters of the period, including his son, Rembrandt Peale, and James Sharples. The marble building where the gallery is housed is one of the finest examples of Greek Revival architecture in America and was designed by William Strickland to resemble the Parthenon in Athens.

The core of the Second Bank collection came from the gallery Peale installed in his home and from the museum he established in 1782 in the Long Room of Independence Hall, then known as the Pennsylvania State House. When you take the public tour of Independence Hall today, the National Park Service guide will show you the Long Room on the second floor, where Peale once had his museum of animal and plant specimens.

Anthony Wayne

(1748-96)

Anthony Wayne's lifelong career as a fighting soldier may have been foreshadowed by an incident as a schoolboy. Wayne rounded up a number of his classmates one day at school and staged a mock battle reenacting the recent capture by the British of Fort Ticonderoga in New England. For this unauthorized escapade, he was roundly disciplined, but his future appears to have been predestined.

He was born in 1745, the only son of Isaac and Elizabeth Iddings Wayne on the family farm, Waynesborough, built by his grandfather in Chester County about twenty miles from Philadelphia. In addition to farming, his father also operated a tannery.

After finishing his schooling at the College of Philadelphia, he took a job as a surveyor working for a group of land speculators who were promoting the settlement of a colony in Nova Scotia. He returned home briefly to marry Mary (Polly) Penrose, the daughter of a Philadelphia merchant. The colony, however, failed within a year.

For the next ten years, he and his father operated the family farm and tannery. By then, Anthony and Polly had two children—a daughter, Margaretta, and a son, Isaac. These years marked a time of growing opposition among the colonists to Britain's policies of increased taxation and restrictions on trade. Anthony Wayne was outspoken in his opposition to the oppressive British taxes. An early patriot, he organized a Committee of Safety in Chester County and in 1775 was elected to the Pennsylvania General Assembly. In 1776, after hostilities had broken out and Congress ordered the formation of a Continental Army, Wayne was made a colonel in charge of one of four Pennsylvania battalions. His military career as a soldier had begun.

After an unsuccessful expedition to the St. Lawrence River, where his force was beaten back by the British, he spent the winter of 1776 as commander of Fort Ticonderoga, now in American hands, the very place where he had visualized himself years earlier as a schoolboy.

Reassigned by Gen. George Washington and promoted to brigadier general, this "troubleshooter of the American Revolution" and his well-trained Pennsylvanians fought in most of the major engagements of the next year, including skirmishes in New Jersey and the Battle of Brandywine. His troops were massacred by a British force at Paoli in September 1777, an attack that resulted in fifty-three men killed and about one hundred wounded.

For this he was severely criticized. To clear his name, he requested a trial by court-martial, which exonerated him. To make matters worse, the British also searched his nearby Waynesborough homestead, kidnapping "poor Robert and James," probably indentured family servants. Although the British could have burned the house as well, they restrained themselves and "acted as gentlemen," according to his wife Polly.

After the Battle of Germantown, he and his men joined those who encamped at Valley Forge for the winter that "tried men's souls," then fought in the Battle of Monmouth in New Jersey the following year.

In the spring of 1779, Wayne was placed in command of a separate light infantry corps formed of hand-picked units from several states. He later earned the nickname "Mad Anthony" for his bold, swift actions and quick temper. Now, with this corps, he carried out an extraordinary exploit—the surprise capture of the British post at Stony Point, an almost inaccessible strong point on the Hudson River. His troops captured the

"impregnable" fort by wading across a sandbar, climbing uphill through a tangle of underbrush, and chopping their way through three rows of redoubts. Forcing their way in, Wayne's men killed twenty redcoats and wounded seventy-four in the fierce fighting, all by bayonet. The Americans lost fifteen men, with eighty more wounded, including Wayne, who had to be carried into the conquered fort. They took 472 prisoners and captured fifteen cannons and stacks of military stores. Wayne reported to Washington that "our officers & Men behaved like men who are determined to be free." Congress presented Wayne with a medal for this unexpected victory, which gave new heart to the American army.

Anthony Wayne, 1796, by James Sharples Sr.
INDEPENDENCE NATIONAL HISTORICAL PARK

When the Continental Army general Benedict Arnold turned traitor and there was danger that West Point might fall to the British, Wayne marched his men sixteen miles at night over mountainous roads in four hours to prevent the loss of this important post.

In Virginia in 1781, Wayne executed another daring battlefield maneuver. When his force of eight hundred men was drawn into a trap and faced with some five thousand British soldiers, instead of retreating, he ordered an attack. This unexpected move confused the superior British force, allowing the Americans to escape the field before they could be overwhelmed. The surrender of Cornwallis and his troops at Yorktown came soon afterward, on October 19, 1781.

The resulting treaty of peace with Great Britain in 1783 left the actual establishment of U.S. authority over the western lands as unfinished business. By provisions of the treaty, the territory south of the Great Lakes was ceded to the United States. It was actually held by unfriendly Indians, however, whom the British encouraged to resist the advance of American settlers. Their hope was to create an Indian buffer state between the United States and Canada. The United States tried to bring these Indians under control and open the Northwest Territory to settlement, first by peaceful means through treaties, and later by military expeditions. But these efforts finally collapsed in 1791, when an army under Gen. Arthur St. Clair was defeated by the Indians.

President George Washington now called on Anthony Wayne to command a new American army, called the Legion of the United States, to force the Indians out of the Northwest Territory. Wayne set up a training camp at Legionville, now present-day Ambridge, near Pittsburgh, and drilled and trained his soldiers into a reliable and effective force. When his army was ready, he advanced slowly, building roads and forts, making sure of his supplies, and sending out scouts. The next summer, he advanced into the heart of the hostile territory, building more forts.

About fifteen miles up the Maumee River from present-day Toledo, Ohio, Wayne's army finally met the main force of the Indians not far from the British post at Fort Miami. He then defeated them in the Battle of Fallen Timbers in August 1794. This battle, together with the British refusal to help their Native American allies, led to the submission of the Indians, an outcome that was confirmed by the Treaty of Greenville, signed in August 1795. Now the entire Northwest Territory—today's states of Ohio, Indiana, Illinois, Wisconsin, and Michigan—lay open to eager American settlers.

On his return from an inspection visit to Detroit, Wayne landed at the Pennsylvania fort at Presque Isle, now Erie. There he fell ill and died on December 15, 1796. He was buried at the foot of the flagpole of the fort, but in 1809, his son removed his bones and returned them home to the family burial plot at Old St. David's Episcopal Church near Waynesborough. A replica of the original fort blockhouse today stands on the site of his first grave on the grounds of the Pennsylvania Soldiers and Sailors Home at Erie.

Historic Waynesborough

When you visit Waynesborough today, you tour the house where Anthony Wayne grew up, the same stone house that became his home shortly before the death of his father. Now the stately mansion, designated a National Historic Landmark, reflects 242 years of ownership and seven generations of Waynes who have resided there. It displays the results of several

Visiting Historic Waynesborough

2049 Waynesborough Rd., P.O. Box 433, Paoli, PA 19301

PHONE: 610-647-1779

WEBSITE: www.madanthonywayne.org

ADMINISTRATION: Owned by Easttown Township and maintained as a park. House administered by the Philadelphia Society for the Preservation of Landmarks and supported by the Anthony Wayne Foundation.

HOURS: Mid-March through December 31, Tuesdays and Thursdays, 10–4; Sundays, 1–4. Closed major holidays.

ADMISSION FEES: $5 for adults; $4 for students and seniors; $3 each for groups with advance reservations.

TOURS: School and group tours with tour guides available with reservations.

TIME NEEDED: At least 1 hour.

SPECIAL EVENTS: December greens sale; spring lecture series.

SPECIAL CONSIDERATIONS: Ground-level access to first floor and carriage house; stairs to second floor.

PARKING: Free on-site parking.

SALES OUTLETS: Gift shop in carriage house offers historical books, maps, craft and children's items.

DIRECTIONS: From Pennsylvania Turnpike, take Exit 24, Valley Forge. Take U.S. Route 202 South to PA Route 252. Follow Route 252 South to Waynesborough Road. Turn right and follow 0.3 mile to site on right. Waynesborough is 4.3 miles from Pennsylvania Turnpike.

Waynesborough was built in 1745 as the home of Anthony Wayne's parents. Seven generations of Waynes, including the general, have lived in the house. PHOTO BY THE AUTHORS

additions to the original 1745 house. Inside, the rooms are furnished to reflect the different time periods of their use, from the eighteenth century of Gen. Anthony Wayne to the Colonial Revival style of later members of the Wayne family. Remarkably, most of the furnishings in the parlor are original pieces used by Anthony and Polly Wayne and their family.

The carriage house on the sixteen-acre estate has been converted to a visitors center and gift shop. A slide show recounts the life of Anthony Wayne and introduces visitors to the house. A chronology of the general's career is displayed nearby.

Original deeds to land grants from the Penn family, the proprietors of Pennsylvania, and the commission appointing General Wayne commander-in-chief of the Legion of the United States, which was signed by President George Washington, decorate the walls of an exhibit room. A uniform coat owned by Wayne is also on display.

Volunteers cultivate a garden just outside the kitchen door. A meeting room and picnic area are also available.

Anthony Wayne is buried a mile away, in the Wayne family plot in the churchyard of the historic 1715 St. David's Episcopal Church in Radnor. His name lives on in history as a county in Pennsylvania and fourteen other states; the towns of Wayne, Waynesboro, and Waynesburg; nine Pennsylvania townships; and Fort Wayne, Indiana.

Stephen Girard

(1750-1831)

Apivotal point in the life of Stephen Girard came on the eve of the American Revolution when, as a French sea captain, he sailed from Martinique to New York. He was forced to put into Philadelphia because of stormy weather, lack of drinking water for his crew, and the threat of lurking British warships.

To repair the storm damage to his ship and avoid the risk of capture by the British Navy, he decided to stay in Philadelphia. In June 1776, he opened a store on the waterfront to sell his cargo and kegs of claret he had imported from France. It was scarcely a month before the resentments boiling up in the colonies provoked the Declaration of Independence, which was read to the public at the Pennsylvania State House, just a few blocks away from Girard's store. The Frenchman, who was sympathetic with the rebels, found himself caught up in the American war with England.

Stephen Girard had been born in Bordeaux, France, the eldest son of a French naval officer. At age fourteen, he had rebelled against his father and was sent to sea as a cabin boy, sailing on several voyages between France and the West Indies. By the age of twenty-three, he had become fully licensed as a ship's captain, although he had sight in only one eye. His first job was as a "supercargo," or trading agent, on a voyage to Santo Domingo in the West Indies, but he left the ship to stay behind and sell the cargo at a higher price. Later he shipped out as first mate aboard a ship bound for New York, where he joined two merchants to form an import-export business with the West Indies. It was in 1776 on the stormy return trip from Martinique that his ship sailed into Philadelphia, then the largest city in the colonies and its busiest trading port.

When the formidable British Army captured Philadelphia in the early stages of the war, Girard and his new wife, Mary, whom he had met in the city, fled to New Jersey. When the British left the city the following year, he returned and took the oath of allegiance to the state of Pennsylvania in order to become a citizen. He and his two partners sold their storm-battered ship, bought another, and resumed a shipping business to the West Indies.

Stephen Girard, 1832, by Bass Otis. STEPHEN GIRARY COLLECTION, GIRARD COLLEGE, PHILADELPHIA

Over the next years, he phased out his partnership and expanded his commerce to Europe and Asia, despite the risk of threatened seizure of his ship in these troubled times of the American Revolution, the French Revolution, and the Napoleonic Wars. Now operating on his own, Girard built his shipping business with hard work, sharp-eyed transactions, and by plowing his profits into improved ships, crews, and cargoes. "To rest is to rust," he said, and proved it by working long hours. He gave detailed instructions to his ship captains and held them responsible for profitable results from each voyage. He was constantly buying, selling, or building ships, or leasing cargo space in other ships, maintaining a healthy mix of calculated risk and thoughtful prudence.

But even as his business ventures prospered, his personal life took a tragic turn. His wife became mentally ill and was diagnosed as incurable. Sadly, in 1790, he placed her in Pennsylvania Hospital, where she would live for twenty-five years, dying in 1815. For companionship, he brought the first of three housekeeper-mistresses into his house on the waterfront, each of whom not only devoted herself to him, but also took care of the various children—some related to other members of his family, some not—that he added to his household.

In 1793, another tragedy befell that illustrated the character of Stephen Girard. Philadelphia, then the capital of the new United States, was struck by a yellow fever epidemic, one of the greatest disasters ever experienced by an American city. Most of the government and many citizens fled, and even President George Washington moved temporarily to nearby Germantown. Girard courageously stepped forward, volunteering to remain behind and run a makeshift hospital for the victims. "The deplorable situation to which fright and sickness have reduced the inhabitants of our city," he wrote, "demands succor from those who do not fear death, or who, at least, do not see any risk in the epidemic which prevails here. . . . If I have the misfortune to succumb, I will at least have the satisfaction of having performed a duty which we all owe to each other." After the epidemic finally abated, Girard and sixteen other brave citizens were honored in a ceremony at City Hall for their courage and mercy.

Girard was the first, or among the first, to develop and maintain American trade on a large scale to many parts of the world, including China, India, Russia, and South America. In the years that followed, his commercial trading business grew, even though the young United States had practically no navy to protect its shipping against British and French privateers. The plundering of cargoes on the high seas by pirates operating from the West Indies and along the Barbary Coast of the Mediterranean Sea had become an increasing problem.

Girard appealed strongly to the federal government to find a way to enforce freedom of the seas for vessels in international commerce. He took a keen interest in contemporary politics, playing an active role in the election of Thomas Jefferson and secretly aiding Simon Bolivar in his overthrow of Spanish colonial rule in South America.

The new nation faced its first great test in the War of 1812. Within a year, the federal government found itself in virtual bankruptcy. Girard had earlier bought the First Bank of the United States and reorganized it as the first privately owned bank in the country, after Congress declined to continue it as a national bank. Its purpose, he proclaimed, was to lend money primarily to ordinary people and small businessmen, making loans to persons of modest means to help them get started in business or farming or to acquire a home.

Now the new federal government was desperate. The U.S. Treasury was out of money, and Congress had declared war on Great Britain. There was no money with which to fight the war. Secretary of the Treasury Albert Gallatin needed to borrow $16 million to keep the nation afloat. Wealthy Americans, including John Jacob Astor, had agreed to put up $2 million. Other citizens had subscribed up to $6 million. Gallatin urged Girard, then the wealthiest man in the country, to help as well. Not only did Girard help, but he agreed to put up the entire remainder—$8 million, more than anyone else. Girard, the patriot, was risking his entire fortune plus his future earnings. He was wagering that his country would win the war and be able to repay its debts—at a time when the outlook was bleak.

By 1814, in spite of a British invasion of the mid-Atlantic states, the tide of war shifted, and Britain and the United States negotiated a peace treaty that ended the conflict and brought the United States increased respect in the world. After the war, the federal government paid all its debts, and Girard got his money back from a grateful nation. A few years later, Congress established another national bank, the Second Bank of the United States. At Girard's suggestion, it was located not in the capital city of Washington, D.C., but in Philadelphia.

Stephen Girard spent his remaining years exploring new areas of business enterprise, most notably banking, coal, and railroads. He clearly foresaw the potential of coal as a fuel and railroads as the means to transport the coal to market. He acquired real estate as far away as Louisiana and built homes in Philadelphia to sell to eager buyers. He was the major investor in the Chesapeake and Delaware Canal, which linked the Delaware Bay with the Chesapeake Bay, reducing shipping time between Philadelphia and Baltimore.

As early as 1807, Girard had become a millionaire, possibly the first in the United States. He was no doubt the richest man in America, but his wealth did not seem to change Girard in any substantial way. In 1797, he had bought a farm in what is now South Philadelphia, and in his later years, he went out to the farm on a daily basis, sometimes pitching in to do the hard farm labor. Even at the Bank of Stephen Girard in the city, customers arriving early would sometimes see the owner in shirtsleeves, pruning vines, nursing a fig tree, or trimming the shrubs.

In the last years of his life, he gave increased attention to the disposition of the wealth he had accumulated. Only after his death, which occurred at his waterfront home on December 26, 1831, did the extent of his legacy become known. He left generous bequests to his mistresses, relatives, colleagues, and the city of Philadelphia for civic improvements. And although he had no children of his own, his largest bequest by far—$6 million—went to establish a boarding school for "poor, white, male orphan children," and he also provided the land on which to build it.

Such a school was, in a sense, an extension of what Girard had been doing for much of his life. He had given room and board and an education to his orphaned nieces, to apprentices in his counting house, and to relatives of his mistresses. Although greedy relatives protested the will, the Supreme Court upheld it. A later decision by the Supreme Court, however, modified the will to also allow black male children to attend Girard College, and the school modified its admission standards so that females could enroll as well. Today a majority of Girard's students are African-American, and half of the students are female. Ten of the thirty-seven pages of Stephen Girard's will are devoted to precise specifications for the layout, architecture, curriculum, and administration of the school, and the results can be seen today when you visit Girard College. More than twenty thousand students have been admitted to the school since it opened in 1848—the living legacy of the old sea captain.

Founder's Hall, Girard College

When you visit Girard College in the Fairmount section of Philadelphia, it is like driving into a green oasis in the midst of a crowded cityscape. The campus of this preparatory boarding school educates children from grades one through twelve. It spreads across forty-three acres and is encircled by its original ten-foot-high stone wall. Virtually all of the school's six hundred students come from single- or no-parent, low-income homes and receive full tuition, housing, meals, uniforms, and books. The campus has eighteen major buildings, including classrooms, dormitories, an armory, student activities building, and chapel. Its central structure, built between 1833 and 1847 in accordance with Stephen Girard's plans, is Founder's Hall. Designed by Thomas U. Walter, the architect of the U.S. Capitol and the Chester County, Pennsylvania, courthouse, it is considered one of the finest examples of Greek Revival architecture in the country.

Founder's Hall is the Greek Revival centerpiece of the Girard College campus. The bronze statuary in front represents Girard's determination to establish a school, although he had no children of his own. PHOTO BY THE AUTHORS

Visiting Founder's Hall, Girard College

2101 South College Ave., Philadelphia, PA 19121

PHONE: 215-787-2680
E-MAIL: elaurent@girardcollege.com
WEBSITE: www.girardcollege.com
ADMINISTRATION: Girard College.
HOURS: Thursdays, 10–2, or group tours by appointment.
ADMISSION FEES: Modest fees for individuals and groups.
TOURS: Founder's Hall and the Stephen Girard Collection of silver, china, furniture, ceramics, and paintings.
TIME NEEDED: 1 hour.
SPECIAL EVENTS: None
SPECIAL CONSIDERATIONS: Entrance to Founder's Hall requires climbing a steep flight of marble steps. Call 215-787-2680 to make special arrangements or for assistance.
PARKING: On-site parking.
SALES OUTLETS: Catalog of Girard collection, postcards, and books about construction of the school.
DIRECTIONS TO REACH SITE: From Vine Street Expressway (Route 676), get off onto 22nd Street North. Turn right on Fairmount Avenue, then first left on Corinthian Avenue. Go four blocks to front gate of Girard College.

When you visit, you will be greeted by a guard at the gate and assigned a parking place on the grounds. A guided tour can be arranged to show you through the massive Founder's Hall. The tour takes you to the marble vestibule, which contains a statue of the founder and his sarcophagus. It continues through the expansive board room, where portraits of the school's presidents are displayed, and two second-floor museum rooms that contain a remarkable collection of the personal possessions of the benefactor. Experts say it is the finest intact single-owner collection from early Philadelphia, including antique furniture, silver, ceramics, and paintings—some pieces imported from Asia and Europe. Even the horse-drawn gig that Girard used to travel around town is on display.

Betsy Ross

(1752-1836)

One of the enduring legends growing out of the Revolutionary War for independence from England is the story of the Philadelphia seamstress who, it is said, made the Stars and Stripes, the first flag of the new nation.

The facts, however, historians say, fall somewhat short of the legend. Betsy Ross was born Elizabeth Griscom in Philadelphia, the eighth child of seventeen children of Samuel and Rebecca Griscom, both devoted Quakers. Her father was a skilled carpenter, a member of the Carpenters Company, and a craftsman who helped build the colony of Pennsylvania's state house, later to be better known as Independence Hall.

Betsy was educated at a school for Quaker children, where as a girl she was taught reading, writing, and sewing. Betsy mastered the art of needlework. Further education for Quaker students often involved serving an apprenticeship, so Betsy apprenticed with John Webster, a talented and popular Philadelphia upholsterer. Upholsterers in the eighteenth century made and sold curtains, rugs, bed linens, and other pieces for the home that required sewing.

While working with Webster, Betsy met and fell in love with a fellow apprentice, John Ross, the son of an Anglican clergyman. This presented the young couple with a problem. Marrying outside their own faith was forbidden by the Quakers. When she and John eloped and married in New Jersey in 1773, Betsy was "read out of the meeting" by her church and was disowned at age twenty-one by her family.

Later the couple opened an upholsterer's shop at the Arch Street house that is now preserved as the Betsy Ross House. Scarcely two years later, Ross, a member of the Pennsylvania militia, died from injuries suffered when a supply of gunpowder exploded on a wharf he was patrolling, leaving the young widow on her own.

In these early days of the Revolutionary War, every colony and many military outfits had their own distinctive flag. The nearest thing to a common banner for the fledgling nation was the Grand Union flag, which had seven red and six white stripes. But in the upper left quarter, called the

Birth of Our Nation's Flag, painted by Charles H. Weisgerber c.1892, is a mythical scene of Betsy Ross presenting the flag to George Washington, George Ross, and Robert Morris. THE STATE MUSEUM OF PENNSYLVANIA (GIFT OF CHARLES H. WEISGERBER II AND FAMILY)

canton, this flag carried a replica of the British national flag, or Union Jack—the red cross of St. George, the symbol of England, with the white cross of St. Andrew, the symbol of Scotland. When flown by American ships, this flag was easily confused with the flag of the hated British East India Company.

On May 23, 1776, George Washington, the commander in chief of the Continental Army in the field, arrived in Philadelphia to report to the Second Continental Congress. The story goes that George Ross, a signer of the Declaration of Independence, who was Betsy's late husband's uncle, had suggested Betsy Ross for the job of making a new flag that would unify the colonial armed forces. A committee of three was chosen that included George Ross, Gen. George Washington, and Robert Morris, a prominent merchant later known as the "financier of the Revolution." The three came to her shop with a rough design for the Stars and Stripes, a design that had been created by Francis Hopkinson, another delegate to the Continental Congress.

Betsy, it is related, suggested that instead of the square shape that was common in those days, they make the flag rectangular. She also suggested that they use five-pointed stars instead of six-pointed ones, because a five-pointed one was easier for a seamstress to cut out. The design was based on one stripe for each of the thirteen original colonies, as well as a white star for each colony. The color red stood for valor; white for hope; and blue, the color of heaven, for reverence for God. This was the tale as it was related by Betsy Ross to her grandson many years later, when she was eighty-four years old.

At this same time, history records, the Declaration of Independence was being drafted. It was adopted by the Second Continental Congress on July 4, 1776, and read to the public in Independence Square on July 8. Authoritative historical records also prove that in May 1777, the Pennsylvania State Navy Board paid "Elizabeth Ross" almost fifteen pounds for making "ships colours etc." Furthermore, on June 14, 1777, the Continental Congress adopted a resolution designating the Stars and Stripes design as the national flag, stipulating that "the flag of the United States be thirteen stripes alternate red and white, that the union be thirteen stars in a blue field, representing a new constellation."

Each state was to supply the flags for its own military units. Because the flag resolution had not described the exact design to be used in the canton, other flagmakers varied the arrangement of the stars. They placed the thirteen stars in circles, squares, or rows with the stars having from five to eight points. Some flags had seven red and six white stripes, while others had seven white and six red. Still others had extra stripes or even blue stripes. Many flagmakers even added eagles, scrolls, the number "76," or other symbols of the new nation. Betsy made her flags with the white stars set in a circle in the blue field, a design that came to be known as the "Betsy Ross flag."

After the death of her first husband, Betsy Ross continued to operate the upholsterer's shop. In June 1777, she married Joseph Ashburn, a seagoing man who had turned to the risky business of privateering. The Ashburns had two daughters, Zillah and Elizabeth. Later, the brigantine *Patty,* on which Joseph Ashburn was first mate, was captured at sea by the British, and he was thrown into prison at Plymouth, England, where he died in 1782.

Word of her second husband's death was brought to Betsy Ross by John Claypoole, a lifelong friend who had been in the same prison as Joseph Ashburn in England. After being released from prison, Claypoole returned to America, where he went back to privateering. However, he agreed to give up this chancy venture after a year to marry Betsy and join her in the upholstery business. His military experience soon brought the shop new business repairing tents and making camp beds, cots, knapsacks, and ships' mattresses. During the War of 1812, the Claypooles sold flags to shipping firms, merchants, and military organizations. Stephen Girard, a wealthy Philadelphian whose ships sailed all over the world, was one of their steady customers.

Betsy and John were married for thirty-four years and had five daughters before he fell ill and died in 1817. Betsy taught sewing to her daughters, granddaughters, and nieces, who continued to run the upholstery shop after her death in 1836 at the age of eighty-four.

American Flag House and Betsy Ross Memorial

You walk through the compact row house on Arch Street in Philadelphia that Betsy Ross later shared with another widow and the widow's two grandchildren after John Ross's death. It was in the front room facing the street that she conducted her upholstery business, making window and bed curtains, drapes, and wall hangings. It would have been in the well-

Betsy Ross operated an upholstery business at her 239 Arch Street residence in Philadelphia. PHOTO BY THE AUTHORS

Visiting American Flag House and Betsy Ross Memorial

239 Arch St., Philadelphia, PA 19106

PHONE: 215-686-1252
WEBSITE: www.betsyrosshouse.org
ADMINISTRATION: Betsy Ross House managed by Historic Philadelphia, Inc.
HOURS: April–September, daily, 10–5; October–March, Tuesday–Sunday, 10–5. Open holiday Mondays.
ADMISSION FEES: $2 donation for adults, $1 for children.
TOURS: Self-guided tours.
TIME NEEDED: 30 to 45 minutes.
SPECIAL EVENTS: Short historical performances daily in courtyard from Memorial Day through Labor Day.
SPECIAL CONSIDERATIONS: Site is on several levels with steep stairs.
PARKING: On-street parking.
SALES OUTLETS: Gift shop offers site-related merchandise and Colonial gift items. Wheelchair-accessible.
DIRECTIONS: Southbound on I-95, take Exit 17 and go west on Market Street. Turn right on Third Street and go one block to Arch Street. Northbound on I-95, take Independence Hall exit. Follow signs for Sixth Street. Take Sixth Street to Market Street, and turn left. At Third Street, turn left and take Arch Street. Betsy Ross House is between Second and Third Streets on Arch Street.

---

furnished parlor behind her shop where she would have received the notable visitors from the Continental Congress.

Several items owned by Betsy Ross are on view for today's visitors: chairs, a chest-on-chest, her eyeglasses, a snuff box engraved with her initials, and a large family Bible inscribed with her name. Inside the Bible, in John Claypoole's handwriting, are listed the names of their children and their birth dates. A marriage certificate for daughter Susanna bears Betsy Ross's signature as Elizabeth Claypoole.

Albert Gallatin

(1761-1849)

lbert Gallatin, who served his country the longest of any U.S. Secretary of the Treasury to date, lived a life filled with contradictions. Born
an aristocrat in Switzerland, he became a fervent proponent of democratic
principles in his adopted country. Longing at first to become a farmer, his
keen intellect and persuasive oratory propelled him into a career as a
politician and diplomat. Although he owned a homestead along the
Monongahela River, at that time on the western frontier, he and his family
lived most of their lives in the sophisticated capitals of Europe and the
United States. Finally, despite his long crusade within the federal government to reduce the national debt, he saw his efforts submerged by the
expenditures needed to fight the War of 1812 against Great Britain.

Although his name is scarcely recognized today, Gallatin stood alongside Thomas Jefferson, James Madison, and James Monroe as they ham-
mered out a political philosophy that defined the U.S. government in its
first decades. Patrick Henry, the Revolutionary leader from Virginia, once
proclaimed Gallatin "a most astonishing man."

Albert Gallatin was born in 1761 in Geneva, Switzerland, to an aristocratic family known for its watchmaking and public service. Both of his
parents died by the time he was nine, and he was raised by a distant relative
who treated him as her son, ensuring that he had a thorough education.

When he finished school, his foster mother suggested he join the German army as an officer and a mercenary, but Gallatin had other ideas. Dis-
liking what he saw of European society, which he felt was permeated with
inequality, he and a boyhood chum ran away from home and took a ship
from France to America to seek their fortunes.

Arriving in 1780 during the dark days of the American Revolution, he
took no part in the fighting, but instead tried unsuccessfully to make some
money by selling a consignment of tea he had brought with him from
Europe. By 1781, the year Cornwallis surrendered to Washington at Yorktown, Gallatin had given up selling tea, sugar, tobacco, and rum and had
taken a job tutoring students in French at Harvard University.

Looking for a more promising livelihood, in 1783 he came up with a plan to buy land on what was then the western frontier. He proposed to sell the land at a profit to European immigrants. He persuaded an agent for French speculators in American real estate to finance his land purchases and began buying 120,000 acres of land along the Ohio River. The following spring, he set out for the Virginia-Pennsylvania backcountry to register and survey his holdings. A chance encounter with George Washington in the Monongalia, Virginia, surveyor's office alerted him that plans were afoot to build a canal along the Potomac River and link it with one or another of the Ohio's tributaries. Betting on a future along the Monongahela River, Gallatin purchased a farm near the confluence with George's Creek in Fayette County, Pennsylvania. There, only a few miles north of today's West Virginia line, he built a small store and office in preparation for the settlers he envisioned would soon come streaming by his front door. Later he built a small glass factory, gristmill, sawmill, and gun factory in what he hoped would become the industrial village of New Geneva.

But Indian troubles and delays on the Potomac canal soon dashed these hopes, and over the next several years, he labored to keep the George's Creek operation going. However, in 1789, he built a house nearby at Friendship Hill for his bride, Sophia Allegre, with whom he had eloped in Richmond, Virginia. But the marriage ended tragically when young Sophia died barely five months later.

To overcome his deep despair over Sophia's death, he became increasingly active in political activities on the frontier. In 1788, he served as a delegate to a Pennsylvania convention that suggested revisions to the new U.S. Constitution. He helped revise Pennsylvania's own constitution in 1789. He was elected to the state legislature in 1790 and reelected in 1791 and 1792. Now a leader in Pennsylvania's homespun democracy, he made a name for himself as a spokesman for the small farmers and entrepreneurs with whom he shared a desire for equal opportunity and economic development. His brilliant reports of the legislature's

Albert Gallatin, 1805, by Rembrandt Peale.
INDEPENDENCE NATIONAL HISTORICAL PARK

committee of ways and means established him as an authority in the field of public finance. In 1793, he was appointed to the U.S. Senate, but he was deprived of his seat because he had not been a U.S. citizen for the full required nine years.

He and his second wife, Hannah Nicholson of New York, with whom he had two sons and four daughters, three of whom died before the age of one, returned to Friendship Hill. They arrived just in time to be caught up in the Whiskey Rebellion, an armed insurrection by western farmers who rebelled against taxes levied by the new federal government against whiskey. Whiskey, distilled from grain and easily shipped, was the main source of income for these western farmers. Gallatin recognized the hardship of the tax on his fellow farmers, but he advocated that nevertheless they should submit to the law rather than risk being forced to do so by federal troops who were even then marching to the scene to enforce it.

In 1794, grateful citizens elected this calm and logical man to the first of three terms in the U.S. House of Representatives, where he became a specialist on financial policy. It was his idea to set up a standing committee on finance, the Ways and Means Committee, to deal with the nation's budget. When Thomas Jefferson became president in 1801, he appointed Gallatin secretary of the Treasury, a post he would hold for thirteen years. As secretary, he was a tireless proponent of reducing the federal debt. Debt, he believed, spawned other evils—corruption, legislative impotence, executive tyranny, social inequality, and financial speculation. His zealous cost-cutting, despite having to finance a war against the Barbary pirates, gave the Treasury a growing surplus.

But he willingly supported spending the money required to buy the Louisiana Territory from France, which added eight hundred thousand acres to the nation. His financing of the purchase without increasing taxation was unique in federal government fiscal history. He followed up by providing the funds that enabled Lewis and Clark to explore these promising new lands. In gratitude, the explorers named a tributary of the Missouri River for him.

He also wanted to see a network of roads and canals that would knit together the expanding country and drew up a plan, which he submitted to President Jefferson. Part of this dream was realized with the construction of the National Road linking the East with the Ohio River.

But British depredations against American ships and crews forced the United States into the War of 1812, at the same time undercutting Gallatin's budget successes. In 1813, President Madison appointed five men—

Albert Gallatin, Henry Clay, John Quincy Adams, Jonathan Russell, and James Bayard—to negotiate an end to the conflict with Britain; the accord signed at Ghent, Belgium, in 1814 was largely a product of Gallatin's perseverance, skill, and patience. Subsequently, he served as ambassador to France from 1816 to 1823, then later as ambassador to Britain from 1826 to 1827.

Returning to the United States, he reluctantly sold his property at Friendship Hill, where his wife had always felt isolated. He then settled with Hannah and his family in New York City, where at age seventy he reentered the world of finance as president of the new National Bank of New York. He was also one of the founders of the New York University and an early president of the New-York Historical Society. It was also during his years in New York that he undertook serious academic studies of the Native Americans and spearheaded the organization of the American Ethnological Society, achievements that earned him the title of "the father of American ethnology."

A dynamic combination of entrepreneur, politician, diplomat, scholar, and financier, he remained active and vigorous until his eighty-eighth year. The shock of the death of his wife in 1849 seriously weakened him, and on August 12 of the same year, he died at the country home of his daughter Frances on Long Island. He and his wife are buried in Trinity Churchyard in New York City.

Friendship Hill National Historic Site

Walking up a winding path, you approach this country home across a broad lawn, passing a bronze statue of Albert Gallatin as a young surveyor. The property is situated high on a bluff overlooking the Monongahela River, sixty miles upstream from Pittsburgh, almost at the West Virginia border.

Inside the mansion, a park ranger greets you in what was formerly the kitchen, now converted into a bookstore and information desk. Gallatin built the original part of Friendship Hill, the brick house, in 1789, and then added a frame addition in 1798. The large, square stone house addition was added between 1821 and 1823, and finally the stone kitchen in 1824. Later additions produced today's L-shaped house. He once wistfully wrote about his beloved Friendship Hill, "I should have been contented to live and die amongst the Monongahela hills."

Visitors take a self-guiding audio tour of the historic home that brings the sparsely furnished rooms to life. Artifacts from Gallatin's day are on

Visiting Friendship Hill National Historic Site

223 New Geneva Rd., Point Marion, PA 15474

PHONE: 724-725-9190

WEBSITE: www.nps.gov/frhi

ADMINISTRATION: Administered by the National Park Service through Fort Necessity National Battlefield.

HOURS: Open year-round. Historic house open daily, 9–5; park grounds open sunrise to sunset. Closed major holidays November–February.

ADMISSION FEES: Free.

TOURS: Ranger-guided tours daily Memorial Day–Labor Day. Self-guided audio house tours and four-minute video program available year-round, as are the 10 miles of walking trails.

TIME NEEDED: At least 1 hour.

SPECIAL EVENTS: FestiFall held last Sunday of September.

SPECIAL CONSIDERATIONS: Handicapped parking area available; uphill trail to house, first floor of house, visitors center, exhibit area, and restrooms are accessible.

PARKING: On-site free parking lot with spaces for buses and RVs, with adjacent picnic area.

SALES OUTLETS: Bookstore in visitors center offers historical books, maps, crafts, and children's items.

DIRECTIONS: Located midway between Uniontown, Pennsylvania, and Morgantown, West Virignia, on PA Route 166, 3 miles north of Point Marion, Pennsylvania.

Several additions have been built on the original Friendship Hill. The brick house was added in 1789, the frame house and front porches followed in 1798, and the stone house was built in 1823. Gallatin lived here from 1789 to 1801. PHOTO BY THE AUTHORS

display—a campaign poster, congressional documents, and products produced by his glass factory at New Geneva. In one room, an innovative graphic exhibit displays a holograph of an actor portraying Gallatin, who recalls the major accomplishments of his career.

Friendship Hill offers ten miles of hiking and cross-country trails that skirt the river's edge. The memorial grave of Gallatin's first wife, Sophia, stands in a wooded glen, a twenty-minute round-trip walk from the house. A nearby gazebo offers an elevated view of the scenic river.

Robert Fulton

(1765-1815)

Robert Fulton, the third of five children of Robert Sr. and Mary Smith Fulton, was born in 1765 in the stone farmhouse you may still visit today, a few miles south of Lancaster. His father, who had previously worked as a tailor, had only recently purchased the farm and moved the family. Soon after Robert's birth, however, a heavy hailstorm devastated their property. The Fultons were forced to sell the place at a sheriff's sale and move back to Lancaster, where his father resumed tailoring but tragically died scarcely two years later.

While his mother kept the family together by taking in sewing, young Robert showed signs of both artistic ability and mechanical inventiveness. When not in school, he painted tavern signs and drew designs that the famed Lancaster gunsmiths etched onto the rifles they made. On the mechanical side, he cleverly devised a hand-cranked paddlewheel boat that he and his friends used to go fishing on a local creek. He was curious, intelligent, and attractive in appearance. And he had an outgoing personality that later won him lasting and productive friendships.

It looked as if the lad were destined for life as an artist when in 1782 he was apprenticed to a Philadelphia jeweler and began painting miniature portraits and cameos, including one of Benjamin Franklin. In 1786, armed with a letter of introduction from Franklin and with only forty guineas in his pocket, he sailed for London to study with the famous portrait artist Benjamin West, himself an expatriate Pennsylvanian and a friend of the Fulton family.

Young Fulton progressed rapidly as an artist, executing drawings and portraits of the English gentry, including a portrait of James Watt, the inventor of the steam engine. He was invited to live for two years at the country estate of Lord Courtenay, duke of Devonshire, to study the duke's paintings and to paint portraits of the duke's friends.

While painting these portraits, Fulton found himself listening to the conversations among the duke and his friends concerning their interest in building a network of canals across England. Intrigued, his interests now turned toward the "useful arts." Putting his portrait painting aside, he turned to his mechanical interests. He designed a marble-cutting machine, then a flax spinner, and a ropemaking device. By 1796, he had British patents on these three devices, as well as on a double inclined plane that could raise canal boats from one water level to the next. He published a treatise that he illustrated himself, describing ways to improve canal navigation. His business card now proclaimed that he was a civil engineer.

Low on income, Fulton went to France in 1797, where he obtained French patents on several canal innovations. By good luck, he met Joel Barlow, a wealthy American residing in Paris, who became interested in Fulton's ideas and lent him generous financial support. Fulton lived with the Joel Barlow family for several years.

Now his restless mind turned to other ideas that would help France prevent its enemy, England, from harassing its ships on the seas. At this time, British warships were blockading French ports. For the next few years, Fulton tried to develop an idea for France's defenses, a submarine that could stealthily approach and place an explosive against the hull of a British ship that would detonate and sink the ship. He built a submersible he named the *Nautilus*. Its crew of two, breathing through compressed air tanks while submerged, hand-cranked a propeller to make the craft move. In September 1800, Fulton's twenty-foot-long "plunging boat" headed toward British warships in the harbor of Le Havre, but the British had been tipped off to the underwater attack and moved their ships safely out of range. Fulton later offered his submarine plans to the British, but after the defeat of the French fleet at Trafalgar, the British lost interest in this new venture.

The inventor now turned his attention to steamboats. Before he left France for England on the submarine project, he had met Robert Livingston, a signer of the Declaration of Independence and now the U.S. ambassador to France under President Thomas Jefferson. Livingston knew that rafts and riverboats had long been restricted to moving

Robert Fulton, 1807, by Charles Willson Peale.
INDEPENDENCE NATIONAL HISTORICAL PARK

downstream. If an engine could be built that would propel a boat upstream, he realized it would revolutionize river travel by replacing sailing ships. Livingston held a monopoly on future rights to operate a commercial steamboat on the Hudson River back in his native New York, if such a boat could be built. But inventor John Stevens, who had been working for Livingston, had been unable to develop a workable steamboat, so Livingston turned to Fulton. In 1802, the two men formed a partnership under which they would share the profits if they could successfully operate such a steamboat service on the Hudson River.

Fulton took the first steps in this venture while he was still in France. He set up a sixty-six-foot-long model tank to determine whether "paddles, skulls [*sic*], endless chains, or water wheels" would be the most efficient for propulsion. In 1803, he built a boat, installed a steam engine in it that had been used to pump water, and successfully navigated the craft up and down the Seine River.

He returned to America in 1806, after a twenty-year absence in Europe. Immediately, he set to work in a New York shipyard on the construction of a narrow, 146-foot-long, flat-bottomed craft that would be propelled through the water by side wheels. It was powered by a Boulton and Watts low-pressure, coal-fired steam engine that he had managed to import from England.

One observer called the boat "an ungainly craft looking precisely like a backwoods saw-mill mounted on a scow and set on fire." Another called it "Fulton's Folly." But the inventor made history by solving the problem of propulsion by combining the English engine with side paddle wheels on his efficiently designed craft.

The public trial of the boat, called the *North River Steamboat of Clermont,* after Livingston's estate on the Hudson, took place on August 17, 1807. The event rated mention in only one newspaper, which said the boat was "invented with a view to the navigation of the Mississippi upward." On that August day, however, the partners only hoped that the ship would be able to complete the journey to Albany.

Forty well-dressed but apprehensive passengers climbed aboard the boat, which boasted three cabins, fifty-four berths, a kitchen, and a bar. When the boat finally got under way, and the creaking and splashing of the side wheels became a consistent sound, the passengers relaxed and returned the salutes of small groups of amazed people who gathered along the banks. When the boat reached Clermont, Livingston proudly announced the engagement of his twenty-three-year-old cousin, Harriet

Livingston, to the forty-two-year-old inventor, and the two married soon thereafter. When the side-wheeler completed its maiden 160-mile trip to Albany the next day, beating the fastest sailing schooner time by two days, Fulton had proved that steamboats were economically feasible. With this accomplishment, the once-obscure painter had become a professional and social success.

Although others before Fulton had built and run steamboats—James Rumsey in 1787 and John Fitch in 1790—neither of their boats could carry enough passengers or cargo to make them commercially successful. Fulton was able to improve on the ideas of others like Rumsey and Fitch, translate their concepts into a commercially working device, and in the case of the steamboat, capture the public's imagination.

He gained more notice the following year when he rebuilt the *Clermont* with a wider hull and set the boat to making regular weekly runs between New York and Albany. This enabled Fulton to enjoy his new life of comfort and wealth. With an aristocratic wife, later a son and three daughters, and an elegant home, he could return to painting not as a struggling young artist, but as a gentleman enjoying a hobby. He was elected to the American Academy of Fine Arts, the American Philosophical Society, and the New-York Historical Society.

His fame as an expert in mechanical fields was now so well established that President Jefferson asked him to investigate and report on the feasibility of building a canal in New Orleans to connect Lake Pontchartrain with the Mississippi River. He reluctantly declined, stating that he was too busy with an experiment. He wanted to demonstrate the power of torpedoes, a new invention, by using them to blow up a vessel in New York Harbor.

Fulton built a second steamboat in 1809 and began to expand his operations. Within five years, the Fulton-Livingston partnership and related stock companies controlled steamboats on the Hudson, Delaware, Potomac, James, Ohio, and Mississippi Rivers and the Chesapeake Bay. They also added other steamboats, steam ferries, a dry dock, and workshop in the vicinity of New York City to their business ventures. Between 1813 and 1815, Fulton also adapted a steam ferry into a steam warship.

On a winter day in 1815 at age forty-nine, Fulton and his lawyer fell through the ice as they tried to board a small boat that would take them across the Hudson River. Fulton pulled his colleague out of the water but developed pneumonia from the exposure. Refusing to stay in bed for long, he insisted on going to the shipyard to check the progress of his warship, the *Demologus*. He suffered a relapse and died. The battle frigate was completed and placed in commission the next year, becoming the first steam-powered warship in the world. Fittingly, the ship was later renamed the *Robert Fulton.* He never relinquished the belief that the "liberty of the seas" would guarantee "happiness of the earth" and that all men could trade freely with one another. He is buried in Old Trinity Churchyard in lower Manhattan.

Robert Fulton Birthplace

Robert Fulton's birthplace remains much the way it looked when the inventor lived here. Built in 1745, the stone structure is one of the oldest houses in Lancaster County. The Pennsylvania Historical and Museum Commission has restored and furnished the house to its appearance during Fulton's lifetime, with furniture of the period filling the front room and the kitchen. Another room holds displays that chronicle the life and accomplishments of the inventor, including miniature paintings he cre-

Visiting Robert Fulton Birthplace

P.O. Box 33, Quarryville, PA 17566

PHONE: 717-548-2679
E-MAIL: SLCHC@aol.com
WEBSITE: www.rootsweb.com/paslchs/index.htmlmail
ADMINISTRATION: Administered by the Pennsylvania Historical and Museum Commission, with the support of the Southern Lancaster County Historical Society.
HOURS: Open Wednesdays, 9–12; Saturdays, 1–4; Sundays, 1–5, or by appointment Memorial Day–Labor Day.
ADMISSION FEES: $1 for adults; children under 12 free.
TOURS: Guided tours from the Southern Lancaster County Historical Society available on request.
TIME NEEDED: About 1 hour.
SPECIAL EVENTS: Craft fair the third Saturday in August; Christmas greens sale the first Sunday in December.
SPECIAL CONSIDERATIONS: Historical Society is handicapped-accessible, but there are a few steps into Fulton's Birthplace.
PARKING: Parking lot at Southern Lancaster County Historical Society, across road from Fulton's Birthplace; more parking behind Birthplace.
SALES OUTLETS: None.
DIRECTIONS: Follow U.S. Route 222 about 6 miles south of Quarryville in Fulton Township. Southern Lancaster County Historical Society is on the left; Fulton's Birthplace is on the right.

Fulton was born in this house in Quarryville, Lancaster County, in 1765. The family moved to Lancaster after a hailstorm devastated the family farm. PHOTO BY THE AUTHORS

ated, illustrated applications of patents for some of his inventions, a portrait of the inventor, and a printed indenture for a servant of his father.

Begin at the nearby visitors center, home of the Southern Lancaster County Historical Society, located in a converted tobacco warehouse once owned by Fulton's relatives. The visitors center features a colorful mural depicting Fulton's life and the evolution of the site through the years and preserves the genealogy records of former county residents.

John James Audubon

(1785-1851)

John James Audubon, born in the Caribbean as the illegitimate son of French parents, linked a brilliant artistic talent with a dogged determination to give Americans a comprehensive view of the panorama of North American bird and animal life that surrounded them. In a life that took him from abject poverty and anonymity to world recognition as an ornithologist, painter, and naturalist, Audubon never lost sight of the dream of his youth to illustrate all the birds and animals of his adopted homeland.

He was born Jean Rabin Fougere in Santo Domingo (now Haiti), the son of Capt. Jean Audubon, a French sea captain, planter, and slave dealer. His mother was Jeanne Rabin, a young Frenchwoman employed as a chambermaid on the island, who died when he was still an infant.

In 1788, fearing worsening conditions in Santo Domingo, Captain Audubon arranged for his son and an illegitimate daughter to be taken to his home in Nantes, France. Here they were brought into the family and raised by his legal wife, Anne Moynet Audubon, since they had no children of their own. Both children were formally adopted by the couple in 1794, as was required if they were legally to inherit Captain Audubon's name and property, and the two were baptized in 1800.

Young Audubon was homeschooled by his stepmother, then spent four years at a naval academy, but he much preferred to roam the woods making sketches of animals and birds. In 1803, probably to avoid having his son conscripted into Napoleon's army, Captain Audubon sent him across the Atlantic to manage an estate he had purchased some years earlier that was twenty-five miles from Philadelphia.

The eighteen-year-old moved into the comfortable house at Mill Grove but paid little attention to his duties or to the agent of his father, who was trying to develop a lead mine on the property. Instead, he turned to nature. It was at Mill Grove that Audubon came up with the idea of shooting a bird he wanted to draw, then propping it up with wires adjusted to hold the bird in a position as if it were alive. Then he would proudly label his bird painting, "Drawn from nature by John James Audubon." By now he had anglicized his name.

He showed even more interest in the girl next door, Lucy Bakewell, and the two were soon taking bird walks in the woods. When his father's agent objected to his plans to marry Lucy, Audubon sailed back to France and got his father's permission to marry. At the same time, his father gave him title to half of the Mill Grove estate. Returning to America with a young hometown friend, Ferdinand Rozier, he promptly sold his half of the estate. To prove to his fiancée that he could support her, he left her behind, took a clerk's job in New York City, and became a naturalized citizen.

After two years as a novice merchant, he formed a partnership with Rozier, and together they headed west by flatboat down the Ohio River to set up a general store at the edge of the wilderness in Louisville. Audubon undertook horseback trips back east to procure new items for the store, sketching birds along the way. Rozier stayed behind and tended the store. Six months later, Audubon married Lucy and brought her to Louisville.

During the next thirteen years, the hard-pressed family moved to four locations along the Mississippi and Ohio Rivers as Audubon sought suc-

John James Audubon, c. 1840, by John Woodhouse Audubon. DEPARTMENT OF LIBRARY SERVICES, AMERICAN MUSEUM OF NATURAL HISTORY (NEG. 335471)

cess in business. During this time, they knew one period of relative prosperity, but his declining business then dissolved into bankruptcy. Now they knew the depths of grinding poverty, which was unrelieved by any support from their relatives. Meanwhile, Lucy gave birth to two sons, Victor and John, and two daughters, both of whom died young. Audubon worked as a store owner and later as a teacher, taxidermist, and itinerant artist, while Lucy worked as a teacher and governess to make ends meet.

Through these difficult years, Audubon doggedly pursued his dream, identifying and painting birds, collecting specimens, and adding paintings to his growing portfolio. But his long absences on bird-hunting trips severely tested Lucy's faith in their future.

Finally, after a separation of fourteen months, the family reunited in New Orleans. The couple made a decision: They would somehow scrape together enough money to send Audubon with his bird pictures to Philadelphia so he could seek competent critics and find the financial support he needed to publish his portfolio.

His foray to Philadelphia and then to New York produced mixed results. On the one hand, he met artists like Thomas Sully, who admired his work and accepted him as an equal, and naturalists who voted him into their professional society. But he also antagonized two other ornithologists, the late Alexander Wilson and Charles Bonaparte.

Two years later, with money he and Lucy had saved from teaching at a plantation, he left to seek financial support in Europe, sailing to Liverpool with a portfolio of two hundred bird pictures. This decision turned his life around. To Audubon's amazement, Liverpool lionized the colorful American backwoodsman and was captivated by his finely drawn pictures. His exhibits in Liverpool, Manchester, and Edinburgh magically generated support from wealthy patrons.

In London, he found a talented engraver, Robert Havell Sr., who had the skill to produce Audubon's long-dreamed-of book, *Birds of America.* Audubon insisted that his birds be printed lifesize on the largest paper then available, and work was begun on an expensive, four-volume "elephant folio." This project eventually took eleven years to complete. To keep the project going financially, Audubon painted oil portraits of people as well as other pictures and took up the task of selling subscriptions to buy his folio.

After more than two years in Europe, where his "immense work" had moved from a dream to a reality, Audubon returned to the United States to see his long-suffering wife and family and to add missing species of birds to his collection. Everything had changed—now he was a celebrity and no longer in poverty. No longer was he a father to be ashamed of and a husband long absent from his family. Lucy believed him when he promised they would never again be apart, and he kept his promise.

With Lucy, he sailed back to England in 1830. The next year, with the help of a collaborator, he published his *Ornithological Biography,* with detailed information on each of the birds in his folio. Between 1831 and 1834, Audubon made additional trips to Florida, South Carolina, and Labrador to collect and draw new species for *Birds of America* and to bring Lucy and their two sons into what had now become a family enterprise. In Charleston, he stayed with John Bachman, a Lutheran minister and amateur naturalist, who later collaborated with Audubon on yet another major project, *The Viviparous Quadrupeds of North America,* a book on mammals that was published after Audubon's death.

A final trip took him back to England in 1837. He remained for two years to oversee the completion of *The Birds of America* and the *Biography,* which were both published to public and professional acclaim in 1838. *The Birds of America* consists of 435 hand-colored folio plates that depict 1,065 birds lifesize. After thirteen long, arduous, and enormously productive years, Audubon could at last sail for home to stay, settling in New York in a home along the Hudson River.

The Audubon and Bachman families became even closer when his son, John Woodhouse Audubon, married John Bachman's daughter Maria in 1837, and his other son, Victor, married Maria's sister Eliza in 1839. Tragically, both young women died of tuberculosis, Maria in 1840, and Eliza a year later. Both sons later remarried, and each named a daughter after his deceased first wife.

In 1843, at age fifty-eight, the old explorer undertook one last expedition, by boat up the Missouri River to the Yellowstone River to collect and paint mammal specimens for the *Quadrupeds* book. But the results were disappointing. Audubon's eyesight began to fail as he aged, and he turned over much of the work on *Quadrupeds* to his sons and Bachman.

Critics of Audubon say he fluctuated between scrupulous scientific accuracy and impressionistic action paintings, which inevitably disconcerted both his artistic and scientific audiences. But the pictures produced by this talented and determined man helped create much of the earliest public appreciation of nature in America, and they remain classics to this day.

Mill Grove Audubon Wildlife Sanctuary

The young Audubon spent the first two years in the United States roaming the wooded hills along Perkiomen Creek and the Schuylkill River. Mill Grove, an estate purchased as an investment by his father, is the only home of the ornithologist-painter that remains in America today.

Both birds and visitors flock to Mill Grove, now a wildlife sanctuary. Miles of trails wind through the grounds. Feeding stations, nesting boxes, and plantings of shrubs and trees attract the birds. Since 1951, some 175 species of birds and more than 400 species of flowering plants have been identified there.

Inside the house, you will find original Audubon prints and plates from his elephant folio. Murals on the walls portray the famous naturalist's

---

Visiting Mill Grove Audubon Wildlife Sanctuary

1201 Pawlings Rd., P.O. Box 7125, Audubon, PA 19407

PHONE: 610-666-5593

WEBSITE: www.montcopa.org/historicsites

ADMINISTRATION: County of Montgomery, Department of History and Cultural Arts.

HOURS: Open year-round. Museum open Tuesday–Saturday, 10–4; Sunday, 1–4. Grounds open Tuesday–Sunday, dawn to dusk. Closed Monday and major holidays.

ADMISSION FEES: None, but donations accepted.

TOURS: Self-guided, although reservations should be made for groups of 10 or more.

TIME NEEDED: 1 hour for museum; 1 hour for trail walk around grounds.

SPECIAL EVENTS: Maple sugar festival, apple festival, holiday open house, a celebration of Audubon's birthday the last Saturday in April. Outdoor education programs offered to school groups grades 1–12.

SPECIAL CONSIDERATIONS: First floor is wheelchair-accessible; written tour descriptions are on all floors.

PARKING: On-site parking, with handicapped parking in front of museum.

SALES OUTLETS: Museum gift shop offers Audubon books, prints, natural-history books, nature-related gifts and toys.

DIRECTIONS: Located at junction of Pawlings and Audubon Roads in Audubon. Follow U.S. Rt. 422 West, and take Audubon/Trooper exit, 363 North. Bear right, then turn left at first traffic light, Audubon Road. Continue to Pawlings Road; Mill Grove is directly ahead.

Mill Grove is the only surviving American home of John James Audubon. MILL GROVE
AUDUBON WILDLIFE SANCTUARY

bird-hunting adventures. The attic of the home has been restored as a studio and taxidermy room, depicting Audubon's working quarters when he lived at Mill Grove. Other rooms in the house are furnished in the style of the early 1800s.

James Buchanan during his presidency, by Matthew Brady. COLLECTION OF THE NEW-YORK HISTORICAL SOCIETY

James Buchanan

(1791-1868)

Although he was one of the most experienced political leaders ever elected as U.S. president, James Buchanan had the misfortune to win the nation's highest office at a time when a rift in the political landscape—the issue of slavery—was disastrously widening.

The question that divided the country was whether to allow landowners in new territories being added to the nation to own slaves, or whether these territories should be brought into the Union as "free states." It was a question neither Buchanan, nor his Democratic party, nor Congress, nor any compromise between the heated adversaries, could resolve. Tragically, no sooner did his one term of office end when federal Fort Sumter was bombarded by the artillery of South Carolina—signaling the eruption of the Civil War.

Like Abraham Lincoln, the man who succeeded him as president, Buchanan had started life in a log cabin. He was born at Stony Batter, an outpost near Mercersburg on the Pennsylvania frontier, in a cabin his Irish immigrant father had bought two years earlier. Here at Cove Gap in the Appalachian Mountains, his father ran a trading post for pack trains that took immigrants to the West. "It was a rugged but romantic spot," he remembered later, "and the mountains and mountain streams . . . were captivating."

Six years later, the family moved to the town of Mercersburg, where James got a good classical education in Latin and Greek at the Old Stone Academy. He graduated in 1809 from Dickinson College in Carlisle, where he excelled as a debater and finished at the top of his class.

For the next three years, he "read for the law" at a lawyer's office in Lancaster, gaining admittance to the bar in 1812. As a young lawyer, he was self-confident, solemn, and precise. Also shrewd in his investments, he soon amassed considerable wealth.

But a personal tragedy intervened. He became engaged to Ann Coleman, but the young woman broke off the engagement due to a misunderstanding, as well as the opposition of her father. She became ill and died suddenly in Philadelphia a short time later, and Buchanan was devastated.

85

He remained a bachelor—our only bachelor president. In 1842, however, he became the guardian of his orphaned niece, Harriet Lane, who remained with him until her marriage to Henry Elliot Johnston in 1866, when she was thirty-six. Harriet served as the hostess and first lady at the White House when her uncle became president. James Buchanan was also the main support of a number of his younger relatives who lived with him at his home in Lancaster.

Buchanan's gregarious nature and skill at speechmaking served him well, and he was elected at age twenty-three to the first of two terms in the Pennsylvania legislature, embarking on what would be a career involvement in politics. He forged alliances, wrote persuasive letters, and took to the stump to promote himself and his party's candidates. Tall and stout, with flowing hair, the meticulously dressed Buchanan presented a distinguished appearance that was reinforced by his courtly manners. In 1821, he was elected a U.S. Congressman. President Andrew Jackson, whom he had supported politically, appointed him ambassador to Russia, where he served from 1832 to 1833, negotiating a commercial treaty under which Russia opened its ports more freely to U.S. merchant ships.

Upon his return, he was elected as a Democrat by the Pennsylvania legislature to the U.S. Senate, where he served from 1834 to 1845. Buchanan strongly urged territorial expansion of the country. "Providence has given to the American people a great and glorious mission to perform, even that of extending . . . liberty over the whole North American continent," he said. On the most divisive issue of the time—slavery—he took a lawyer's ambivalent position. Although he considered it morally wrong to hold another human being as a slave, he saw no practical resolution, since slavery was now so firmly established in the South. He defended the right of a citizen to keep any property he had lawfully acquired, even slaves, and therefore opposed outside interference with the property rights of Southerners.

Buchanan sought the Democratic nomination for president in 1844, but a dark horse from Tennessee, James K. Polk, received the nomination and was elected instead. Polk appointed Buchanan secretary of state, and in that capacity he negotiated the entry of both Texas and Oregon into the Union. In the aftermath of the Mexican War, Buchanan arranged a peace treaty that added New Mexico and California to the United States.

After unsuccessfully seeking the Democratic presidential nomination again in 1848, "Old Buck" went back to his Lancaster law practice. He bought and moved into Wheatland, a handsome home on the city's outskirts, and enjoyed his life as a country squire. He made yet another unsuccessful bid for the presidential nomination in 1852, losing to a younger man, Franklin Pierce, who then appointed him ambassador to Great Britain.

In 1856, with the nation embroiled in arguments about extending slavery into western territories, Buchanan finally won his party's nomination, due in large part to his reputation as a conservative and a compromiser. He defeated the Republican nominee, John C. Fremont, as well as ex-President Millard Fillmore, a third-party candidate, to win the election by a plurality of votes. "The great object of my administration," he promised, "will be to arrest, if possible, the agitation of the slavery question at the North, and to destroy sectional parties."

But no sooner was he elected than the slavery issue boiled up again. The Supreme Court handed down the Dred Scott decision, which stated that slaveholders had the right to take their human property anywhere they chose, and ruled unconstitutional the Missouri Compromise, which had been the guideline for slave and free territories. This ruling reinforced the concept that slaves were considered property and opened up territories like Kansas and others in the West to the extension of slavery. The decision gratified Southerners but inflamed many in the North who wanted to stop the spread of slavery. What's more, the people in the territory of Kansas, in a controversial referendum, had voted for a constitution that allowed slaveholding if and when the territory should become a state.

By 1858, Buchanan was being stymied by the inaction of Congress, his own party was split, and his administration was near paralysis. Several of his cabinet officers resigned, and another, Secretary of War John Floyd, was caught misusing government funds. To add fuel to the fire, in 1859, abolitionist John Brown carried out the capture of the federal armory at Harpers Ferry, stirring fears of a possible insurrection of slaves and further hardening Southern hostility toward all Northern antislavery partisans. To try to reach an agreement between North and South, Buchanan proposed a constitutional convention to devise an amendment to the Constitution that would affirm the right to hold slaves as property, let territories decide whether they would become slaveholding or free, and return fugitive slaves to their owners. Congress never considered the proposal.

The presidential election of 1860 brought the crisis to a head. Although Buchanan had declined to run for reelection, the slavery issue so bitterly divided his party that the Democrats offered both an antislavery candidate and a proslavery candidate. This split allowed the Republican candidate, Abraham Lincoln, to win the election with far less than a popular majority.

During Buchanan's remaining four months in office, he made repeated but fruitless attempts to soften the stance of antislavery Northerners and to compromise with Southern states who threatened to secede from the Union. He steadfastly refused to recognize the legality of secession or to negotiate the surrender of federal forts in the South. Two Southern members of his cabinet resigned, and rumors flew, including one that the Confederates intended to capture Washington, D.C. He announced his determination to protect federal property in the South and attempted to resupply Fort Sumter in South Carolina, but the ship was fired upon and driven back by South Carolina artillery.

Buchanan's last days in office were filled with indecision, and in March 1861, with relief, he turned the crisis over to the newly elected Abraham Lincoln and returned to his home in Lancaster. Here he sadly watched as seven Southern states seceded from the Union and his country became engulfed in the tragic Civil War he had tried so hard to avert.

In his retirement years, he wrote a full account of his presidency. James Buchanan died in 1868 at his beloved Wheatland. Ignoring his desires for a simple ceremony, some twenty thousand people attended the state funeral at the mansion. He is buried at Woodward Hill Cemetery in Lancaster.

James Buchanan's Wheatland

At Wheatland, the large brick mansion of James Buchanan, the stage is still set much the way it was when top officials of the Democratic Party came here in 1856 to offer Buchanan his party's nomination for presi-

Wheatland was built in 1828 and purchased by James Buchanan for $6,750 in 1848 when he was secretary of state under James K. Polk. Buchanan returned to Wheatland after his presidential term in 1861 and remained there until his death in 1868. PHOTO BY THE AUTHORS

Visiting James Buchanan's Wheatland

1120 Marietta Ave., Lancaster, PA 17603

PHONE: 717-392-8721
E-MAIL: jbwheatland@aol.com
WEBSITE: www.wheatland.org
ADMINISTRATION: Purchased by the Junior League of Lancaster in 1936 and administered by the James Buchanan Foundation for the Preservation of Wheatland.
HOURS: April–October, open daily, 10–4. Group tours available by appointment.
ADMISSION FEES: $5.50 for adults; $4.50 for seniors; $3.50 for students; $1.75 for children.
TOURS: Tours begin in carriage house visitors center with videos and displays; tours of house led by costumed guides; self-guided tours of landscaped grounds and outbuildings.
TIME NEEDED: At least 1 hour.
SPECIAL EVENTS: Christmas candlelight tours, Buchanan mansion mystery tours, a summer family festival. Educational programs include children's hands-on tours, family history day camps in summer, and school programs, including teacher's resource guide and traveling trunks.
SPECIAL CONSIDERATIONS: The carriage house visitors center is handicapped-accessible, as is the first floor of Wheatland; stairs to second floor of mansion.
PARKING: Free on-site parking.
SALES OUTLETS: Gift shop offers books, pamphlets, and videos about Buchanan, Victorian-style gifts, and Buchanan memorabilia.
DIRECTIONS: From Lebanon Exit of Pennsylvania Turnpike, follow PA Route 72 south into Lancaster. Turn right on Columbia Avenue, PA Route 462 West, and then turn right on Marietta Avenue. Go two blocks to Wheatland on your left.

dent, the prize he had sought for so many years. During the campaign, Buchanan used the library as his campaign headquarters, leaving Lancaster only rarely to make personal appearances. Here he corresponded with numerous supporters and wrote his inaugural address and later his memoirs, *Mr. Buchanan's Administration on the Eve of Rebellion.* A campaign flag bearing stars of thirty-one states in a blue canton hangs on a wall, and his books line the study.

The restored building, Federal style in architecture, was built in 1828 for a wealthy lawyer and banker who named it The Wheatlands because of its rural location overlooking wheatfields. In 1848, Buchanan purchased the twenty-two-acre farm, which he owned for twenty years. He praised "the comforts and tranquility of home as contrasted with the troubles, perplexities, and difficulties" of public life.

In those days, visitors dismounted from their carriages and climbed the steps to the front door to be greeted in the hallway by a servant. They enjoyed lively conversation and piano music played in the parlor by Buchanan's niece, Harriet Lane. Friends or family would gather around the "grand old mahogany table" to enjoy leisurely meals. In the elegant dining room, Buchanan once entertained Andrew Johnson, who later became president. The owner possessed a well-stocked wine cellar, of which one bottle remains unopened for today's visitors to admire. Much of the statesman's original furniture and silverware remain in the house and are on display. A lithograph of Queen Victoria and Prince Albert, presented by the prince of Wales, looks down from the wall. An enormous porcelain bowl was a gift from a Japanese delegation.

Upstairs visitors view the bedrooms, a bathroom with a huge tub, and servants' rooms. Outbuildings include a brick privy and a smokehouse. The former carriage house has been converted into a visitors center that features a video presentation, exhibits, and a collection of President Buchanan's memorabilia.

Another nearby site, Buchanan's Birthplace State Park, is an 18.5-acre park located along picturesque Buck Run between McConnellsburg and Mercersburg, near the village of Cove Gap along Pennsylvania Route 16. A monument, provided by Harriet Lane Johnston's will, marks the site of his birth. The original Buchanan cabin from Stony Batter is preserved and displayed on the Mercersburg Academy campus.

Asa Packer

(1805-79)

Few would have predicted that a poor farm boy from Connecticut would one day achieve the status of America's third-wealthiest man. Or that this rough-edged youngster who got no further than eighth grade in school would establish a distinguished university. Or that this entrepreneur would risk his hard-won fortune to build a railroad that colleagues warned him might never be profitable.

All of these achievements lay in the future for Asa Packer. As a seventeen-year-old, he left his family's farm in Mystic, Connecticut, threw a knapsack over his shoulder, and walked more than 150 miles to reach the home of his cousin Edward Packer, a carpenter, who lived in the town of Brooklyn in Susquehanna County, Pennsylvania. Edward hired him as an apprentice and taught him the trade of carpentry. A quick and enthusiastic learner, Packer completed his apprenticeship within a year. To prove his proficiency, he rented a nearby farm owned by Zopher Blakeslee, an early settler in the region, and followed the carpentry trade for several years. He even took a job for a year in faraway New York City while still keeping his farm near the Susquehanna River.

No one knows for sure, but it was probably a girl, Sarah, daughter of Zopher Blakeslee, who attracted him back to Pennsylvania, although he also told friends he didn't like life in the big city. In January 1828, he married Sarah, and together the couple turned to farming the land. To make ends meet, he put his carpentry skills to work by building canal boats at Tunkhannock, a town twenty miles away on the Susquehanna River.

After four years of raising and selling crops during the growing season and building boats during the winter, he answered a newspaper advertisement that offered a job as a canal boat captain on the Lehigh River, another nearby river system. The Lehigh provided a water highway from the rich anthracite coalfields to the Delaware River and from there downriver to the rapidly industrializing city of Philadelphia.

Anthracite was finding increasing use as a fuel to heat homes and to power steam engines. To exploit this natural resource, the Lehigh Coal

Asa Packer, 1878. JIM THORPE LIONS CLUB/ASA
PACKER MANSION

and Navigation Company built a canal along the fast-running Lehigh River that enabled canal boats to safely haul loads of coal from the Mount Pisgah field near the town of Mauch Chunk to markets downstream.

Asa Packer shrewdly saw opportunities for himself as he observed this coal boom. In 1833, he gave up farming and moved to Mauch Chunk. He first became the owner and master of a coal barge, and then added a second barge, which his brother Robert captained. In 1835, he turned over operation of the barges to others but retained part ownership. Meanwhile, he and his brother purchased a general store, which they called A & R Packer, to supply the needs of the fast-growing coal town of Mauch Chunk.

Saving part of his earnings, he soon opened a boat-building business, constructing barges rather than operating them. He and Robert then extended their influence to yet another river system when they won a contract to build canal boats in Pottsville on the Schuylkill River. Next he undertook the task of building a series of canal locks on the Lehigh Canal.

Ever alert to new opportunities, Packer now branched out into mining and coal trade speculation, which flourished as a result of the great demand for energy in Philadelphia. He mined and shipped anthracite for the Lehigh Coal and Navigation Company, the major firm in the region. Eventually he opened his own coal-mining business in the nearby Nesquehoning area, the location from where he hauled coal to Philadelphia. During the 1840s, Packer expanded the scope of these activities sufficiently to earn the title of coal dealer, and by 1850, he had accumulated $100,000 in real and personal property.

Although many men would have been satisfied with these accomplishments, this entrepreneur could not resist a challenge. With typical foresight, he envisioned that railroad freight cars would eventually replace the slower and seasonal canal boats in hauling bulk coal. So in 1853, he bought the charter of a prospective railroad whose owners had failed to lay even a foot of track. Confronted with a deadline by which construction had to start, he persuaded companies and friends to buy stock in the future railroad, and then risked all of his own considerable assets to raise the capital. His workmen began building the first section of his Lehigh Valley Railroad just seventeen days before the charter was due to be withdrawn.

In spite of dire predictions of failure, engineering difficulties, high payroll costs, slumping stock prices, and even an outbreak of cholera, work continued on the railroad, which followed roughly the same route as the canal. Within two years, he completed a forty-mile section from Mauch Chunk to Easton at the confluence of the Lehigh and Delaware Rivers. He secured railroad cars on lease from the Central Railroad of New Jersey. Within the first year alone, the company added fifteen locomotives, six passenger cars, two baggage cars, and more than eight hundred coal cars that hauled more than four hundred thousand tons of coal. The success of the railroad attracted people to the area, and soon new towns and businesses developed. After four years, the rail line was capable of hauling four million tons of coal a year. By the time of his death in 1879, Asa Packer had built the Lehigh Valley Railroad into 650 miles of track from New York State to the New Jersey seaboard.

He also gained political power. As a Democrat, he was elected to the state legislature in 1842 and 1843, and helped Carbon County become a separate Pennsylvania county in 1843. That December, he was named associate judge of the first county court, and he was thereafter known as Judge Packer. Although regarded as taciturn and a man of few words, he was elected in 1852 to the U.S. Congress, where he served two terms. At the National Democratic Convention of 1868, Judge Packer was nominated for president as Pennsylvania's favorite son, and in 1869, he was his party's candidate for governor but lost in a close election race.

Meanwhile, he shifted the headquarters of the railroad to Bethlehem, a larger and more centrally located city. He invested in the Bethlehem Iron Company, which produced rails for his railroad. Together the railroad and iron industries greatly spurred the growth of Bethlehem.

By now the foremost industrialist of the region, Asa Packer turned his attention not so much to making money as to giving it away. For many years, he had been a philanthropist, donating generously to help build St. Mark's Protestant Episcopal Church in Mauch Chunk, where he served as a vestryman for forty-four years.

Now, at the end of the Civil War, he wanted to establish an institution for the education of the youth of the region. He donated fifty-six acres of land and $500,000 to found a new university, the technically oriented Lehigh University. When his oldest daughter, Lucy, died in 1873, he donated a new library in her name, and in 1875, he gave another fifty-two acres of land. Later, in his will, he left the university $1.5 million in railroad stock, the income to be used for maintenance and support of the university. Through this and his other philanthropies, he set an example of giving for other industrialists of his time.

Asa and Sarah had two sons, Robert and Harry, and two daughters, Lucy and Mary, as well as an adopted daughter, Marion. Three other daughters died in infancy. Within five years of Packer's death, both of his sons died without heirs. Sarah died in 1882, four years after the couple had celebrated their golden wedding anniversary with a huge party at their Mauch Chunk mansion. Both husband and wife are buried in a family graveyard on the property. Mary continued to live in the mansion until her death in 1912. She willed the family homestead to the borough of Mauch Chunk.

Asa Packer Mansion

The imposing Packer Mansion, built in the Italianate style by Asa Packer with profits from his successful railroad venture, sits high on the slope of the Lehigh Gorge above the town of Jim Thorpe, renamed from the former Mauch Chunk.

When you climb the sloping walkway and enter the home, you feel as though you have stepped back into the Victorian era of opulence. The mansion and its contents appear to have been frozen in time since daughter Mary Packer Cummings willed the property to the borough, which kept it "in mothballs" until 1954. Then the Jim Thorpe Lions Club took over management of the house and grounds and opened the mansion to the public.

The railroad entrepreneur had spared no expense in building and furnishing his elegant home. Many windows are stained glass, and some floors are paved with Minton tiles. Wood paneling was carved by European artisans, who made fifteen hundred rosettes, each one different from the others. The dining room is decorated with gold leaf wallpaper. Atop the house is a tower, or belvedere, that looks out over the town and the valley, giving Asa Packer a view of the river and his railroad operation.

Visitors are fascinated by the library, which served as an office for Packer and his male secretary. Beneath a patterned ceiling, the walls are covered with ornate heavy wallpaper. An 1878 typewriter has seven

Visiting Asa Packer Mansion

P.O. Box 108, Jim Thorpe, PA 18229

PHONE: 570-325-3229

ADMINISTRATION: Jim Thorpe Lions Club.

HOURS: Memorial Day–Labor Day, open daily, 11–4:15; April, May, and November, open weekends.

ADMISSION FEES: $5 per person; $3 for children and seniors.

TOURS: Tours leave every 15–20 minutes. Group reservations are recommended.

TIME NEEDED: 40 to 45 minutes.

SPECIAL EVENTS: None.

SPECIAL CONSIDERATIONS: A historic home not adapted for handicapped access.

PARKING: County-owned parking lot across street, and more parking available downtown.

SALES OUTLETS: Museum and sales outlet at nearby railroad station.

DIRECTIONS: Jim Thorpe is located a few miles from Exit 34 off the Northeast Extension of the Pennsylvania Turnpike (I-476). Follow U.S. Route 209 South through Lehighton into Jim Thorpe. Asa Packer Mansion is on the hilltop to the right.

While living in this ornate Italianate mansion, Packer developed the Lehigh Railroad, founded Lehigh University, and held several state and national political offices. PHOTO BY THE AUTHORS

changeable fonts. A letterpress copying machine made perfect copies but printed backward so that correspondence had to be held up to a mirror to be read. A gasolier, or tabletop lamp, has blue satin glass globes and won first prize for "best home lighting" at the famous 1876 Centennial Exposition in Philadelphia.

In the hallway of the second floor stands an orchestrion, an unusual instrument more than six feet high. It contains 187 pipes, snare and base drums, a cymbal, and a triangle that produce music when prompted by rolls like those used in a player piano. The volume is adjusted by opening and closing its glass doors. Visitors get to hear the sound of this rare instrument, brought from Europe to the United States by Mary Packer Cummings and thought to be the only one in the world still in working condition.

Behind the mansion is an icehouse that held blocks of ice cut from the Lehigh River during the winter and packed in sawdust. During the summer, air blowing across the ice was led through ducts into the house. Warm air was exhausted upward through the belvedere, thus providing an early air-conditioning system.

Next door is another impressive mansion owned by son Harry that the Packers built for him as a wedding present. The mansion today serves as a four-star bed-and-breakfast inn and as the scene of a "Murder in the Mansion" weekend for invited guests.

A half mile away in the town of Jim Thorpe is St. Mark's Episcopal Church, the notable Gothic structure that Asa Packer's philanthropy made possible. Its unique altar, given by his wife, Sarah, in memory of Asa Packer, is white Italian marble carved by European craftsmen with biblical scenes. Minton tiles form the floor, and the pews are of black walnut. The rose window behind the choir balcony is one of several Tiffany windows. An elegant iron elevator, one of the oldest operating elevators in the country, was installed by Mary Packer Cummings. Both the church and the Packer Mansion are designated as National Historic Landmarks.

Edgar Allan Poe

(1809-49)

The six years Edgar Allan Poe spent as a writer in Philadelphia, from 1838 to 1844, were the most productive of this author's fruitful but tragic life. While working as a freelance writer, then as a magazine editor, he created a hallmark form of American literature—the modern detective story.

Sitting in a small, second-floor room of a house open to visitors today, Poe worked late into the night, the words before him illuminated by a dim light. On the floor above, his teenage wife, Virginia, lay suffering from tuberculosis. His mother-in-law, Maria Clemm, known as Muddy, kept house for the three of them.

In these cramped conditions, he wrote or published some of his best-known works, including *The Fall of the House of Usher,* a tale that set the stage for horror stories to follow. Soon thereafter, he wrote *The Murders in the Rue Morgue,* in which he created the character of C. Auguste Dupin, a detective in Paris who solves crimes by piecing together the clues he finds. With this story, Poe inaugurated what was to become one of the most popular and captivating forms of fiction.

Other horror stories came out of this Philadelphia period: *The Gold Bug, The Pit and the Pendulum, The Tell-tale Heart,* and *The Black Cat.* At his day job as an editor for *Graham's Lady's and Gentleman's Magazine,* he wrote poetry, literary criticism, and book reviews that appraised the works of current authors such as William Cullen Bryant, Washington Irving, and Henry Wadsworth Longfellow.

Poe's writing often reflected the unsettled and unloved life he had led since childhood. His mother, Elizabeth Arnold Poe, known as Eliza Poe, was a favorite young actress and dancer who performed in theaters along the eastern seaboard. Eliza died when Edgar was only two, by which time his father, David Poe, had already deserted the family. Young Edgar never really knew his mother or enjoyed any affection from his father. Frances Allan and her husband, John, a tobacco exporter, who lived in Richmond, where Eliza had last appeared on stage before she died, raised him as a foster child. Frances loved the boy, but John never adopted him or fully accepted him as a member of the family.

Poe lived from ages six to eleven with the Allans in England, where he attended boarding school. Returning to Richmond, he later enrolled at the University of Virginia. His year there was marked by distinction in Latin and French, as well as athletics and campus leadership, but he had trouble keeping up socially and financially with his well-to-do classmates. After his foster mother died, he ran up heavy gambling debts, and his foster father forced him to leave college.

At eighteen, Poe rebelled and set off for Boston, where he published his first volume of poems, many of them dealing with death, loss of a loved one, or terrifying circumstances. To earn a living, he enlisted in the army for two years and earned the rank of sergeant major. Following a brief reconciliation with John Allan, he obtained an appointment to the U.S. Military Academy at West Point. When Allan remarried, Poe lost all hope of his continuing support.

Poe was court-martialed for neglecting his duties and was expelled from the academy, but not before 131 cadets had contributed $1.25 each to enable him to publish another small book of poems. After leaving West Point, he spent the next four years in Baltimore living with his aunt, Maria Clemm, and her daughter, Virginia. Although Poe romanticized the accomplishments of his forebears, it is clear that from the age of twenty-two, he faced a life of struggle and poverty.

In 1831, Poe managed to publish a new collection of poems, but his letters at the time reveal that these were difficult years. He feared imprisonment for his debts and was desperate for financial support. He sometimes took refuge in bouts of drinking. During this time, Poe was writing tales and selling them to journals in Baltimore and Philadelphia.

Edgar Allan Poe, 1848, an engraving from a daguerreotype. EDGAR ALLAN POE NATIONAL HISTORIC SITE

Magazines were becoming increasingly popular at the time, and Poe was hired as editor, critic, and contributor to the *Southern Literary Messenger* of Richmond, whose circulation promptly grew as a result of his contributions. Poe married the fourteen-year-old Virginia in 1836 and, with Maria Clemm, formed a household that in 1837 moved from Richmond to New York, thence to Philadelphia, then back to New York. "We lived only for each other," Clemm later wrote. She and Virginia worried when Poe traveled because of his occasional erratic behavior when he was on his own.

Poe contributed articles and poetry to a New York newspaper, the *Evening Mirror.* In its January 29, 1845, issue, the editor published Poe's *The Raven,* today considered one of the most famous poems ever written. The poem was an instant literary hit, although he received only $9 for it. Within a month, it had been reprinted at least ten times. People loved its catchy sound effects and read it aloud to each other. The resulting acclaim by the public was one of the only times in Poe's life that his intense desire for recognition was fully realized.

But his popularity with literary society in New York was soon dimmed by the harsh criticism he leveled at fellow authors such as Henry Wadsworth Longfellow and Nathaniel Hawthorne. When his literary criticism as well as his personal behavior reached extremes, Poe's popularity faded as quickly as it had grown.

In New York, Poe briefly owned his own journal—a lifelong dream—but soon lost it because of precarious financing. He was forced to sign over half his interest to his creditors, and the magazine folded a month later. Among all of Poe's writings, only his volume *Tales of the Grotesque and Arabesque,* a collection of horror stories, achieved some commercial success. He never profited from the copyrighting of his material, much of which was republished by others without any compensation to the author.

It was in New York that Virginia died of tuberculosis at the age of twenty-four in 1847. Following Virginia's death, Poe rapidly disintegrated, returning to Richmond in 1849, still preoccupied with the goal of owning his own journal. Setting off for New York to seek patrons and to visit Mrs. Clemm, Poe traveled no farther than Baltimore. There he died in a delirium from what a doctor said was "acute congestion of the brain." Edgar Allan Poe, one of the most innovative writers in the annals of American literature, lies buried in the Westminster Presbyterian Church Cemetery at Fayette and Green Streets in Baltimore, along with Virginia and Maria Clemm.

Edgar Allan Poe National Historic Site

As you tour this townhouse that Poe rented in 1843 on Seventh Street in Philadelphia, a National Park Service interpreter recalls events of Poe's tragic but productive life. The restored house is unfurnished, leaving it to the visitor's imagination to picture each room as it would have been when the author, his young wife, Virginia, and his mother-in-law, Maria Clemm, lived here.

You are helped to visualize Poe, a freelance writer endeavoring to support his family, writing at a table lit only by a gas lamp while his wife, suf-

---

Visiting Edgar Allan Poe National Historic Site

532 N. Seventh St., Philadelphia, PA 19106

PHONE: 215-597-8974 (visitors center) or 215-597-8980 (Poe house)
WEBSITE: www.nps.gov/edal
ADMINISTRATION: Administered through Independence National Historical Park of the National Park Service.
HOURS: June–October, open daily, 9–5; November–May, Wednesday through Sunday, 9–5. Closed New Year's Day, Thanksgiving, and Christmas Day.
ADMISSION FEES: Free.
TOURS: Ranger-guided tours of the three-building complex include exhibits, audio-visual programs, and bookstore.
TIME NEEDED: 1 to 2 hours.
SPECIAL EVENTS: Educational and entertaining events are scheduled throughout the year, such as a 90-minute "Poe in Philadelphia" program for groups; a one-act play, "Remembering Poe"; and a celebration of poetry during National Poetry Month.
SPECIAL CONSIDERATIONS: Wheelchair-accessibile first floor, which includes exhibits, audiovisual programs, and bookstore. Braille text available.
PARKING: Adjacent parking lot, entered from Spring Garden Street.
SALES OUTLETS: Bookstore offers books, videos, audiocassettes, and posters.
DIRECTIONS: Poe house is located at the corner of North Seventh Street and Spring Garden Street in Philadelphia. From I-95 North, take Historic Area Exit. At bottom of ramp, turn left at traffic light onto Delaware Avenue and follow to Spring Garden Street (about 1.5 miles). Turn left on Spring Garden Street and proceed to Seventh Street. From I-95 South, take Independence Hall/Historic Area Exit. At bottom of ramp, turn right on Callowhill Street. Follow to Seventh Street and proceed to Spring Garden Street.

Though Poe only lived in this Philadelphia house for a short time, he created some of his best-known works here, including *The Fall of the House of Usher, The Murders in the Rue Morgue,* and *The Tell-tale Heart.* NATIONAL PARK SERVICE

fering from tuberculosis, for which there was no known cure, lay in her third-floor bedroom. The tour leads eventually to the basement, a setting that might easily have inspired Poe as he wrote the short story *The Black Cat,* one of the horror tales for which he is famous.

The Park Service has imaginatively combined the restored Poe house with two houses next door to provide visitors with a reception area where tours gather and a small auditorium where an eight-minute video of Poe's life is presented. A furnished Victorian-style reading room allows visitors to peruse a complete set of Poe's writing, books of his poetry, and books written about him as one of America's most influential authors.

Other homes and museums associated with Edgar Allan Poe are located in Baltimore, the Bronx, and Richmond.

St. John Neumann

(1811-60)

Few foresaw that John Neumann, an immigrant priest who spent much of his life ministering to fellow immigrants, would become a saint. Diminutive in stature, quiet in manner, modest in appearance, he arrived in the United States from his native Bohemia (now the Czech Republic) in 1836, ready for whatever God had in store for him as a Catholic priest.

Neumann grew up in the small town of Prachatitz. He came from a strict Catholic family, did well in his school studies, and graduated in 1835 from the Catholic seminary in nearby Budweis, the town that later gave its name to Budweiser beer. Adept at languages, he learned to speak not only his native German, but also Czech, Italian, French, English, and Spanish. Later in life, he even learned Gaelic so he could converse with Irish immigrants.

Faced with the fact that he could not be ordained in his local diocese because it had no need for additional priests, John Neumann determined to go to the United States, where German-speaking priests were needed. So in 1836, he left his family and boarded a ship for America. Years later, he remembered his difficult voyage. His clothing was nearly worn out, his shoes had holes in them, he was down to his last pennies, and someone on the ship had stolen his hat.

But he was right about the need for priests in America. The bishop of New York immediately ordained the young Bohemian and assigned him as a pastor to serve the many immigrants who were pouring into upstate New York. Many of these immigrants had been drawn to the area by construction jobs on the recently completed Erie Canal. Here between Rochester and Buffalo, he ministered to some four hundred Catholics, three-fourths of them German immigrants, riding horseback between his rural parish churches.

After four years of riding the rural circuit, he applied for and was accepted as a novice in the Redemptorists, a religious congregation that ministered to the "poor and most abandoned." A year later, in Baltimore, he became the first person in the United States to profess the vows of a

Redemptorist. He was assigned to construct and become the pastor of St. Philomena's Church in Pittsburgh. In 1848, scarcely five years after he had became a Redemptorist, Father Neumann was selected to be the superior of the Redemptorists in the United States.

In 1852, he was appointed bishop of Philadelphia, a large diocese that covered two-thirds of Pennsylvania, parts of Delaware and Maryland, and half of New Jersey, supporting a Catholic population of about 170,000, many of them German-speaking. Surprised and humbled by the announcement, he begged the archbishop to withdraw his name because he felt unworthy of the responsibility. Pope Pius IX, however, informed Father Neumann that he must accept the appointment.

Philadelphia, the second-largest city in the nation, had the largest Catholic diocese in the country at that time. Many of the wealthier Catholics expected a different kind of bishop—one who was more cultured, refined, polished, and well-bred. Instead, they received a dedicated, hard-working priest who poured out his energies day and night for his flock.

One of Bishop Neumann's most notable accomplishments in Philadelphia was the establishment of a parochial school system with lay board members that would provide Catholic children "an education based on religious principles" so they would not be "led astray by false and delusive theories . . . which leave youth without religion." During his eight years as bishop, he began thirty-four schools, in spite of the fact that the diocese was strapped for money and the nation was suffering through a national financial crisis. He founded the Sisters of Saint Francis of Philadelphia and assisted in establishing the Sisters of the Immaculate Heart of Mary. He encouraged the Sisters of Notre Dame to come from Germany to staff the new Catholic schools.

In 1854, nineteen years after he first arrived in America, Bishop Neumann found an opportunity to return to his native land. The pope had invited all bishops to come to Rome for a cere-

St. John Neumann, a rendering on a prayer card. NATIONAL SHRINE OF ST. JOHN NEUMANN, PHILADELPHIA

mony. After his duties in Rome were completed, Neumann made his way to what was then Bohemia. When he arrived at a village near his hometown, he later wrote, all the townspeople turned out to greet their native son, and there was nothing he could do but spend the night there.

Next morning, trying to avoid publicity, he suggested that he walk the last few miles to his home village by a back road. The people wouldn't hear of it. Instead, he emerged from the rectory where he was staying to find awaiting him the personal sleigh of a prince, equipped with four horses and a liveried coachman. As the astonished bishop neared Prachatitz, with bells ringing in the steeple and the town band playing, a salute of cannon fire greeted him. There to welcome him were his proud father and his youngest sister. When he left a week later, however, he managed to slip away from his hometown at daybreak, avoiding what he knew was a planned gala send-off.

As the Diocese of Philadelphia gained more parishioners, the pope appointed a bishop coadjutor to assist Bishop Neumann with his increasing duties. But the "Little Bishop," as many called him, continued to visit outlying parishes, hearing confessions and saying Mass. No village was too remote, no farmhouse too isolated for him to visit. Meanwhile, Bishop James Wood took over responsibility for the diocese's finances.

Bishop Neumann always lived a spartan life. His room contained only the barest of necessities, and he often had but one suit of clothes to his name. Though he tried to conceal it from even his closest associates, he often slept on a bare floor. On January 5, 1860, as he was walking near his office to mail a chalice as a gift to a poor pastor in an outlying parish, he suffered a massive heart attack or stroke and died just two hours short of his forty-ninth birthday. His funeral procession was the largest seen in the history of Philadelphia to that time. He lies buried in St. Peter the Apostle Church in Philadelphia, which has been under the care of the Redemptorists since its founding.

In 1921, Pope Benedict XV declared John Neumann's virtues to have been heroic. In 1963, Pope Paul VI beatified him in a ceremony at St. Peter's Basilica in Rome, and in 1977, the same pope declared John Neumann a canonized saint, the first male citizen of the United States to be so honored.

National Shrine of St. John Neumann

People of all faiths are welcome to visit the National Shrine of St. John Neumann at St. Peter the Apostle Church at the corner of Fifth Street and Girard Avenue in the northeastern part of Philadelphia. As a priest of the

St. John Neumann's body lies in a modern chapel beneath the main sanctuary of the Redemptorist St. Peter the Apostle Church, where he was bishop of Philadelphia in the 1850s. PHOTOS BY THE AUTHORS

Redemptorists, Father Neumann considered the St. Peter Church his home during the period from 1852 to 1860, when he served as bishop of the Diocese of Philadelphia.

Visitors enter through the public entrance on Fifth Street next to the church and proceed to the shrine office, where tours are arranged. The chancel of the large upper church, built in 1845, is encircled with stained-glass windows from Vienna and Innsbruck in Austria.

In the "lower church," once the basement of the original structure, is a contemporary chapel. The body of St. John Neumann, preserved in a lifelike manner, rests within a transparent sarcophagus beneath a striking mosaic depicting events in the saint's life. Encircling the chapel are colorful scenes of the life of

---

Visiting National Shrine of St. John Neumann

**St. Peter the Apostle Church,
1019 N. Fifth St., Philadelphia, PA 19123**

PHONE: 215-627-3080
E-MAIL: Neumann@philanet.com
WEBSITE: www.stjohnneumann.org
ADMINISTRATION: The Redemptorists of St. Peter the Apostle Catholic Church.
HOURS: Shrine open Monday–Saturday, 7:30–5:30; Sunday, 7:30–5:00.
ADMISSION FEES: Free.
TOURS: Group tours of the shrine, museum, and upper church of St. Peter the Apostle available.
TIME NEEDED: 1 to 2 hours.
SPECIAL EVENTS: Worship services, special scheduled pilgrimages, and celebrations of St. John Neumann.
SPECIAL CONSIDERATIONS: Lower church, shrine, and gift shop are ramp-accessible.
PARKING: On-site parking.
SALES OUTLETS: Gift shop open Monday–Saturday, 9–4; Sunday, 10–4.
DIRECTIONS: From I-95 North, take Exit 17 (Callowhill Street). Stay right; turn right on Fifth Street. Follow to Girard Avenue, turn right, and then right on Lawrence Street into parking lot. From I-95 South, take Girard Avenue Exit, and follow to Fifth Street. Turn left on Lawrence Street, one block after Fourth Street, and turn right into parking lot.

St. John Neumann depicted in stained-glass windows designed by a fellow Bohemian, Herbert Gunther.

To one side of the chapel is a small museum that contains St. John's personal possessions, such as a notebook he once used, church proclamations, and religious relics. Nearby is the Chapel of the Blessed Sacrament, where devout parishioners meditate and offer prayers.

Stephen Foster

(1826-64)

Stephen Foster was a bundle of contradictions. This troubadour of the South and one of America's first songwriters was not a southerner, but a Yankee who was born and lived most of his life in Pittsburgh. Only once did he venture into the Deep South, when a group of friends joined him and his wife on their belated honeymoon, a riverboat cruise from Pittsburgh to New Orleans to take in the Mardi Gras celebration.

Foster had little musical training, although he played several instruments. His choice of occupations made him the despair of his family and of his long-suffering wife. And he earned only a meager income during his lifetime from the more than two hundred songs he wrote, although some of these tunes were on the lips of millions.

Stephen Foster seems to have been born with a song in his heart, poetry in his mind, and an overwhelming desire to share his music with others. From an early age, it was music that motivated him. His inspiration came from the sentimental parlor songs his sisters played on the piano at home and the minstrel shows that moved from one river town to the next as they played in local theaters. He also was intrigued by the singing of the black stevedores who manned the riverboats that churned up and down the Ohio River near his home.

Stephen Foster, America's first professional composer, was born in Pittsburgh on July 4, 1826, the ninth child of William and Eliza Foster. The day he was born was the very day that two of the nation's founding fathers— Thomas Jefferson and John Adams—died, exactly fifty years after the Declaration of Independence.

He received a good education at private academies in Pittsburgh and in northeastern Pennsylvania. In his spare time, the boy liked to tramp in the woods and write poetry. In a letter written when Stephen was fifteen, his father wrote that "he seeks no associates and his leisure hours are all devoted to musick, for which he possesses a strange talent." Stephen eagerly taught himself to play the flute, his principal instrument, as well as the family piano, the clarinet, violin, and guitar. He spent hours at a local music store, where he got to know the proprietor, Henry Kleber, a German immigrant and musician. At age fourteen, he composed his first song, "Tioga Waltz."

Although he enrolled in college in 1845, he returned home after only a few days. At loose ends, he and several other young men formed a club that met twice a week at Foster's home to sing the popular songs of the day. Whenever they ran out of songs, Foster would simply compose a new one.

But Foster's father soon decided it was time for this "idle dreamer of a son" to get a paying job, so he sent him off to an older brother, Dunning, in Cincinnati, who gave him a job as a bookkeeper for the steamboat company where he worked. At the time, the waterfront of this busy shipping port teemed with a kaleidoscope of southern planters, rivermen, African-American roustabouts, and gold seekers bound for California. Like Pittsburgh, it was also a popular stop on the minstrel circuit. Foster soon found himself keeping books by day and writing songs at night.

Carrying compositions like "Lou'siana Belle" and "Uncle Ned" under his arm, he made the rounds of the local music publishers with little success. Then in 1848, he appeared with "Oh, Susanna," a song he had written earlier in Pittsburgh. A publisher paid him $100 for the song, with which he was delighted. "Oh, Susanna" immediately appeared in the repertoire of nearly every minstrel group and soon became the marching song of the

Stephen Foster, c. 1860. FOSTER HALL COLLEC-
TION, CENTER FOR AMERICAN MUSIC, UNIVERSITY
OF PITTSBURGH

hordes of forty-niners who were following the siren call of the California gold rush. It became the unofficial theme song of the wagon trains then heading west across the prairie. It was a windfall for his publisher, who sold some one hundred thousand copies of the sheet music. Suddenly, it seems, everyone was singing "I come from Alabama with a banjo on my knee," and Stephen Foster vaulted to popularity as a songwriter.

With this musical success under his belt, Foster now determined to do what he had always wanted to do—become a full-time songwriter—at a time when this job title did not even exist. He would, in fact, become the first person in the United States known to earn his living solely through the sale of his musical compositions to the public, but because neither he nor anyone else had a sense of the value of his songs, he made little money from his melodies. Most of his songs sold only a few thousand copies each. It was his minstrel songs that brought the most income. He even allowed one of his songs to be published in return for a mere fifty copies of the sheet music and occasionally gave one away.

In the next years, he wrote a handful of songs, including the memorable "Old Folks at Home," a song that made blackface songs fit for singing in the parlor. Shortly thereafter, he wrote the equally memorable "My Old Kentucky Home" after he supposedly took a brief trip to Bardstown, Kentucky, to visit a relative.

He now signed a contract with a New York music publisher, Firth, Pond & Co., to produce his songs, and then returned to Pittsburgh to marry Jane McDowell, the daughter of a physician. A servant of the McDowells later inspired Foster to write the song "Old Black Joe." It was the couple's delayed honeymoon in 1852 that took them on the steamboat trip to New Orleans. In 1853, he produced "The Social Orchestra," a collection of seventy-three of his own and other composers' melodies arranged as instrumental solos, duets, trios, and quartets. He arranged his most popular songs for guitar accompaniment, focusing on ballads like "Jeanie with the Light Brown Hair," which he wrote for his wife; "Hard Times Come Again No More"; and "Come Where My Love Lies Dreaming."

Recognizing the popularity of Christy's Minstrels, the headliners of the day, Foster offered E. P. Christy first rights to introduce some of his newly written songs—a privilege for which Christy paid him the small fee of $10 for performing each song. Foster even allowed Christy to claim that he was not only the performer, but the composer of what became Foster's most famous tune, "Old Folks at Home" ("Swanee River"), although the song was later correctly attributed to Foster. "Old Folks at Home" became an immediate hit. Within a year, the publisher sold 130,000 copies. In return for such generous treatment by the new composer, the minstrels spread his name wherever they went, spurring sales of his published sheet music. When Christy's Minstrels went to England, they made "Old Folks at Home" almost as famous in that country as in the United States. Thousands of Englishmen sang about Florida's Suwannee River, which Stephen Foster had never seen.

Now acclaimed as "America's Songwriter," Stephen Foster, Jane, and their infant daughter, Marion, were induced by their publisher to move to New York, where they rented a house across the Hudson River in Hoboken. But

Foster seems to have been homesick for Pittsburgh and his family and friends, and in 1854, he and Jane impetuously sold all their furniture and moved back to the homestead in Pittsburgh, where they lived once more with Foster's parents. The composer was heartbroken when his mother died in 1855 and his father six months later. Within a year, Stephen's older brother, Dunning, who had obtained the job for him in Cincinnati, also passed away.

Foster now all but ceased writing, producing only a single song during 1856 and 1857. His debts mounted, and he was forced to sell the future rights to his previous works and to appeal to his publisher for cash advances against his future earnings. Jane later took a job as a telegrapher for the Pennsylvania Railroad to help support the family.

In 1860, Foster moved back to New York to be near his publisher, leaving Jane and little Marion behind. He composed a number of songs the following years in New York. Actually, more than half of his tunes were issued after 1860, but few of them were as memorable as his earlier works. He needed the income, however, and music stores were eager to sell any sheet music that had the name Stephen Foster on it.

As his situation became more desperate, he turned more and more to alcohol, and the quality of his tunes declined. He dashed off and sold one song for $25. His longtime publisher, Firth, Pond & Co., was bought out by another music company. When the Civil War broke out, he wrote a number of songs proclaiming the Union cause.

In January 1864, suffering with a fever, he fell in his rooming house and lay bleeding on the floor until he was discovered by a maid. He was taken to Bellevue Hospital, where he died three days later, at age thirty-eight. The composer was buried in the Allegheny Cemetery in Pittsburgh. More than twenty-five songs he had written were published posthumously, including the haunting "Beautiful Dreamer."

Stephen Foster's songs are deeply embedded in America's musical consciousness. "My Old Kentucky Home" was designated the official state song of Kentucky, and "Old Folks at Home" the official song of Florida, earning Stephen Foster the honor of being the only songwriter to have written the official songs of two states. It is likely that many who hum his melodies may not even know who wrote them. A fellow songwriter, George F. Root, credits Foster with creating the "people's song," seemingly simple words and music combined in such a way "that it will be received and live in the hearts of the people." *Harper's New Monthly Magazine* proclaimed two months after his death that "the air is full of his melodies. They are our national music."

Center for American Music—
Stephen Foster Memorial and Foster Hall Collection

You will find the Stephen Foster Memorial, an elegant Gothic structure, on the city campus of the University of Pittsburgh, next to the university's most prominent building, the forty-two-story Cathedral of Learning.

It is the only memorial of its kind in the United States devoted to an American composer. It contains a six hundred-seat auditorium that is used for concerts and theater productions. Its west wing houses the Center for American Music, which includes a library and exhibit room, both devoted mainly to Stephen Foster and his times. Encircling the twelve-sided exhibit room are copies of the first editions of many of Foster's 286 known works. Alcoves around the room hold Foster memorabilia, including booklets, advertisements, broadsides of performances of his music, and songsters (booklets that contained the lyrics to songs but no music). Visitors see a piano from Foster's home, his flute, a barrel organ, and a music box, as well as the first draft of "Old Folks at Home." Also on display are photographs and letters from the composer. Above each alcove is a stained-glass window that depicts one of his songs. Familiar Stephen Foster tunes play in the background as you stroll through the museum.

The handsome paneled library serves as the principal repository for materials concerning the life and music of America's first professional

The Stephen Foster Memorial is the world's only concert hall, museum, research library, and archives devoted to an American composer. PHOTO BY THE AUTHORS

Visiting Center for American Music— Stephen Foster Memorial and Foster Hall Collection

**Stephen Foster Memorial, University of Pittsburgh,
4301 Forbes Ave., Pittsburgh, PA 15260**

PHONE: 412-624-4100
E-MAIL: amerimus@pitt.edu
WEBSITE: www.library.pitt.edu/libraries/cam/cam.html
ADMINISTRATION: Administered by University of Pittsburgh.
HOURS: Open Monday–Friday, 9–4; weekend and library hours by appointment. Closed for university holidays.
ADMISSION FEES: General admission is free. Guided tours $1.50 for adults; $1 for seniors and students.
TOURS: Guided tour for up to 50 people available by reservation two weeks in advance.
TIME NEEDED: 1 hour.
SPECIAL EVENTS: January 13 ceremony on anniversary of Stephen Foster's death.
SPECIAL CONSIDERATIONS: Handicapped ramp available; restrooms accessible only by chairlift.
PARKING: Paid parking lots and metered spaces available near site.
SALES OUTLETS: Bookstore offers music, recordings, postcards, and books about Stephen Foster.
DIRECTIONS: From Pennsylvania Turnpike, take Exit 3 and follow I-79 South to I-279 South, then follow I-279 South to I-376 East to Exit 5, Forbes/Oakland. Follow signs to University of Pittsburgh.

songwriter. Much of this material was gathered between 1931 and 1937 by Josiah Lilly, a pharmaceutical manufacturer from Indianapolis who became fascinated with Foster and his contributions to American music. He and a research team identified, acquired, and authenticated all of Foster's known works, then donated the entire collection to the University of Pittsburgh. Under the leadership of John Bowman, chancellor of the university from 1921 to 1945, and members of the Tuesday Musical Club, $500,000 was raised to construct the building, which opened in 1937. Contributions and an endowment fund now maintain the museum and its collection. A statue of the composer stands across from the museum on Forbes Avenue.

Elsewhere, you may wish to visit Stephen Foster State Folk Culture Center, on the banks of the Suwannee River in White Springs, Florida; My Old Kentucky Home State Park, in Bardstown, Kentucky; and Stephen Foster State Park, along the Suwannee River in Georgia.

Andrew Carnegie

(1835-1919)

Andrew Carnegie's talent lay not in inventing new industrial machines or processes. Instead, his skill was in recognizing how a new development in technology could be put profitably to use, and then backing up his vision with what money he had.

As a young working man, he foresaw the market for attaching sleeping cars to passenger trains. He anticipated the impact oil would have on the economy and bought an oil well. He concluded that bridges made of iron would replace those built of wood. And he clearly saw that steel was tougher and better suited to make rails for the expanding railroad system, just as steel was also better for framing city buildings than cast iron.

There were only a few hints of such insights in the boy born in Dunfermline, Scotland, the son of a hand loom weaver and his wife. Young Andrew, although a bright lad, had only four years of schooling when the mechanization of weaving in Scotland forced his poor family to make the arduous journey to America, where they joined other family members in Pittsburgh. His father took a job in a cotton textile factory, and twelve-year-old Andrew went to work in the same factory as a bobbin boy, earning $1.20 a week.

Young Andrew next became a steam engine tender, then a messenger for a local telegraph office. Here he earned the reputation of being the company's fastest delivery boy, memorizing the location of every business office in the city of Pittsburgh. To expand his knowledge, he borrowed books from a kindly businessman, thus developing a lifelong pursuit of knowledge and a love of books and libraries.

Hanging around the telegraph office, Carnegie learned to decipher incoming messages by the sound of the clicking key, rather than waiting for the entire message to be printed out on a tape. As a reward, his supervisor promoted him, and he became a telegraph operator.

Then came his big break. His skill at telegraphy caught the attention of one of his customers, Thomas A. Scott, superintendent of the Western Division of the growing Pennsylvania Railroad, who promptly hired him

Andrew Carnegie, c. 1905. LIBRARY OF CONGRESS

to be his personal telegrapher and secretary at the handsome salary of $25 a month.

As the protégé of one of the most able and daring railroad executives in the country, Carnegie received valuable lessons in business management and stock investment. So rapidly did he learn the details of managing a railroad line that when Scott returned to Philadelphia in 1859 to become general manager of the Pennsylvania Railroad, Carnegie was appointed his successor as superintendent of the Western Division at the young age of twenty-two. When the Civil War broke out, Scott was appointed assistant secretary of war to take charge of military transportation. He brought Carnegie with him to Washington to head up telegraphic communications with the army.

Now that Carnegie had money of his own to invest, he put that money into a company that made sleeping cars, which at that time were an innovation for the railroads. He also invested in an oil well in western Pennsylvania, as well as the Pacific and Atlantic Telegraph Company, which he later sold to Western Union at a great profit. He organized the Keystone Bridge Company to build iron railway bridges. In 1865, with the war over, he resigned from the Pennsylvania Railroad to further his other interests and made several trips to Europe as an agent to sell railroad bonds on behalf of a New York investment banker.

On one of these trips, he watched a demonstration of inventor Henry Bessemer's converter, which turned iron into steel by blowing cold air on red-hot pig iron. He quickly realized the potential that this tougher metal would have in the manufacture of all-steel rails for railways. In spite of the economic depression that then gripped the United States, Carnegie risked everything by plowing profits from his other investments into a state-of-the-art steel mill along the Monongahela River near Pittsburgh. He brought experts from England and Wales to build and operate his plant, and acquired rich deposits of iron ore in the Lake Superior region. Soon the Edgar Thomson Works, cannily named for a leader of the Pennsylvania Railroad, a sought-after customer, was producing excellent steel and underselling the steel rails then being imported from England.

Carnegie continually followed two policies: keeping production costs low and hiring able managers to run the plants. He advised his managers to "cut the costs, run the mills full, and let the profits take care of themselves." It was these policies that now brought Henry Clay Frick into the Carnegie Steel Company. Frick, the "Coke King" of Pennsylvania, became a partner, assuring Carnegie an ample supply of coke to fuel his converters. With Carnegie's support, Frick was soon supervising Carnegie's steel empire while Carnegie himself concentrated on obtaining new orders.

Under Frick's direction, the steel enterprise in the 1880s made spectacular advances. The Homestead Works, a competitive rival, was purchased in 1883. Carnegie Steel embraced the latest steel technology and was the first to employ a chemist on its staff. The company paid above-average wages, promoted from within, and provided a number of educational and recreational benefits to its employees. Its innovations paid off handsomely, and by 1890, the company's profits had reached $4.5 million.

In his personal life, Andrew Carnegie lived with his mother until she died in 1886. Only then, in his fifties, did he marry Louise Whitfield, whom he had known for fifteen years. The Carnegies had one daughter, Margaret.

But in 1892, an event occurred that would besmirch the reputations of both Carnegie and Frick—the Homestead strike. This efficient plant had produced steel for much of the nation, including notable structures such as the Panama Canal and ships like the USS *Maine*. Carnegie, who wanted to reduce labor costs and install labor-saving devices, told Frick, his second in command, not to renew the contract of the Amalgamated Association of Iron and Steel Workers, since they represented only a minority of the mill's workmen. Then he left for his usual long summer vacation in Scotland. The workers refused Frick's demand that some of the higher-paid workers accept a cut in wages and that they disband their union. Negotiations turned to violence when Frick brought in three hundred Pinkerton security agents to secure the property so he could hire strikebreakers to operate the plant. A furious day-long pitched battle ensued in which four workers and six Pinkerton agents died, the workers seized the plant, and the governor was forced to send in the state militia. Carnegie, in a cable from Scotland, supported Frick's adamant stand. The militia permitted company officials to occupy their offices once more, but several days later, Frick was shot, stabbed, and almost killed by an anarchist who was not even a worker at the plant. Frick, while still recovering from his wounds, brought in strikebreakers, reopened the mill, and ended unionization of the plant—actions that embittered many former steelworkers and cast a gloom over the town that lingers even to this day.

Ironically, it had been only three years prior to the Homestead strike that Carnegie had published an article entitled "Gospel of Wealth," setting out a philosophy that those who accumulated great wealth in a modern industrial society should consider themselves merely trustees of that wealth and should return most of it to society in ways they deemed most beneficial. By 1901, after he had broken off his partnership with Frick and had sold his huge steel company to financier J. P. Morgan, Carnegie began to earnestly practice what he had preached. He was fond of saying "A man who dies wealthy, dies disgraced."

First were libraries. He had profited from using a library and wanted others to gain from them as well. Over the years, he provided no less than 2,811 libraries to the English-speaking world, including 1,946 in the United States, 660 in Great Britain, and 156 in Canada, at a cost of more than $50 million. He donated only the buildings, however, insisting that the communities share the responsibility by taxing their citizens to pay for the purchase of books and the cost of the buildings' maintenance. Use of the libraries was to be free to everyone.

In addition to libraries, he established the Carnegie Foundation for the Advancement of Teaching, and among his first gifts following his retirement were pension funds for his former steelworkers and for college teachers. The Carnegie Institution of Washington, D.C., was created in 1902 to advance scientific research and discovery. Even churches, which ranked last on his list of institutions to help, were remembered with gifts of 7,689 pipe organs.

Carnegie then raised his sights to worldwide problems. In pursuit of international justice and the abolition of war, he created the Endowment for International Peace. He also built what he called his three "Temples of Peace": the Pan-American Union building in Washington for the promotion of peace in the Western Hemisphere; the Central American Court of Justice in Costa Rica to arbitrate differences among those frequently quarreling countries; and The Hague Peace Palace in the Netherlands to house the World Court.

It was a cruel twist of fate that Andrew Carnegie, the peacemaker, died in 1919 even as his countrymen were fighting and suffering in World War I. His widow, Louise, wrote that "the world disaster was too much. His heart was broken."

Carnegie Museums of Pittsburgh

What you see at the Carnegie Museums of Pittsburgh has less to do with Andrew Carnegie himself and more to do with the people he intended to benefit—the people of Pittsburgh. The resources that he endowed illustrate Carnegie's belief that education and culture can make any person's life better, as they had his own.

An immense complex of sandstone buildings that fills more than a city block in the Oakland section of the city, the museums have been referred

Visiting Carnegie Museums of Pittsburgh

4400 Forbes Ave., Pittsburgh, PA 15213

PHONE: 412-622-3131 or 412-622-3236

WEBSITE: www.carnegiemuseums.org

ADMINISTRATION: The Carnegie Museums of Pittsburgh, a nonprofit corporation, maintains 40 buildings for the Carnegie Museum of Natural History, Carnegie Museum of Art, Carnegie Science Center, and Andy Warhol Museum. The Carnegie Library of Pittsburgh, a public trust supported by local financial resources, includes the Main Library, 20 branch libraries, bookmobile, services for blind and handicapped, and film center. Carnegie Music Hall is part of the Carnegie complex.

HOURS: Tuesday–Saturday, 10–5; Sundays, 1–5; closed Mondays and major holidays, but since each museum maintains separate schedules, call first.

ADMISSION FEES: $6 for adults; $5 for seniors; $4 for children and students with ID for each museum.

TOURS: Group tours and exhibition tours available upon request.

TIME NEEDED: Most visitors come to one of the museums for enjoyment, research, or special events, so times vary. Allow 6 to 8 hours to visit the Carnegie complex, which includes the Museum of Natural History, Art Museum, Carnegie Library, and Music Hall. The Science Center and Andy Warhol Museum are at two other locations in Pittsburgh, and visitors should allow at least 2 hours each.

SPECIAL EVENTS: Both on-site and community outreach programs are offered throughout the year, including special exhibits, programs, lectures, and film series at the Art Museum and Andy Warhol Museum; performances, science and research, Omnimax Theatre, and planetarium at the Science Center; exhibits, programs, lectures, film series, family overnight adventures, and more at the Museum of Natural History.

SPECIAL CONSIDERATIONS: Wheelchairs and strollers available at no charge; selected tours presented in sign language. All museums meet ADA requirements.

PARKING: Various paid lots near the complex.

SALES OUTLETS: Each museum maintains its own store with books, toys, maps, gifts, jewelry, and children's items. Food service is available at each of the museum sites.

DIRECTIONS: From downtown Pittsburgh, follow I-376 (Penn Lincoln Parkway) along the Monongahela River to Forbes Avenue Exit. Follow Forbes Avenue 0.5 mile to 4400 Forbes Avenue and Carnegie Complex, which is across from the 42-story Cathedral of Learning of the University of Pittsburgh.

The Carnegie complex of museums is a legacy in Pittsburgh that was developed through an endowment from Andrew Carnegie, the Scottish immigrant who became the richest man in the world through his steel business. CARNEGIE MUSEUMS OF PITTSBURGH

to as the cultural heart of Pittsburgh. Within this dynamic set of buildings, as its founder planned, are the Museum of Art, including its Architecture Hall; the Museum of Natural History; the Carnegie Library of Pittsburgh; and the Music Hall. It fulfills the promise engraved on its façade to serve as a center for art, science, literature, and music. Two other parts of the complex are located on the city's North Side across the Allegheny River: the Carnegie Science Museum and the Andy Warhol Museum.

One remarkable room in the main complex, the foyer for patrons of the Music Hall, is a glittering chamber filled with black marble columns, a mosaic marble floor, and a gold coffered ceiling lit by a dazzling array of chandeliers. The chandeliers, hung in 1907, were one of the first major electric lighting displays to be installed in Pittsburgh. At one end of this magnificent hall stands a bronze statue of Andrew Carnegie.

Another remarkable room is Architecture Hall, where replicas of classic architectural buildings and sculptures are displayed. Visitors may admire a full-size replica of the Erechtheum ("Porch of the Maidens"), famous landmark of the Acropolis in Athens, and a full-size replica of the façade of the Abbey Church of Saint Gilles du Gard. The nearby Hall of Sculptures exhibits 140 plaster casts of renowned sculptures and is itself modeled after the interior of the Parthenon. About one and a half million people visit these Andrew Carnegie museums each year.

Henry Clay Frick
(1849-1919)

Like many a poor boy growing up in rural Pennsylvania, Henry Frick—known to his family and friends as Clay—made up his mind at an early age that one day he was going to be rich. He was going to be richer, he vowed to himself, than his grandfather Abraham Overholt, who operated a distillery on a prosperous farm and whom he admired. The difference between Clay Frick and scores of other young people who may have nurtured the same daydream was that Frick figured out a practical way to reach his goal and had the nerve, personal discipline, and drive to take the risks that would get him there.

Frick was born in West Overton, forty-five miles southeast of Pittsburgh, the son of a miller who gave him the name of the then-leader of the Whig political party, Henry Clay. His birthplace and boyhood home was a small, converted springhouse his grandfather Overholt had leased to his father. At the age of eight, he was able to help with chores on his father's farm and to attend school during the winter months. His lifetime schooling consisted of only thirty months at the Classical and Scientific Institute at nearby Mount Pleasant, additional business schooling in Pittsburgh, and later a few months at Otterbein University in Ohio.

Frick, however, had little interest in the classical curriculum of the liberal arts college and at seventeen quit his studies for a job back home working in an uncle's store. He soon took another job at a department store in Pittsburgh but contracted typhoid fever and had to return home to recuperate.

After his recovery, his grandfather employed him as the chief bookkeeper at another distillery he owned, offering his grandson the possibility of eventually taking over its management. But Frick was looking in a different direction, at the extensive deposits of coal that lay buried in the region. With some money he had saved, in 1869 he joined a partnership with two cousins and another partner to buy six hundred acres of bituminous coal land in nearby Connellsville.

Frick had the vision to foresee that the newly introduced Bessemer process of making steel would generate a demand for coke, a fuel made by subjecting bituminous coal to high heat in an oven. The resulting coke, composed largely of carbon, is then fed into a Bessemer converter along with iron ore, limestone, and forced air to rid the ore of its impurities and produce molten steel, a metal that is harder and easier to shape than cast iron. He recognized that the plentiful soft and sulfurous bituminous coal could be slowly baked into "coal cakes"—coke—then shipped by rail to fuel the modern Bessemer furnaces of Pittsburgh's growing steel industry. Borrowing money, he and his partners bought 123 more acres of coal land and formed Overholt, Frick and Company, later to become the H. C. Frick Coke Company.

To finance the construction of fifty beehive ovens to turn coal into coke, Frick took the train to Pittsburgh and applied for a loan of $10,000 at the new bank of T. Mellon and Sons. Its founder, Judge Thomas Mellon, sent an agent to investigate the young entrepreneur. The agent's report reveals the practical, down-to-earth judgment of a nineteenth-century Pittsburgher. "Lands good, ovens well built, manager on job all day, keeps books evenings," observed the agent tersely. "May be a little too enthusiastic about pictures but not enough to hurt; knows his business down to the ground; advise making the loan."

Despite the financial panic that overtook the country in 1873, Clay Frick sold more and more coke in Pittsburgh, and he used the profits to buy more and more coalfields at depressed prices. He bought out his chief competitors. When his partners worried that he might be overextended, he bought out their interests as well, thus becoming the sole proprietor.

He never wavered in his belief that steel was the key product in industrial development and that coke was the key ingredient in the manufacture of steel. He lived frugally and gambled on the return of better times, continuing to build hundreds of new coke ovens. By the late 1870s, when the tide of depression finally ebbed and the price of a ton of coke rose from 90 cents to $1, then $2, then $3, then $5 a ton, the Frick firm dominated the coke market. It now

Henry Clay Frick, an engraving from *Magazine of Western History.* LIBRARY OF CONGRESS

had nearly a thousand employees and as many ovens. It shipped a hundred freight carloads of coke a day to the Pittsburgh mills. In 1879, on his thirtieth birthday, Henry Clay Frick reached the goal he had set for himself: He had a fortune of $1 million, twice that of his grandfather's estate.

In 1881, Frick married Adelaide Childs of Pittsburgh. While in New York City on their wedding trip, the Fricks were invited to a dinner by Andrew Carnegie and his mother. Much to his surprise, Carnegie offered him a partnership in his steelmaking company. The deal gave Carnegie an assured source of supply of coke for his furnaces and gave Frick the investment capital he needed to further expand his coke empire.

Thus began a partnership that would last two decades. Carnegie soon brought Frick, with his excellent business skills, into the top management of his steel operations. By 1892, Frick had organized Carnegie's interests—mills, mines, and transportation facilities—into the largest steel company in the world, the Carnegie Steel Company, returning rich profits to Carnegie, Frick, and the other partners.

But this steady progress was dealt a severe blow in 1892 with the strike of steelworkers at the Homestead plant on the outskirts of Pittsburgh, whose workers were turning out tons of high-quality steel at this state-of-the-art mill. As it turned out, this year proved to be a tumultuous one for Frick, both professionally and personally, and clouded his reputation and that of Carnegie.

Carnegie, always cost conscious, was determined to reduce labor costs at the Homestead plant. He gave Frick orders not to renew the labor contract of the union workers, a minority of the plant's employees, when it came due for renegotiation. Then he left for Scotland for his usual summer vacation. Going even beyond Carnegie's instructions, Frick demanded that some workers take a pay cut and also refused to renew the union's contract, locking the workers out of the plant when they called a strike in retaliation.

To break the strike, he planned to bring in strikebreakers to get the plant running again. As he had done in other labor disturbances, Frick attempted to bring in three hundred Pinkerton security agents under cover of darkness. Shots rang out, and before the all-day battle ended, four steelworkers and six Pinkertons were dead. The workers seized the plant, and the governor of Pennsylvania was forced to send in the state militia to quell the violence.

Although the militia permitted the company officials to occupy their offices once more, Henry Frick was physically attacked in his office downtown by a crazed anarchist who shot and stabbed him repeatedly. Frick barely escaped death. Recovering from his wounds, Frick ordered in other strikebreakers to run the plant, reopened the mill, and disbanded the union. But management's unyielding actions at the Homestead plant cost many steelworkers their jobs, embittered the townspeople for years thereafter, and besmirched the reputations of both Carnegie and Frick.

As if this assassination attempt were not enough, eleven days later Frick's twenty-six-day-old baby boy, Henry Clay Frick Jr., died, the second of two children he and his wife had lost. An adored six-year-old daughter, Martha, had died only a year before.

Although Frick continued to lead the steel company for seven more years, relations between Carnegie and Frick were never the same. Eventually Carnegie demanded that Frick sell his 11 percent interest in the company. Frick sued Carnegie over the value of his interest and won a court judgment, conceding only that he would never again hold any office in the steel company. When Carnegie sold his company to a syndicate headed by the banker J. P. Morgan the following year, Frick's interest in the resulting billion-dollar United States Steel Corporation had more than doubled in value, and much to Carnegie's chagrin, Frick was invited to serve on the board of directors of the new corporation.

In later years, the Fricks moved from Pittsburgh to a mansion on East 70th Street in New York City. The mansion was especially designed to house the art collection that the coal and steel baron had accumulated over the years, a world-famous collection of 1,350 works that is now open to the public. Here he died just short of his seventieth birthday. He was buried in Pittsburgh at Homewood Cemetery, only a few blocks from his beloved home, Clayton.

Frick Art and Historical Center

Visitors are invited to tour Clayton, the Victorian mansion where Henry Clay Frick and his wife, Adelaide, lived for twenty-three years and raised their family. The mansion is the only one left standing along what used to be Pittsburgh's "Millionaire's Row." The Fricks remodeled the gray stone mansion when they purchased it in 1882, even requesting that their neighbor, George Westinghouse, help install the electric wiring. From the elegant leather-backed chairs in the dining room to the numerous oil paintings on the walls, most of the furnishings are original. All of this was carefully preserved first by his daughter, who lived here in her later years, then by the Helen Clay Frick Foundation, which she established.

Personal photographs of the Frick family are still in place; even some of their personal calling cards remain in a silver tray in the parlor.

Visitors are welcome to walk the paths of the nearly six-acre estate, a green oasis in the Point Breeze section of the city now designated as the Frick Art and Historical Center. In addition to the mansion, you may tour the visitors center, art museum, greenhouse, café, and car and carriage museum. This museum displays Frick's 1914 Rolls-Royce Silver Ghost touring car, as well as more than thirty other classical autos that brought Pittsburgh recognition as an early automobile manufacturing center.

Helen Clay Frick built the Frick Art Museum in 1969, an impressive Italian Renaissance building, as a legacy for her father. It displays Italian, Flemish, and French paintings, sculpture, and decorative arts from the

Visiting Frick Art and Historical Center

7227 Reynolds St., Pittsburgh, PA 15208

PHONE: 412-371-0600

WEBSITE: www.frickart.org

ADMINISTRATION: Frick Art and Historical Center is a nonprofit organization established by Helen Clay Frick.

HOURS: Tuesday–Saturday, 10–5; Sunday, 12–6; closed Mondays.

ADMISSION FEES: Art museum, car and carriage museum, museum shop, and visitors center are free. House tours of Clayton are $10 for adults; $8 for seniors; $8 for students; $9 for one parent and one child.

TOURS: Self-guided except for docent-led tours of Clayton scheduled every 15 to 30 minutes depending on season; group tours available upon request.

TIME NEEDED: 4 hours.

SPECIAL EVENTS: Several art exhibitions with related educational programs throughout the year. "Clayton in Holiday Dress" at Christmastime; summer garden tour.

SPECIAL CONSIDERATIONS: Specialized tours of Clayton available. Art museum, car and carriage museum, café, visitors center, and first floor of Clayton are handicapped-accessible; wheelchairs available on loan.

PARKING: Free on-site parking.

SALES OUTLETS: Museum shop in visitors center offers gifts, children's toys, books on Henry Clay Frick, postcards, and jewelry.

DIRECTIONS: From downtown Pittsburgh, follow Fifth Avenue through Oakland and Shadyside to Penn Avenue. Bear right on Penn Avenue, proceed four lights, and turn right on Homewood Avenue. Go one long block to traffic circle, and follow signs to parking lot.

Frick's restored twenty-three-room Victorian home, Clayton, is part of the Frick Art and Historical Center, a six-acre complex of museums. Ninety-three percent of the furnishings and artifacts are original. FRICK ART AND HISTORICAL CENTER, PITTSBURGH

early Renaissance period through the eighteenth century and offers traveling exhibitions of various artists. As its founder intended, it continues to be free to the public.

The visitors center and gift shop are housed in what used to be the Frick family's two-story playhouse, which had its own bowling alley. A former garage on the grounds houses a popular café.

West Overton Museums

A short drive southeast of Pittsburgh brings you to Scottdale, site of the two-room springhouse where Henry Clay Frick was born. The restored small stone structure is open to the public as part of West Overton Village, an intact rural industrial village built by Abraham Overholt, Frick's maternal grandfather. Overholt, a hardworking Mennonite entrepreneur, operated a farm, two distilleries, and a gristmill.

The springhouse was built in 1800 to refrigerate food as part of Abraham Overholt's homestead. Visitors may view the pool in the basement

Abraham Overholt built this three-story brick home when he was the proprietor of a farm, gristmill, and two distilleries.

The centerpiece of the West Overton Museums in Scottdale is the Overholt Distillery established by Abraham Overholt, grandfather of Henry Clay Frick. Inside is the Distillery Museum, with displays of the coke and coal business that brought Frick to prominence.
PHOTOS BY THE AUTHORS

Visiting West Overton Museums

West Overton Village,
PA Route 819, Scottdale, PA 15683

PHONE: 724-887-7910

E-MAIL: womuseum@westol.com

WEBSITE: fay-west.com/westoverton

ADMINISTRATION: West Overton Museums is a nonprofit educational organization established by Helen Clay Frick as her father's legacy.

HOURS: May–October, Tuesday–Saturday, 10–4; Sunday, 1–5.

ADMISSION FEES: $6 for adults; $4 for seniors; $3 for children ages 7–12; free for children under 6.

TOURS: Self-guided tours of distillery, carriage house, springhouse, summer kitchen, smokehouse, garden, hay barn, chicken coop, stock barn, brick barn, and blacksmith shop; guided tour of the Overholt Homestead.

TIME NEEDED: At least 2 hours.

SPECIAL EVENTS: Parlor talks, January–April; quilt show in June; Civil War encampments in midsummer; heritage musical play third and fourth weekends in September; holiday season candlelight tours.

SPECIAL CONSIDERATIONS: Main floors of all buildings handicapped-accessible; first-floor restrooms available.

PARKING: Free on-site parking.

SALES OUTLETS: Gift shop offers souvenirs and books on Henry Clay Frick, mining and coke production, and southwest Pennsylvania.

DIRECTIONS: From Pennsylvania Turnpike, take Exit 8, New Stanton. Follow U.S. Route 119 south for 10 miles to PA Route 819 South (Scottdale exit). Turn right and follow Route 819 for 1 mile. West Overton Museums are on the right.

This small stone cottage was the birthplace of Henry Clay Frick in 1849. PHOTO BY THE AUTHORS

where spring water cooled the perishable food kept for the "big house." Two rooms were constructed above the pool for the John Frick family. Today these rooms are filled with photographs and memorabilia of Henry Clay Frick; his parents, John and Elizabeth Frick; and his grandparents, the Overholts.

A guided tour leads you through Abraham Overholt's three-story homestead, with its summer kitchen, washhouse, springhouse, blacksmith shop, and carriage house. You may also tour the five-story distillery itself. Now converted to a museum, it houses exhibits explaining the making of coke and contains two floors of furniture, craft implements, and displays illustrating eighteenth- and nineteenth-century life in western Pennsylvania. On display are the original chair, desk, and office equipment used by Frick to run his coke and steel empire. A video explains the process of turning bituminous coal into coke.

George Westinghouse

(1846–1914)

Early in life, George Westinghouse displayed the curiosity and mechanical aptitude that later made him one of the most prolific inventors the United States has known.

When he was but thirteen, growing up in the small town of Central Bridge in upstate New York, his father assigned him the task of cutting a pile of metal pipes into equal lengths. His father estimated that the job would take the boy the rest of the week, but young George ingeniously rigged a cutting tool to a power machine and cut all the pipes into lengths within a few hours.

In later years, the inventions and innovations that germinated in the mind of George Westinghouse would change the face of the United States, providing important building blocks of progress in the nation's industrial history. The ideas that sprang from the mind of this impetuous tinkerer laid the foundation for the electrification of the country, improved the heating and lighting of homes, and introduced revolutionary changes in the nation's rail, road, and sea transportation systems. His contributions earned him a place beside Thomas Edison and Alexander Graham Bell in this country's golden age of invention, the latter half of the nineteenth century.

In his youth, Westinghouse divided his time between going to school and tinkering in the workshop where his father fabricated agricultural products such as threshing machines. He produced his first invention, a rotary engine, when he was only fifteen and earned a U.S. patent for it by the time he was nineteen.

With the outbreak of the Civil War in 1861, he followed the example of two older brothers and ran away from home at age fifteen to join the Union army, but his father found him and brought him back. When he finally reached the legal age of seventeen, he joined a cavalry regiment for a year, and then switched to the Union navy, where he became acting third assistant engineer on the USS *Muscoota* and the USS *Stars and Stripes*.

At war's end, he returned home and went to Union College in Schenectady, but for only a few months, dropping out when the college's classical curriculum did not offer the practical subjects he wanted. Instead, he went to work in his father's machine shop.

On a railroad trip back home from Albany, his train was detained because two cars of the freight train ahead of them had jumped the track, a common occurrence in those days. Workmen were laboriously trying to get the cars back on the track using levers and jacks. As Westinghouse watched, he had a better idea. By the next day, he had put together plans, specifications, and a drawing of a car replacer. His father, unimpressed, wasn't interested in financing its manufacture, so the young inventor found two local businessmen with whom he formed a partnership. Selling his car replacer brought him in contact with other railroad men, and he soon came up with another innovation, an improved frog, the device that joins intersecting tracks together.

Another rail accident inspired the invention for which Westinghouse became best known. To stop a train in those days, brakemen atop the cars had to turn a brake wheel, then leap to the top of the next car and turn that wheel. The procedure was not only slow, but dangerous. So dangerous, in fact, that six of every ten brakemen were either killed or seriously injured on the job. A speeding train might travel a half mile before it could be halted. The Westinghouse air brake used compressed air, piping, hoses, couplings, and brake shoes in a complex system that could be controlled by the engineer in the locomotive cab.

On a notable day in April 1869, the first train to be equipped with the new air brake left the station in Pittsburgh, where Westinghouse now lived. Aboard the train were railroad executives and the twenty-two-year-old inventor. Unexpectedly, a horse and wagon suddenly appeared astride the track ahead, and a collision seemed imminent. The engineer grabbed the handle of the air brake, and the train screeched to a stop only a few feet short of the horse and wagon. After this successful demonstration of his air brake, none of his detractors called him "Crazy George" any longer.

George Westinghouse, 1906. GEORGE WESTING-HOUSE MUSEUM, WILMERDING, PENNSYLVANIA

The air brake gained immediate acceptance, and its impact was enormous. By the following year, Westinghouse had formed the Westinghouse Air Brake Company to manufacture the new safety product, for which orders came pouring in from the fast-expanding railroad system. He also revolutionized railroad signaling, developing a system of electric power signal devices, many of which are still basic to railways today.

Working on railway signaling equipment got Westinghouse deeply interested in electricity. He tackled the problem of generating electric power and getting it to where customers needed it, thereby bringing about the great alternating current versus direct current controversy of the mid-1880s between George Westinghouse and Thomas Edison. Edison's inventions depended entirely on direct current, which could be distributed only at a low voltage over short distances. Westinghouse demonstrated that alternating current could be transmitted over long distances at a higher voltage. All that was needed was a transformer to step down the higher voltage so that it was suitable for everyday use. To fill this need, he bought the patent for a transformer that had been developed by a French electrician and a British engineer, then improved upon it.

Now the stage was set for a showdown between the DC advocates and the AC partisans—a contest that would determine who would build the hydroelectric power generating plant to harness the mighty Niagara Falls. When Westinghouse won the contract to build three five thousand-horse-power generators at the falls, the die was cast in favor of alternating current. The first AC electricity to be produced from Niagara Falls in 1896 was used for street and home lighting in Buffalo, New York, and to power the multitude of new plants that quickly opened around Niagara Falls. This very successful Westinghouse alternating current power plant became the model that was used to electrify the world. AC electricity also rapidly accelerated the industrialization of the United States and many other countries by providing a versatile and powerful new source of energy.

Not only was George Westinghouse an inspired inventor, he also became a competent entrepreneur. To convert his innovations into marketable products, he formed no fewer than sixty companies, either wholly owned or associated with him. By 1889, the Westinghouse Electric Company alone operated around the world and employed some fifty thousand people. The electric company as well as Westinghouse Air Brake Company concentrated their operations in the Pittsburgh area, where the founder built a company town called Wilmerding.

An ideal community in many respects, the town was an outstanding example of Westinghouse's benevolent employment practices. He developed a reputation for paying fair wages and providing generous benefits. His workmen responded by avoiding the labor strife that plagued many of Westinghouse's competitors. He inaugurated paid vacations for his employees and was among the first to give them a half day off on Saturdays, a move that infuriated fellow Pittsburgh entrepreneurs Andrew Carnegie and Henry Clay Frick. He introduced apprentice training programs for new employees. Conditions at Westinghouse were so good that labor leader Samuel Gompers once said that more employers like Westinghouse would put labor unions out of business.

Westinghouse showed few signs of slowing down as the years passed. He returned to work with engines around 1895, when he learned about a workable steam turbine that had been developed by an Englishman, Charles Parsons. He bought the rights to Parsons's design and installed the experimental turbine to generate electric power for his Pittsburgh plant. By 1900, he had installed a similar unit in Hartford, Connecticut, the first steam turbine electric power generating plant in the United States. Today steam turbines produce the major portion of the nation's electricity, and they power navy ships as well as commercial cargo vessels.

In 1913, Westinghouse developed heart disease, and he died the following year in New York City. Widely honored for his many-sided career, he was one of the most productive inventors on record and owner of 361 patents.

In the economic bad times that followed, several of his companies failed to survive, and others were sold or merged. Surprisingly, few products on the market today still carry a Westinghouse trade name, although many bear its pedigree.

The many achievements of George Westinghouse, however, never overcame his innate modesty. "If some day they say of me that in my work I have contributed something to the welfare and happiness of my fellow men," he said, "I shall be satisfied."

George Westinghouse Museum

Visitors step back in time when they enter The Castle, the imposing chateaulike stone building that crowns a broad lawn atop a hill in Wilmerding, fourteen miles north of Pittsburgh. In a wood-paneled office, now carefully preserved, George Westinghouse made risk-taking decisions that determined the success of his diverse industrial empire, which

The George Westinghouse Museum is housed on one floor of the building known as The Castle, which was the general office of Westinghouse Air Brake Company for nearly one hundred years.

The Appliance Room is a step back in time to when household products carried the slogan "You can be sure if it's a Westinghouse." PHOTOS BY THE AUTHORS

Visiting George Westinghouse Museum

Castle Main,
325 Commerce St., Wilmerding, PA 15148

PHONE: 412-823-0500
WEBSITE: www.georgewestinghouse.com
ADMINISTRATION: The museum is an independent, volunteer, nonprofit organization, established solely as a memorial to George Westinghouse, his achievements, and his contributions to society. Support for the museum comes primarily through voluntary contributions. The building is now owned by the APICS Educational and Research Foundation.
HOURS: Open year-round, Monday–Friday, 10–4; Saturday, 11–3. Closed Sunday and major holidays.
ADMISSION FEES: $3 per person; $5 per couple; children free.
TOURS: Tours for groups of 10 or more are available by reservation. A 45-minute impersonation of George Westinghouse in period dress of the 1890s is available for groups by appointment, either at the museum or off-site for a donation.
TIME NEEDED: 2 hours.
SPECIAL EVENTS: George Westinghouse Days Festival in early June.
SPECIAL CONSIDERATIONS: Wheelchair access available by telephoning in advance.
PARKING: Free off-street parking.
SALES OUTLETS: Small sales outlet for souvenirs.
DIRECTIONS: Traveling west on U.S. Route 30, turn left at East McKeesport onto PA Route 148 (Fifth Avenue). Go downhill to Wilmerding, and follow Station Street to Herman Avenue. Turn left. Turn left again onto Commerce Street. The Castle is in full view.

manufactured products ranging from the complicated air brake to the everyday electric iron.

The original Castle was built of wood in 1890 as the centerpiece of the company town. More than a hundred homes grew up around the industrial plant that fabricated the air brake. As well as the company business office, the building housed a library, reading rooms, restaurant, gymnasium, swimming pool, and bowling alleys—all for the use of employees.

After a fire gutted the building in 1896, Westinghouse rebuilt the present building of solid stone to be the headquarters for his expanding industrial empire. In the interim, however, a local YMCA had been constructed that now provided for the recreational needs of the neighborhood. He added a tower that holds a four-way clock whose four faces are cleverly operated by a single mechanism. A later addition provided more office space for the Westinghouse Air Brake Company, which continued to occupy the building until 1986, when the company was sold.

The results of the inventive mind of the founder are displayed in the four large rooms of the museum on the Castle's first floor. Visitors see a kaleidoscope of ingenious inventions created by George Westinghouse or his talented engineers: the air brake, an electric wheelchair, a robot, early circuit breakers, radio equipment, and a time capsule designed for the 1939 New York World's Fair. Would-be inventors will be fascinated by his original notes and detailed drawings. One room displays a collection of Westinghouse consumer products, ranging from an early electric stove to a toaster. Another room includes Westinghouse family photographs and memorabilia, including the inventor's many honors and awards.

Henry Mercer

(1856-1930)

You might say that Henry Mercer was born with a silver trowel in his hand. The son of a retired naval officer in Doylestown near Philadelphia, he had the unusual good fortune of having a wealthy aunt, his mother's sister, who had no children of her own but wanted to help her nephew fulfill his life's dreams. Those dreams were history and archeology and a strong desire to study the past and learn from it. You can chart humanity's course, he was convinced, by studying the tools that people used.

Graduating from Harvard University in 1879 with a bachelor's degree in liberal arts, he studied law at the University of Pennsylvania Law School for a year, then read law in an uncle's law firm for most of another year. In 1881, he was admitted to the Philadelphia County bar, but at that point in his life, he seems to have decided that a law career was not for him.

He left immediately for Europe, financed by his devoted aunt's generosity. His mother's sister, Lela, widow of a wealthy diplomat, had returned to Doylestown and spent much of her life sharing her fortune with the Mercer family. Henry spent much of the 1880s on scholarly excursions through England, Yugoslavia, Bulgaria, Turkey, and Egypt, sometimes traveling along rivers in a houseboat. On his travels, he took photographs, kept detailed journals, and collected cultural artifacts. It is believed that one reason for his protracted stay abroad was that he had contracted a venereal disease, which he felt prevented him from marrying or having children. It is a fact that he never married.

Returning home, he turned to archeology as a "gentleman scholar." He explored caves in a number of eastern states, searching unsuccessfully for evidence that early man had inhabited these regions. In 1894, he became assistant curator of American and prehistoric archeology at the University of Pennsylvania, where he served until 1897, when he quit over policy differences. During this time, he joined an expedition that investigated caves in Yucatan and published its findings.

Now he transferred his intellectual curiosity to the Bucks County Historical Society, which he had helped establish. Here he introduced a novel idea in archeology. Instead of concentrating on the remote past by unearthing primitive tools, as archeologists do, he suggested collecting and studying the tools of the recent past, then deducing how these tools had been used in earlier times. It was his belief that these tools often had not changed much over the centuries. Thus began his collection of trade and craft tools of the American pioneers, the tools you now find displayed at the Mercer Museum. Before he was through, he had amassed more than fifty thousand items, some as small as a needle, others as large as a stagecoach or whaleboat. He pioneered the method of visible storage, in which he arranged artifacts in open display, thus making the entire collection accessible for study. He continued collecting, cataloging, and exhibiting these implements, as well as writing and lecturing about them, until his death in 1930.

Searching for these old tools led him into another venture. While collecting potters' tools, Mercer discovered that the making of redware pottery traditionally fashioned by Pennsylvania Dutch potters was becoming a lost art. So he decided to build a pottery factory specializing in handmade ornamental tiles. As with all of his enthusiasms, he then made an exhaustive study of the art of tilemaking, consulting European experts to learn their techniques of kiln construction, glazing, and firing. He soon discovered that his local Bucks County clay was ideal for tilemaking and in 1898 began to produce a dazzling variety. Many of the tile designs were drawn from historic incidents. Probably to his own surprise, the artfully designed tiles produced by his Moravian Pottery and Tile Works were an immediate artistic and commercial success. Mercer tiles became status symbols at some notable places: the John D. Rockefeller Jr. estate in Pocantico Hills, New York; the U.S.

Henry Mercer, c. 1900, with his dog.
MERCER MUSEUM OF THE BUCKS COUNTY HISTORICAL SOCIETY

Military Academy at West Point; and the Pennsylvania State Capitol at Harrisburg. The business quickly developed into a profit-making enterprise.

In 1908, the unconventional Mercer introduced another surprise, this time for the architectural community. He began to build a residence for himself out of exposed, reinforced concrete, a material that could be molded and shaped. He designed the house from the inside out, one room at a time, letting the interior design determine the exterior appearance. This was Fonthill, a structure inspired by his "literary and artistic dreams and memories of travel." The house resembled a medieval manor, but it also possessed modern conveniences—electricity, central heating, even an elevator.

In 1911 and 1912, he replaced his original tile works with a new factory modeled after early Spanish missions. In 1916, he completed and presented to the Bucks County Historical Society a fireproof museum, also constructed of exposed concrete, in which to house his vast collection of tools. Construction took three years and involved only eight workmen and a horse named Lucy.

Eventually his peers recognized the innovative talent of Henry Mercer. The Society of Arts and Crafts in Boston, of which he was a master craftsman, awarded him its bronze medal for excellence in 1913. In 1916, he received an honorary doctor of science degree from Franklin and Marshall College. In 1921, the American Institute of Architects awarded him its gold medal for distinguished achievements in ceramic art. He continued his active life as a scholar, collector, and writer while still creating designs for his thriving tile works.

After his last European trip in 1904, he became more reclusive and was periodically beset with illnesses. James Michener, who was a paperboy in Doylestown, remembered seeing Mercer, his black cloak swirling behind him, riding his bicycle into town. It was reported that he took two naps daily, ate supper late in his bedroom, and often worked until after midnight, rising the next morning at 7 A.M. Until the end, he criticized any neglect of the past and any economic system that wasted natural resources.

At the close of his life, Henry Mercer could lay claim to being an archeologist, collector, scholar, ceramist, architect, and benefactor. "Research, discovery, investigation, the longing to open a new door and find out something never known before," he once wrote, were what motivated him. A friend described the squire of Doylestown simply as a "discoverer of the past"—a past whose craftsmanship is vividly illuminated for all those who today visit the three Mercer museums.

He died at the age of seventy-four at Fonthill, his concrete castle, and is buried in the Mercer family plot at the Doylestown Presbyterian Church Cemetery.

Fonthill Museum

When you enter Fonthill, Henry Mercer's dream house, it is like entering a dimly lit medieval castle. Built entirely of hand-mixed concrete, this imposing structure has forty-four rooms, twenty-one chimneys, eighteen fireplaces, thirty-two stairwells, and more than two hundred windows of varying sizes and shapes. Its interior walls are elaborately adorned with an incredible array of Mercer's colorful handcrafted tiles, as well as nine hundred prints and wall hangings. Unexpected doorways appear on every level. A guide leads you on a fascinating tour through the winding hallways and rooms.

Visiting Fonthill Museum

East Court St. and PA Route 313, Doylestown, PA 18901

MAILING ADDRESS: 84 S. Pine St., Doylestown, PA 18901
PHONE: 215-345-0461
E-MAIL: info@mercermuseum.org
WEBSITE: www.fonthillmuseum.org
ADMINISTRATION: Bucks County Historical Society administers Fonthill, the Mercer Museum, and the Spruance Library.
HOURS: Open year-round, Monday–Saturday, 10–5; Sundays, 12–5.
ADMISSION FEES: $7 for adults; $6.50 for seniors; $2.50 for youth.
TOURS: Guided tours available; reservations required. Fees and hours may vary, so call to verify.
TIME NEEDED: 1 hour.
SPECIAL EVENTS: Fonthill Fourth of July, special behind-the-scenes tour available.
SPECIAL CONSIDERATIONS: The concrete castle has many sets of stairs.
PARKING: Available on-site.
SALES OUTLETS: Shop offers a video on American castles and a book on Fonthill.
DIRECTIONS: From Philadelphia, take I-95 North to Street Road, PA Route 132 West. At Old York Road, PA Route 263 North, turn right. Turn left onto PA Route 313. At the second traffic light, turn left on East Court Street. Fonthill is first driveway on right. Follow tree-lined driveway to parking lot.

Fonthill, home of Henry Mercer, was built between 1908 and 1910 and is constructed entirely of hand-mixed concrete. Mercer's imaginative design includes forty-four rooms, eighteen fireplaces, thirty-two stairwells, and more than two hundred windows. The interior walls, floors, and ceilings are decorated with hundreds of Mercer's hand-crafted tiles. MERCER MUSEUM OF THE BUCKS COUNTY HISTORICAL SOCIETY

Visiting Moravian Pottery and Tile Works

130 Swamp Rd., Doylestown, PA 18901

PHONE: 215-345-6722

WEBSITE: www.mptw.go.to

ADMINISTRATION: Administered by the Bucks County Park and Recreation Department.

HOURS: Open daily, 10–4:45; except major holidays.

ADMISSION FEES: $3 for adults; $2.50 for seniors; $1.50 for youth.

TOURS: 45-minute tours begin every half hour from 10–4.

TIME NEEDED: 1 hour.

SPECIAL EVENTS: Annual Tile Festival the third Saturday in May. Ceramist apprenticeships and workshops.

SPECIAL CONSIDERATIONS: First level is accessible, but second level has limited accessibility.

PARKING: Available on-site.

SALES OUTLETS: Shop offers tiles made on-site and a selection of books.

DIRECTIONS: Moravian Pottery and Tile Works is at the same location as Fonthill Museum (see above).

Visiting Mercer Museum

84 S. Pine St., Doylestown, PA 18901

PHONE: 215-345-0210
E-MAIL: info@mercermuseum.org
WEBSITE: www.mercermuseum.org
ADMINISTRATION: Bucks County Historical Society administers the Mercer Museum, Fonthill, and the Spruance Library.
HOURS: Monday, Wednesday–Saturday, 10–5; Tuesday, 10–9; Sunday 12–5. Open year-round, but not heated.
ADMISSION FEES: $6 for adults; $5.50 for seniors; $2.50 for youth.
TOURS: The museum is self-guided, with printed and audiotape guides available. Educational programs from preschool to ninth grade, plus a portable teaching tool consisting of artifacts, tapes, and a teacher's manual.
TIME NEEDED: 1 to 2 hours.
SPECIAL EVENTS: Folk Fest on Mother's Day weekend.
SPECIAL CONSIDERATIONS: The museum has elevators, but some exhibits are reached only by steps.
PARKING: Available on-site.
SALES OUTLETS: Shop offers handcrafted items, pottery, jewelry, educational toys, and books.
DIRECTIONS: From Philadelphia, take I-95 North to Street Road, PA Route 132 West. Then take PA Route 611 North to Doylestown, avoiding the Route 611 Bypass. Take Doylestown exit on right. Follow the blue-and-white Cultural District signs to the first traffic light, and turn right on Ashland Street. Immediately turn left on Green Street. Museum is on left.

Moravian Pottery and Tile Works

Near Fonthill is the Moravian Pottery and Tile Works, which Mercer built to produce his artistic tiles and mosaics. It, too, is constructed of poured concrete and is built around a courtyard in the Spanish Mission style. A videotape presentation summarizes Mercer's life and describes the tile-making process, which continues today at this working museum. The tile works is now operated by the Bucks County Department of Parks and Recreation, which sells its handsome tiles to the public.

Mercer Museum

The third Mercer-related structure is the Mercer Museum, located a mile away in downtown Doylestown. Walk into this towering seven-story reinforced concrete building, and you are dwarfed by its atrium-style central court. Many of the fifty thousand antique objects that Mercer collected are suspended from the ceiling or hung on the walls of this huge room. Surrounding the central court are alcoves and exhibit rooms on every level that hold a variety of implements used by artisans and craftsmen of the eighteenth and nineteenth centuries. Each alcove is devoted to a different trade or craft. More than sixty American trades are represented. Discover not only tools of woodworking, metalworking, textile weaving, and dairying, but also a whaleboat, a Conestoga wagon, an antique fire engine, even a hangman's gallows.

All three of these Mercer buildings have been designated by the National Park Service as National Historic Landmarks.

Milton S. Hershey

(1857-1945)

Both as a young apprentice and in his early life, Milton Hershey was convinced he knew how to make delicious candy, but for many years he could not find enough people to buy it.

The man whose name later became synonymous with the chocolate bar was born on September 13, 1857, into a Mennonite family descended from immigrants from Germany and Switzerland. Their home was a farm in Derry Township, near present-day Harrisburg. His father, who failed at running a fruit farm and nursery, permitted Milton only four years of schooling before apprenticing him to the editor of a German-language newspaper. When Milton showed little talent for printing, his hardworking mother, Fannie, found him a job with a candy and ice cream maker in Lancaster, where he spent four years learning the basics of candymaking.

In 1876, he decided to move to Philadelphia, where a celebration was taking place to mark the hundredth anniversary of the Declaration of Independence. Hoping to profit from the thousands of people coming to the city, he borrowed money from his family and set up shop. Cooking his candy at night, he sold his fresh caramels and taffy to the exposition crowd from a pushcart. For the next six years, with the assistance of his mother and her generous sister Mattie, who came to help, he struggled to keep his fledgling company alive. Finally, however, he was forced to close it to pay off his creditors.

Next Hershey went to Denver, where his father had gone after he drifted away from the family, and the young man went to work for a candy manufacturer. Although not able to go into business for himself, he learned a valuable lesson: Add fresh milk to your caramels, and you greatly improve their quality. He then tried his luck in New York City, but lack of capital and high sugar prices doomed his business yet again.

Downhearted, he returned in 1886 to his Pennsylvania roots—to Lancaster, close to where he had grown up as a farm boy. But he was now twenty-nine years old and penniless. His extended family, which had been

Milton S. Hershey with Robert Schaeffer, one of the students at the Hershey Industrial School, 1920. HERSHEY COMMUNITY ARCHIVES, HERSHEY, PENNSYLVANIA

so generous at first, now no longer wished to help him in his candymaking venture.

A friend, William Henry Lebkicher, lent him some money so Hershey could salvage the kettles and candymaking slabs he had used in New York. He rented a small room in an unused factory and, undaunted, began making and peddling caramels through the Lancaster streets with a basket on his arm. Every day he had to hike several miles to a farm to get the five gallons of milk he needed to add to his candy mixture.

One day an English importer came to town and tasted Hershey's Crystal A milk caramels and, marvel of marvels, placed an order, the first large order the Lancaster Caramel Company had received. It was five hundred English pounds, enough to provide a foundation for the company's growth. This order and succeeding orders from abroad provided the collateral he needed to negotiate a $250,000 loan from a New York City bank, which he used to expand his candy business. Now orders seemed to magically show up in every mail delivery.

By 1893, he had opened plants in Mount Joy, Pennsylvania, and Chicago and Geneva, Illinois, all of which joined the original Lancaster plant in producing his trademark Crystal A caramels. He added other confections, giving them fanciful names like Uniques, Melbas, Empires, and Scarlets, and introduced mass production. In 1894, a book about Lancaster County stated that Hershey's business "has grown to wonderful proportions . . . a million dollars worth of business a year. These goods are shipped to all parts of the world, including Japan, China, Australia and Europe." For Hershey, it had been an amazing turnaround, a vindication of his perseverance, and a confirmation of his determination not to compromise on quality.

Once he found his economic footing, Milton Hershey proved that he was a born entrepreneur. Visiting the World's Columbian Exposition in Chicago in 1893, he became fascinated by some innovative German chocolatemaking machinery. Hershey bought the entire exhibit, along with the right to use it, and installed it in his Lancaster plant, where he began producing chocolate candy. At first he simply chocolate-coated his caramels, then later added novelties like chocolate cigars and cigarettes.

Now he hit his stride. He displayed boldness both in business and in his personal life. In 1897, while making a sales call at Jamestown, New York, he met an attractive, red-haired Irish Catholic shop girl at a confectionery and soda fountain. The forty-one-year-old bachelor and Catherine "Kitty" Sweeney surprised friends and family alike by marrying the next year, and Kitty came to live in the big house in Lancaster that Hershey had purchased with his profits.

His other surprising decision was to sell the now-profitable caramel business in 1900 for $1 million. But he had an ace up his sleeve—he had developed a formula for milk chocolate. A few months before the sale, he had test-marketed a milk chocolate bar. He was convinced that he could now offer the ordinary consumer an inexpensive chocolate product that had heretofore been available only as a luxury item from Switzerland and Germany. He was right, and the Hershey Bar became an immediate success.

Encouraged, Hershey set about building a state-of-the-art factory to produce the new line of chocolate candy. Its location was his old hometown of Derry Township, twenty miles north of Lancaster in the midst of Pennsylvania Dutch dairy farms, convenient to transportation, and surrounded by rural Pennsylvanians, who he believed would be energetic workers.

He visualized not only a factory, but a factory within a model town. His architects laid out streets and water and sewer systems. They built homes to sell to Hershey employees at a reasonable price, as well as recreational facilities and cultural venues. He incorporated a bank, public

Chocolate Avenue in Hershey, Pennsylvania, c. 1925. HERSHEY COMMUNITY ARCHIVES, HERSHEY, PENNSYLVANIA

library, hospital, zoo, park, inn, laundry, men's and women's clubs, and a trolley line to bring workers easily from nearby towns.

Both the company and the community prospered. In 1908, the Hershey Chocolate Company incorporated, and by 1915, the plant covered thirty-five acres. Company sales rocketed from $600,000 in 1901 to $20 million twenty years later.

Determined to keep his employees working during the lean years of the Depression, Hershey launched a large-scale building project in the 1930s that added a hotel, high school, community building, sports arena, and innovative windowless, air-conditioned office building.

His concern for his community went even further. He and Kitty were childless, so together they founded a school for needy orphans, which is now recognized as one of the most generous of its kind in the country. In 1918, three years after the death of his wife, Hershey donated an estimated $60 million in trust to the school. Today the Milton Hershey School provides kindergarten through twelfth-grade education and free room and board to twelve hundred needy children whose family life has been disrupted.

In yet another bold move, the chocolate entrepreneur built or bought six sugar mills in Cuba to guarantee his supply of that important product. East of Havana, he built a town for his workers named Central Hershey. Just as he had in Pennsylvania, he brought in doctors, dentists, and teachers and built a free school for the children, as well as a golf course and baseball diamond.

Hershey's persistence, innovative ideas, emphasis on quality, and concern for his employees and those in the community were both the reasons for, and the hallmarks of, his success. His abilities to judge the market and produce a fresh, affordable taste treat were evident in both his original 5-cent Hershey Bar and his later successes. During World War II, Hershey again demonstrated his inventiveness by developing the Field Ration D for the U.S. Army. This four-ounce energy bar packed six hundred calories and did not melt in the heat when soldiers carried it into the field. His factory was soon turning out five hundred thousand bars every day. "He was never satisfied with the conventional way of doing things," one of his managers summed up. "He was always wanting to experiment."

His beloved wife, Kitty, died in 1915 after a lengthy illness. Milton Hershey lived for an additional thirty years, dying at age eighty-eight in 1945. Both are buried in the Hershey Cemetery along with his parents.

Hershey Museum, Milton Hershey School, and the Town of Hershey

The Hershey Museum offers innovative displays that illustrate Milton Hershey's career and describe chocolatemaking, as well as exhibits that portray Native Americans and Pennsylvania Dutch antiques. Today the Pennsylvania town that Hershey built is not only a manufacturing center, but a tourist attraction as well, due in part to a fun-filled amusement park also built by Hershey. Hersheypark is a popular theme park with sixty rides and a zoo. In Hershey's later years, his employees remember, the founder liked to step into the park after all the visitors had left, get on the merry-go-round, mount one of the gilded horses, and take several turns on the carousel for his own enjoyment.

The town today has many dimensions. The original chocolate factory is still here, as well as a newer plant at the western edge of town. The factories are not open for tours, but at Chocolate World, automated cars take visitors on a free ride that tells how cocoa beans make their way into chocolate bars. The Milton Hershey School lies east of town on an impressive nine thousand-acre campus. You may drive through the grounds, passing some of its eighty individual student cottage residences and the town center of classroom and recreational buildings, then visit Founders Hall, whose gleaming white marble rotunda towers seventy-two feet above the surrounding countryside. Inside Founders Hall, a video relates the story of

Founders Hall at the Hershey School tells the story of Milton S. Hershey with photographs, memorabilia, and a video presentation. PHOTO BY THE AUTHORS

Visiting Hershey Museum

170 W. Hersheypark Dr., Hershey, PA 17033

PHONE: 717-534-3439
E-MAIL: info@hersheymuseum.org
WEBSITE: www.hersheymuseum.org
ADMINISTRATION: Administered by the M. S. Hershey Foundation.
HOURS: Memorial Day–Labor Day, daily, 10–6; Labor Day–Memorial Day, 10–5.
ADMISSION FEES: $6 for adults; $3 for youth ages 3–15.
TOURS: Self-guided tours. Discovery Room for children. Information is available about visiting Chocolate World, the Hershey Mansion, the Homestead, the Milton Hershey School, Hersheypark, Hershey Arena, Zooamerica, Hotel Hershey, Hershey Lodge and Convention Center, and the Hershey Medical Center.
TIME NEEDED: Allow at least 2 hours for the museum.
SPECIAL EVENTS: Exhibits, classes, lectures, excursions and tours, historical displays, and special programs for visitors, area residents, and schools throughout the year.
SPECIAL CONSIDERATIONS: Museum is handicapped-accessible. Special needs may be met by making prior arrangements with museum staff.
PARKING: $6 or free, depending on season, for Hersheypark or Hershey Arena. The Hershey Museum is located across from Chocolate World and next to Hershey Arena.
SALES OUTLETS: Museum store carries a variety of books, videos, and items about Milton Hershey and the town, as well as chocolate specialties and souvenir items.
DIRECTIONS: From the Pennsylvania Turnpike, take Exit 20. Follow PA Route 72 North to U.S. Route 422 West. This becomes Chocolate Avenue, leading into the town of Hershey. Turn right on Park Avenue by the chocolate factory, and left on Park Boulevard. Follow signs to Chocolate World parking.

the founding of the school, whose mission it is to serve children "in social and financial need."

Nearby, you may visit the Homestead, built as a farmhouse in 1826 by Hershey's great-grandfather, the house where Milton Hershey was born. In one room are displays describing his life and memorabilia such as his top hat, passport, and a cigar box. Today the building provides alumni services and visitor information.

The elegant and historic Hotel Hershey sits high above the town. An adjacent twenty-three-acre botanical garden features seasonal displays.

Visiting Homestead at Milton Hershey School

P.O. Box 830, Hershey, PA 17033-0830

PHONE: 717-520-2200
ADMINISTRATION: Administered by Milton Hershey School.
HOURS: Monday–Friday, 8–4:30.
ADMISSION: Free.
TOURS: Self-guided.
TIME NEEDED: One-half hour.
SPECIAL EVENTS: None.
SPECIAL CONSIDERATIONS: Homestead is handicapped-accessible.
PARKING: On-site.
SALES OUTLET: None.
DIRECTIONS: Exit from Hershey Museum. Turn right on Hersheypark Drive. Turn right on Cocoa Avenue. Turn left on U.S. Route 422; turn right on Homestead Lane to Homestead.

Hershey was born on the first floor of this farmhouse in 1857 and lived there until 1866. New owners added the framed wings. In 1896, Hershey purchased the homestead back again and made it available to his father, who lived there until his death in 1904. PHOTO BY THE AUTHORS

The extensive Hershey Lodge on U.S. Route 422 attracts group meetings to its elaborate convention center. The Hershey Bears professional ice hockey team plays in the nearby arena. Hershey is also home to the Milton S. Hershey Medical Center, a state-of-the-art treatment, educational, and research center for central Pennsylvania. This medical center, made possible by a $50 million grant from the M. S. Hershey Foundation, serves as Penn State University's College of Medicine.

St. Katharine Drexel

(1858-1955)

Growing up in a mansion in Center City Philadelphia in the mid-1800s, Katharine Marie Drexel seemed to have it all. Her father, Francis A. Drexel, a partner of financier J. P. Morgan, had made a fortune as a Philadelphia banker. Instead of attending a parochial school, Katharine was tutored at home, and servants filled the house. The family took frequent trips to Europe, and at age twenty-one she was treated to a lavish debutante ball.

But beneath this veneer of a society aristocrat, young Katharine grew up a deeply religious person who seemed to take little pleasure in the joys of this elegant life. As a devout Roman Catholic, she pleaded to receive her first communion at age nine; she was allowed to receive it at eleven, rather than wait until the traditional age of thirteen. At fourteen, she was praying forty-five minutes a day and attending Mass daily.

Her mother, Hannah Langstroth Drexel, had died about five weeks after giving birth to Katharine. Her father remarried in 1860, when Katharine was two years old, and she was raised by her stepmother, Emma Bouvier Drexel, whom she loved dearly. She took her cue from her devout stepmother, who was known for her efforts to help the poor. Emma established a dispensary for those in need at the family's fashionable townhouse, and Katharine, her older sister, Elizabeth, and her stepsister, Louise, all helped care for those who came.

In 1883, when Katharine was twenty-four, Emma died of cancer after an agonizing illness during which Katharine helped care for her. After his wife's death, Francis Drexel took his daughters to Europe to comfort them, but Katharine's grief was profound. "When dear Mamma went to our true home," she wrote to her spiritual advisor, "I felt life to be too serious a passage into eternity to wish to spend my odd minutes reading of the joys of this world. I am not happy in the world. There is a void in my heart which only God can fill."

Scarcely two years later, her father caught a cold that developed into pleurisy, and he died in February 1885. Her father's death so soon after her stepmother's seemed to shatter Katharine. The grieving Katharine and her sisters were visited by two priests, who told them of the mission work the church was doing among the western Indians on the reservations. Katharine's sympathy for the outcasts of society was awakened. She and her sisters began to contribute thousands of dollars to Catholic Indian missions from the income of the huge trust funds their father had bequeathed to each of his daughters.

Weak, tired, and jaundiced, Katharine was taken by her sisters to the health spas of Europe in 1886. Her health improved, but her outlook was still bleak. A breathtaking Alpine view merely reminded her that "man [is] an atom in the great creation. . . . I felt as if standing at the Day of Judgment. How have you passed your life?"

In 1887, the Drexel sisters took a third trip to Europe. While in Rome, Katharine Drexel had an audience with Pope Leo XIII, who, after hearing her concerns about missionary work among the Indians, challenged her to become a missionary herself and serve them.

She returned to the United States fully recovered, and in the fall of 1887, she took a trip to survey Catholic Indian missions in North Dakota, Minnesota, and South Dakota. At Holy Rosary Mission in South Dakota,

St. Katharine Drexel, a portrait on a prayer card. ARCHIVES OF THE SISTERS OF THE BLESSED SACRAMENT

she met with Chief Red Cloud. The trip reinforced her awareness of the needs of the Indians and the vital work of missionaries. Subsequent trips to Indian missions convinced her that she must do something more than contribute money.

Bishop James O'Connor, a former pastor and family friend, suggested that Drexel establish an order of women explicitly devoted to the needs of both Native Americans and African-Americans. By 1889, she had decided that she did indeed have a calling to the religious life and that she would establish such an order. Her decision to "enter religion" seems to have transformed her alienation from the world into a worthy purpose that she thenceforth pursued with vitality.

She entered as a novice with the Sisters of Mercy in Pittsburgh. After completing her eighteen-month novitiate, she established a new religious community, calling the new order the Sisters of the Blessed Sacrament for Indians and Colored People. She vowed to be the "mother and servant" of the Native American and African-American races "and not to undertake any work which would lead to [their] neglect or abandonment."

In its first year, the new order occupied the Drexel summer home in Torresdale near Philadelphia. The next year, Sister Katharine Drexel, using her own funds, built a motherhouse for herself and her first twenty-one novices on part of her family's extensive property in Bensalem. This building now forms part of the campus complex of St. Elizabeth's Convent, which continues as the motherhouse of the Sisters of the Blessed Sacrament.

After three more years of study and training, nuns of the Blessed Sacrament were ready for the mission field. In 1894, five sisters made the trip west to Santa Fe, traveling part of the way in a freight car, to take over the administration of St. Catherine's boarding school for Indians.

In subsequent years, Mother Katharine surveyed numerous sites for building projects and supervised the planning and construction of new convents and schools throughout Indian territory in Arizona, Washington, the Dakotas, Montana, and Wisconsin, and in twenty-six Catholic dioceses across the country. She established numerous schools and convents for African-Americans in Virginia, Ohio, New York, Massachusetts, Pennsylvania, Illinois, Tennessee, and Louisiana.

Perhaps Mother Katharine's most important and lasting achievement among blacks came in 1925 with the establishment of Xavier University in New Orleans, the first and only Catholic university for African-Americans. In the rigidly segregated South of that time, her purchase of the site of an earlier college brought a storm of protest. Despite the opposition, she opened a training school for black teachers. The institution grew, later adding a college of pharmacy. By 1932, Xavier had reached university status. As segregation was gradually overcome, Xavier in 1954 was integrated and now accepts students without regard to race, creed, or color; however, it is still predominantly African-American.

During her sixty-four years as a member of the new religious order, Drexel distributed more than $20 million of her wealth in building these schools, convents, hospitals, and social agencies and to supply teaching staff for the schools.

Mother Katharine's years of devoted but strenuous physical exertion eventually caught up with her. In 1935, she suffered a heart attack, which forced her retirement in 1937, when she gave up the leadership of her order. As a resident in her motherhouse for the remaining eighteen years of her life, she lived a life of contemplation and prayer. When she died, she left a legacy of sixty-five missions in twenty-one states, forty-nine elementary and twelve high schools, Xavier University, three houses of social service, and more than five hundred sisters who served these institutions.

The process of canonization involves three steps: servant of God, beatification, and canonization. Beatification requires recognition by the church of an extraordinary event that cannot be explained according to the laws of human science and is attributed to divine intervention through the mediation of the servant of God. The cause for canonization was begun in 1964, and Pope John Paul II completed the canonization on October 1, 2000. Katharine Drexel is the fourth American to be canonized as a saint; the others are Elizabeth Ann Seton, Francis Cabrini, and John Neumann.

St. Katharine Drexel Shrine

Green lawns and stately stone buildings greet you at the fifty-four-acre St. Elizabeth Convent built by St. Katharine Drexel as the home base for

her Order of the Sisters of the Blessed Sacrament. The buildings, constructed in Spanish Mission style, have distinctive red tile roofs reminiscent of European monasteries. The complex is located in Bensalem, nineteen miles north of central Philadelphia.

Tours start at the visitors center with a video on the life of Katharine Drexel. Exhibits portray the widespread activities of the order among Native Americans and African-Americans throughout the United States.

From the visitors center, it is a short walk to the chapel and shrine. The long

St. Elizabeth Chapel is located above the St. Katharine Drexel Shrine. Both are parts of the Motherhouse of the Sisters of the Blessed Sacrament. ARCHIVES OF THE SISTERS OF THE BLESSED SACRAMENT

Visiting St. Katharine Drexel Shrine

1663 Bristol Pike, Bensalem, PA 19020

PHONE: 215-639-7878
E-MAIL: kathdrexel@aol.com or sbs@libertynet.org
WEBSITE: www.katharinedrexel.org
ADMINISTRATION: Order of the Sisters of the Blessed Sacrament.
HOURS: Open daily, 10–5.
ADMISSION FEES: No admission fee, but donations accepted.
TOURS: Pilgrimages for 10 or more available by appointment from 10–12 and 1–3.
TIME NEEDED: 2 hours.
SPECIAL EVENTS: Feast Day on March 3.
SPECIAL CONSIDERATIONS: Only the shrine is handicapped-accessible; handicapped parking available.
PARKING: Available close to Shrine.
SALES OUTLETS: Gift shop in the visitors center offers books, jewelry, religious items, and craft items from the missions, as well as from the sisters.
DIRECTIONS: From I-95 North or South, take the Woodhaven Road Exit (PA Route 63). Stay in right lane. Take Bristol Pike Exit (U.S. Route 13). At traffic light, turn left on Bristol Pike North. The Sisters of the Blessed Sacrament is on right in 0.25 mile. Make the second right on Drexel Drive. Follow the signs for the shrine and parking.

and narrow St. Elizabeth Chapel, funded by Katharine Drexel, contains features donated by her father and sisters and was built in memory of her older sister, Elizabeth. It features a high, timbered roof and ranks of carved oak benches facing inward to seat the nuns at prayer. A finely carved oak altar is topped with a walnut figure of Jesus on the cross. In

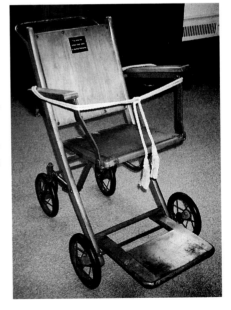

Katharine Drexel was a frugal woman who spent the last twenty years of her life in prayerful retirement at the motherhouse. Her wheelchair was constructed from two folding chairs with wheels attached. Despite her wealth and education, she led a life of austere poverty.
PHOTO BY THE AUTHORS

the back of the chapel hang banners portraying our Lady of Guadalupe; St. Martin DePerres, an African-American; and Blessed Kateri Tekakwitha, a Native American.

In the shrine beneath the chapel, a small room holds possessions of the diminutive and frugal St. Katharine, including the makeshift wheelchair that she insisted be fashioned out of two ordinary folding chairs using wheels from a baby carriage. Also on display are threads she used to patch her shoes and a collection of pencils she had worn down to stubs. A simple granite sarcophagus contains her remains.

Gifford Pinchot

(1865-1946)

Gifford Pinchot and the profession of forestry in the United States grew up together. As the first chief forester of the federal government, he played a key role in shaping the policies that today regulate use and conservation of the nation's forest resources.

At the beginning of the twentieth century, this country's forests were viewed by most citizens as an inexhaustible resource. Trees were felled to provide open fields for farming, lumber for home and building construction, logs for heating and cooking, and exports to other countries. Little attention was paid to replanting trees to assure an adequate supply of timber for the future.

It was Pinchot's father, a large estate owner near Milford, Pennsylvania, whose fortune had come from selling wallpaper, who suggested that his son might choose to become a forester so he could help correct these destructive forest practices. Gifford earned a degree from Yale University in 1889, and then sailed to Europe to learn how forestry was being practiced there. In Europe, he met a professor who directed him to a forestry school in Nancy, France. After a year of study and observation, he returned to the United States and traveled to the West, talking with lumberjacks and learning the ways of the woodsmen.

At this time, the wealthy George Vanderbilt was developing his extensive Biltmore estate in Asheville, North Carolina. The eminent landscape architect Frederick Law Olmsted, who had been hired by Vanderbilt, recommended young Pinchot to take charge of Biltmore Forest, some three thousand wooded acres of the estate. "Here was my chance . . . to prove what Americans did not yet understand," Pinchot wrote later, "that trees could get cut and the forest preserved at one and the same time. It was the first piece of woodland in the U.S. to be put under a regular system of forest management whose object was to pay the owner while improving the forest."

The practice of forestry as Pinchot developed it at Biltmore involved selectively cutting only the mature trees, while leaving in place younger

157

trees and other species that would rejuvenate the cut-over area. The common practice of the time was to slice a swath through the forest, cutting every tree in sight, thus leaving the land barren, subject to erosion, and susceptible to the growth of other species of trees that would produce poor lumber. "Forest butchery," Pinchot called it.

After Biltmore, the young forester surveyed for the state of New Jersey and for owners of private estates in the Adirondacks. In 1896, he was appointed by President Grover Cleveland to the National Forest Commission, established by the National Academy of Sciences to make recommendations on the national forest reserves in the western states. Acting on the commission's report, President Cleveland added thirteen new forest reserves to the western mountain region.

Pinchot was appointed as head of the Division of Forestry in the Department of Agriculture in 1898. His German-born predecessor, Bernhard Fernow, had not paid much attention to the national forest reserves and did not believe the country was ready for applied forestry. He had confined the work of his agency to advising private landowners on forestry techniques. Pinchot had other ideas. From the beginning, he had his eye on the publicly owned national forest reserves. These reserves were under the control of the General Land Office, a bureau of the Department of Interior, which made no effort to develop their commercial potential. Backed by now-President Theodore Roosevelt, and supported reluctantly by the economic interests of mining, grazing, lumbering, railroads, and irrigation, which had long pushed for development of the reserves, Pinchot achieved success in 1905 with the passage of an act that transferred the reserves to his agency's control. The Forest Service, as it was named, became a force to be reckoned with as Pinchot moved rapidly to transform his bureau into a regulatory agency.

Unlike national parks, national forests were available for timbering, mining, and cattle and sheep raising. Today national forests continue to provide raw

Gifford Pinchot, 1905. USDA FOREST SERVICE

materials for many synthetic products

considered essential for modern life, including plastics, fibers, and medicines. The Forest Service began to permit regulated tree cutting, theoretically not to exceed annual growth rates. It allowed regulated grazing that would not be destructive to watersheds. It also permitted hydroelectric power development. All of these activities were accompanied with a modest scale of fees.

Pinchot was a strong advocate of a government that stood above contending forces. His ideal was a government manned by experts loyal to the realities of their discipline, rather than to the narrow and selfish ends of special interests that governed under the mantle of an enlightened president selected "by the people" to rule in their name.

The policies he implemented for the forest reserves went to the heart of the great public issues of the time—the expansion and centralization of federal power, the control and regulation of large-scale enterprises, and the resolution of conflicts between large and small industries. This explains the influence Pinchot wielded on the national scene. He became a close colleague of Theodore Roosevelt, and as a member of Roosevelt's informal "tennis cabinet," he could always get the president's ear.

In the final days of the Roosevelt administration, Pinchot was involved in the White House Governors Conference, which showcased conservation methods; the National Conservation Commission; and the North American Conservation Conference with Mexico and Canada, which met in the White House in 1909.

Roosevelt's successor, however, William Howard Taft, was no enthusiast of conservation. After several differences of opinion with the new president, Pinchot was dismissed within Taft's first year.

After his years as a federal employee, Pinchot decided to tackle politics on his own and ran unsuccessfully in Pennsylvania for the Republican nomination for the Senate in 1914, 1920, 1926, and 1934. In 1914, he married Cornelia Bryce, a crusader for women's suffrage who later ran unsuccessfully for Congress and for governor of Pennsylvania.

In 1922, Pinchot ran for governor of Pennsylvania and won. Applying the same organizational skills he had shown as chief of the U.S. Forest Service, he inaugurated the state's first annual budget, reorganized the state government, instituted a new administrative code, and regulated electric power utilities.

Forbidden by law to succeed himself, Pinchot sat out a term, until disarray in party ranks made possible his election to a second term as governor in 1930, during the Depression. Under his administration, many miles of dirt country roads were paved, helping farmers take their crops to market and providing jobs for many of the unemployed.

But Pinchot's major legacy relates to conservation of natural resources, a phrase he helped make a household term. "Conservation means the wise use of the earth and its resources for the lasting good of men," he wrote. "Conservation is the foresighted utilization, preservation, and renewal of forests, water, land, and minerals for the greatest good of the greatest number for the longest time."

Gifford Pinchot died in New York City in 1946, having lived what he preached. He is buried in a tree-covered family plot of the Milford Cemetery, located in the town near his home.

Grey Towers National Historic Landmark

A winding entrance road takes you past the gatehouse and up to what was once the country estate of Gifford Pinchot. The three towers of the stone mansion reflect its name, Grey Towers, given by Gifford's father, James, when he built it in 1886. Its design is reminiscent of a French chateau of medieval times.

A recent $15 million renovation has restored the nineteenth-century elegance of the mansion. Hand-painted designs decorate the walls. A paneled entrance hall leads visitors through the spacious interior. Many

Grey Towers, the family residence of Gifford Pinchot, was built in 1886 as the home of his parents. USDA FOREST SERVICE

Visiting Grey Towers National Historic Landmark

P.O. Box 188, 151 Grey Towers Dr., Milford, PA 18337-0188

PHONE: 570-296-9630
E-MAIL: gtowers@pinchot.org
WEBSITE: www.pinchot.org/gt
ADMINISTRATION: USDA Forest Service.
HOURS: June–October, 10–4.
ADMISSION FEES: Free, but donations accepted.
TOURS: Guided tours daily on the hour, June–October.
TIME NEEDED: 1 hour.
SPECIAL EVENTS: Programs on conservation, forestry, and life of Pinchot scheduled periodically.
SPECIAL CONSIDERATIONS: Handicapped-accessible; handicapped parking available.
PARKING: On-site parking.
SALES OUTLETS: Books, postcards, memorabilia, and posters available, as well as publications about Pinchot, conservation, and the Forest Service.
DIRECTIONS: From I-84, take Exit 43 and follow signs to Milford. As you descend the hill and enter the town, Apple Valley Restaurant is on the right. Just past the restaurant, make a sharp right turn at Grey Towers sign. Entrance to Grey Towers is on the left on this road.

pieces of elegant furniture bequeathed by several generations of Pinchots fill its rooms.

Visitors may tour the first-floor rooms, terrace, and gardens. A feature not to be missed is the wisteria-covered "Fingerbowl," an elevated pool on the terrace that was used as a table by the Pinchots for outdoor dinners. Waiters around the pool floated wooden bowls of food across the water to guests on the opposite side.

Several rooms of the mansion have been converted into a museum that exhibits the furnishings and decor of the Pinchot family during the 1920s and 1930s.

Grey Towers is administered by the U.S. Forest Service and is frequently used for conservation conferences and for meetings of the Pinchot Institute, an independent, nonprofit organization committed to "leadership in conservation thought, policy, and action."

Another site worth visiting is the Cradle of Forestry located in the Pisgah National Forest near Brevard, North Carolina. This site includes an interpretive museum and historic complex where Gifford Pinchot founded one of the first schools to train forest rangers.

Zane Grey

(1872-1939)

In his early years, Zane Grey was encouraged to become a dentist like his father. But when he began to practice, he discovered his interests lay in other directions. He preferred spending his time writing fiction.

After six years practicing dentistry in New York City, he married Lina Roth, and that changed everything. Lina, or Dolly, as Zane called her, could see that writing was her husband's passion, and she encouraged him to pursue it. Even before they were married, she used money from her grandfather's inheritance to allow him to publish his first novel, *Betty Zane,* when no one else would take the chance. And in 1905, the year they were married, the couple made a life-altering decision: Zane forsook his dental practice for the risky career of freelance writing.

He had grown up as Pearl Zane Gray in Zanesville, Ohio, a town founded by his great-great-grandfather after the Revolutionary War. When the family moved to Columbus, Ohio, in 1890, his father changed the spelling of their last name to Grey. Later, he himself dropped his first name, going by the more masculine-sounding Zane.

After school, he did odd jobs at his father's dental office, even occasionally extracting teeth. But at that time, fishing and baseball were more important to him. A good athlete, his baseball skill won him a scholarship to the University of Pennsylvania. He pitched and played outfield on the Penn teams from 1893 to 1896. Off the field, he was an indifferent student, quick to anger, and an independent person who was something of a loner socially. After graduating with a degree in dentistry, he set up practice in Manhattan but yearned for the out-of-doors he had known back in Zanesville. He continued to play baseball with a local semiprofessional league and went fishing at every opportunity.

He had always been an avid reader. Now, after seeing patients during the day, he began to write. Two years after meeting Dolly during a summer vacation, he wrote an article on fishing, "A Day on the Delaware," which, much to his delight, was published by an outdoor magazine. This acceptance fired his ambition to begin a novel about his Revolutionary War ancestors, the book he published with Dolly's financial support.

The year 1904 was a pivotal one. It was the year Zane and Dolly married. It was also the year the Grey clan—Zane, and Dolly, Zane's widowed mother, his brother, and his sister—decided to buy property along the Delaware River in Lackawaxen and build houses for the family there. And it was the year Zane began writing full-time.

At first he wrote magazine articles, mostly on fishing, camping, and outdoor adventures, but sales were scarce. In two years, he sold only two articles and a photograph to *Field & Stream* and two short stories to *Recreation* magazine. In the meantime, he had written three novels. Dolly painstakingly made a neat longhand copy of each one to send to the publisher. His first, *Betty Zane,* was self-published. His second, *Spirit of the Border,* he placed with a publisher but received only modest royalties as compensation. His third, *The Last Trail,* was rejected by several publishers. The couple exhausted their savings and had to borrow from Zane's brother, Romer, known as R. C.

At a meeting of a New York City outdoorsmen's club in 1907, Grey met C. J. "Buffalo" Jones, an adventurer and rancher who wanted to raise money to experiment with crossbreeding buffalo with cattle. Grey offered to accompany Jones to his ranch in Arizona and write a book about him to encourage financial interest in his experiments. To pay for Zane's travel costs, Dolly willingly contributed the rest of her modest inheritance.

This horseback adventure in the West changed Grey's life—but not immediately. The tenderfoot from the East asked Jones the name of every feature of terrain, every plant, and every animal. He absorbed the western dialect. He listened to the innumerable tales told around the campfire. He learned of the outlaws, the rangers, and the wild-horse hunters. He absorbed the lore of the Indians. He took copious notes and forgot nothing.

He returned to his home in Lackawaxen glowing from his experiences,

Zane Grey. ZANE GREY MUSEUM

with a burning desire to weave them into stories. His forte from here on would be the western story. He had learned to love the West, and he wanted to bring these wide-open spaces to life for others.

But the resulting western novel he wrote, *The Last of the Plainsmen,* was rejected brusquely by Harper and Brothers, the editor cruelly telling Grey that he didn't think he was equipped to "write either narrative or fiction." Dolly, who throughout her life was indispensable to Zane Grey as a loving and supportive wife, advisor, editor, critic, and business manager, sent the book to a dozen publishers, finally allowing one publisher to print it with only minimal royalties to the author. She and Zane again had to rely on loans from R. C. to live in their sparsely furnished house.

Finally, in 1908, he sold a children's book, not about the West, but about baseball, to a Chicago publisher. The same publisher also agreed to reprint *The Last of the Plainsmen.* Several other magazine articles brought some much-needed income.

By 1909, now thirty-seven years old, he had written conscientiously every day but had published very little. Now he drew on his western knowledge and experience for yet another novel, *Heritage of the Desert,* a fast-moving action tale about Mormon settlers, cowboys, outlaws, and horses. He submitted it to the same editor at Harper and Brothers who had turned down his previous effort. This time, however, the editor praised the author and offered him a contract. Coincidentally, that same day another New York publisher offered to buy serial rights to the novel. Zane Grey had finally arrived as a novelist.

His next novel, *Riders of the Purple Sage,* the book for which Zane Grey is best remembered today, almost met the same fate as his first one. Several editors at Harper turned it down because of its controversial view of Mormon life. But Grey went over their heads to the Harper vice president and pleaded with him to read the story as well. The executive liked it and agreed to publish it. The novel drew glowing reviews, sold thousands of copies, and brought handsome profits to the publisher and the author.

After years of adversity, Grey hit his stride. "After all these years of effort, agony, study, reading, reading, reading . . . and writing about the great outdoors," he wrote in his diary, "I am about to come into my own." In succeeding years, he wrote *Desert Gold* (about Mexico), *The Light of Western Stars* (New Mexico), and the *U. P. Trail* (the transcontinental railroad). Now that his books had become popular and his finances more secure, Grey took frequent trips searching for story ideas to the West and to prime fishing areas, often accompanied by R. C.

He authored a dozen books and numerous magazine articles on fishing, and was well qualified to do so. He had become a world-renowned fisherman, at one time holding ten world records, more than any other individual. He was the first angler to catch a fish over 1,000 pounds with rod and reel, a 1,040-pound blue marlin.

His novel *The Lone Star Ranger,* published in 1915, elevated Zane Grey to the best-seller list, and *The Rainbow Trail,* published the same year, barely missed the list. His novels often ran as serials in popular magazines before they were published in book form. He had been selling regularly to the top magazines, and now the movie studios were interested. He sold the motion-picture rights to *Riders of the Purple Sage* and *The Light of Western Stars* to a Hollywood producer in 1917, and the following year, the Grey family with their three children moved to a new home in Hollywood, California. More than forty-five of Grey's books were made into motion pictures, and many of them have been remade two, three, or four times.

Over the next twenty years, Zane Grey wrote and published novels, serials, and magazine articles, interspersed with trips throughout the West and fishing expeditions. He reveled in his new prosperity. The family had homes all over the United States—in Lackawaxen, Pennsylvania; Altadena and Avalon, California; a cabin in Arizona; and a fishing camp in the Florida Keys. He and his family periodically cruised the Pacific on their large yacht.

Zane Grey suffered a sunstroke while fishing in Oregon in 1937, followed by a paralyzing stroke the next day. He suffered a fatal attack in 1939 and died at home with Dolly at his side. By the time of his death, this prolific writer had written eighty-nine books, including fifty-six novels of the West. Many had been serialized in large-circulation magazines that brought his stories to thousands of additional readers. He was popular throughout the English-speaking world and also found readers in Germany, France, Spain, and even Eastern Europe. Twenty-four other books he had completed were published by Dolly after his death.

Zane Grey wrote for the common person who enjoyed reading a good yarn. By his own admission, he wrote historical romances, not historical novels. A historical romance, he felt, should be true to the spirit of history but may juggle the facts to accentuate the spirit. He was a man of action who loved the West, so he wrote adventure stories set in the western United States to describe the region he loved and to spread his ideals.

Zane Grey Museum

When you walk across the broad porch and into the interior of the house where Zane and Dolly Grey lived from 1914 to 1918, you enter the study where the writer endured his lean years and wrote a number of his early novels and magazine articles. Here is the Morris chair equipped with a large board that he used to write on, as well as a desk and a trunk he took on his travels. A mounted bass recalls Zane Grey's love of fishing, which originally drew him to this spot where the Lackawaxen River meets the Delaware River.

Encircling each room at the ceiling line are figures reminiscent of Navajo sand paintings and Hopi kachina figures, western motifs painted by Dolly's cousin to decorate the rooms. Photographs on the walls depict Zane Grey the traveler, the fisherman, the baseball player, and the cowboy. His antiquated dental drill and other dental equipment stand in one corner, reminders of his early dental practice.

Another corner reflects Dolly Grey's role in the success of the celebrated author: a theme she wrote in college as an English major; an original manuscript of a fishing story that Zane wrote and she edited; and

Zane Grey, father of the western novel, lived in this house along the Upper Delaware River from 1914 to 1918. ZANE GREY MUSEUM

Visiting Zane Grey Museum

Scenic Dr., Lackawaxen, PA 18435

PHONE: 570-685-4871

WEBSITE: www.nps.gov/upde

ADMINISTRATION: Administered by the National Park Service as part of Upper Delaware Scenic and Recreational River. R.R. #2; Box 2428, Beach Lake, PA 18405

HOURS: Memorial Day–Labor Day, Thursday–Sunday, 10–5.

ADMISSION FEES: Free admission; fee for tours.

TOURS: Tours of museum offered every 30 minutes from 10–4:30.

TIME NEEDED: 1 hour.

SPECIAL EVENTS: Zane Grey's birthday celebrated last weekend in January from 12–4.

SPECIAL CONSIDERATIONS: There are some entrance steps and stairs.

PARKING: Small parking lot at museum.

SALES OUTLETS: Gift shop offers Zane Grey books and movies, as well as items of local interest.

DIRECTIONS: From I-84, exit at PA Route 739 North. Follow about 1 mile, and turn right on SR 1001 (Well Road). Cross U.S. Route 6, and follow PA Route 434 about 2 miles. Turn left on PA Route 590, and follow to Lackawaxen and the museum.

photographs of her life. Near the house is the church graveyard where both Zane and Dolly Grey were buried.

Another nearby historic site is the Delaware Aqueduct, built in 1848 by John Roebling, architect of the Brooklyn Bridge. The aqueduct once carried the Delaware and Hudson Canal across the river from Pennsylvania to New Jersey. Constructed from 1825 to 1829, the canal was built to transport anthracite coal from mines in northeastern Pennsylvania to markets on the Hudson River.

The Wyeth Family

The Wyeth family of Chadds Ford in southeastern Pennsylvania represents the most creative dynasty of painters in the United States since the talented Peale family of the eighteenth and early nineteenth centuries.

N. C. Wyeth
(1882-1945)

The patriarch, N. C. (Newell Convers) Wyeth, came to southeastern Pennsylvania from New England to study under the famed illustrator Howard Pyle, married Carolyn Bockius, a girl from Wilmington, Delaware, and embarked on a career as an illustrator. In 1911, he and Carol, as he always called her, bought eighteen rolling acres near the village of Chadds Ford and there built a small, two-story brick house and a white clapboard studio, thereby planting a seedbed that has produced three generations of creative artists.

N. C. Wyeth developed into one of the country's foremost illustrators in a day before radio, motion pictures, and television, when it was books and magazines that provided the prime means of communicating exciting stories. He produced some three thousand works of art, including illustrations for 112 books and countless magazine articles of the day. Generations of Americans have imagined Jim Hawkins in *Treasure Island* and David Balfour in *Kidnapped* the way N. C. Wyeth imagined and portrayed them.

Both at his easel and in the midst of his growing family, Wyeth radiated vitality and enthusiasm. With him there were no small passions, no passive reactions. He systematically stoked his children's imagination, even joined in their youthful games. He imbued them with his respect for history and abiding love of nature.

Although he depended on the income from his illustrations to support his growing family, he always yearned to be recognized as a fine artist and painted a large number of landscapes and still lifes in various styles that at the time captured popular attention. But in teaching his children, he concentrated on the basic techniques of painting, bringing each child into his studio for sessions of endless artistic practice. Until his untimely death in a tragic railway accident in 1945, Wyeth managed a hothouse of creativity, developing each child's talents to the utmost. In this he succeeded to an extraordinary degree.

Henriette Wyeth, the eldest daughter of N. C. and Carol, had a distinguished career as a portraitist, especially of young children. She married the artist Peter Hurd, who himself had been a student of N. C.'s. They settled on a ranch in New Mexico, where they both painted scenes of the Southwest. There she died in 1997.

Daughter Carolyn Wyeth established herself as a painter of intense originality. Her paintings were prized for what critics called their "brooding, abstract power." She opened an art school in N. C.'s old studio after his death and passed along her father's principles. She died in 1994.

Nathaniel Convers Wyeth, the only one of N. C.'s children who did not pursue art as a career, used his tutored imagination and creativity in the field of science instead, becoming the first senior engineering fellow at the DuPont Company, the highest technical position in the company at that time. The holder of twenty-five patents, he invented the prototype of

N. C. Wyeth. BRANDYWINE RIVER MUSEUM

The N. C. Wyeth painting of William Penn in the Mural Room of the N. C. Wyeth Studio.
BRANDYWINE RIVER MUSEUM

the plastic bottle used today for carbonated drinks. He died at age seventy-eight in 1990.

Daughter Ann Wyeth married John McCoy, another of her father's students, and together they raised three children in Chadds Ford. She is a painter whose pictures follow the Brandywine tradition, as well as an accomplished composer of music.

N. C.'s youngest child, Andrew Newell Wyeth, born in 1917, is also a world-renowned painter, and the legacy continues into succeeding generations. Twelve of N. C.'s thirteen surviving grandchildren work in the arts, including Andrew's son Jamie; two of Ann's daughters, Robin McCoy Bent and Ann Brelsford McCoy; Nathaniel's son Andrew; and Henriette's son Michael. Andrew's older son, Nicholas, is an art dealer specializing in family art.

Andrew Wyeth
(1917–)

In his works, often done in muted earth colors, Andrew Wyeth portrays what his biographer Richard Meryman, in his book *Andrew Wyeth: A Secret Life,* characterizes as "the commonplace, the remote, peculiar side of nature hidden from most eyes." Meryman continues, "He has achieved the nearly

Andrew Wyeth, by Peter Ralston. BRANDYWINE
RIVER MUSEUM

impossible, broad popularity while
assured of a major place in the history
of American art. He is the quintessen-
tial painter, obsessed and undistractible.
His contained, often poignant, often
eerie pictures—combining romanticism
and realism—have touched so deep a
chord in Americans that he is a household name."

In recognition of his many achievements, he has been honored with exclu-
sive one-man shows at prestigious
museums such as New York's Metropolitan Museum of Art, Washington's
National Gallery of Art, and London's Royal Academy of Arts. He was
elected a member of the American Academy and Institute of Arts and
Letters and the Academie des Beaux Artes and in 1990 was awarded a
Congressional Gold Medal.

Andrew Wyeth caught the attention of the art world in 1948 when he
released *Christina's World* and *Karl,* paintings done in precise detail of two

Andrew Wyeth Gallery in the Brandywine River Museum. BRANDYWINE RIVER MUSEUM

friends and neighbors of the artist. The paintings stood out as examples of vivid realism at a time when most painters were leaning toward abstract art.

In the years since, Andrew Wyeth's brush has produced painting after painting in watercolor, oil, and tempera, a technique he perfected. In his choice of subjects, he shows a special tenderness for unappreciated people who struggle to build a life. He has sometimes waited patiently for years until a person was willing to pose for him, and for fifteen years he kept secret a series of paintings he did of Helga Testorf, a German woman who worked for a nearby farm family. Of his art, he says: "I think one's art goes as far and as deep as one's love goes. I see no reason for painting but that. If I have anything to offer, it is my emotional contact with the place that I live and the people I do."

Though art collectors eagerly await his latest painting, Wyeth resists many of the demands of fame. His wife, Betsy, long his most influential critic and mainstay, handles all contracts and sales of his works, freeing the painter to do what he likes to do best—roam the countryside of southeastern Pennsylvania or coastal Maine, painting the subjects that catch his artistic eye. Maine, with its rugged seascapes, has long been the summer gathering place for members of the Wyeth family.

James Wyeth. BRANDYWINE RIVER MUSEUM

James Wyeth
(1946–)

Andrew's younger son, Jamie, as he is known, became a nationally recognized painter at age nineteen, when he was introduced to the art world with a one-man exhibition in New York City. He painted a posthumous portrait of President John F. Kennedy and has since served on the National Council of the Arts. Though Jamie continues to broaden his interests, his work remains in the tradition of N. C., with its adherence to realism, the sense of a story behind the images, a touch of humor, strong images and sharp contrasts in his landscapes and portraits. He is known especially for his unconventional animal portraits, includ-

James Wyeth's *Portrait of Pig* hanging in the Heritage Gallery of the Brandywine River Museum. BRANDYWINE RIVER MUSEUM

ing *Portrait of Pig* and *Raven.* An exhibit, "One Nation: Pirates and Patriots," in which Jamie's paintings were displayed alongside those of his grandfather, underlined the continuing Wyeth tradition.

Brandywine River Museum
and N. C. Wyeth House and Studio

Visitors gain an up-close understanding of the talented Wyeth family when they visit the Brandywine River Museum in Chadds Ford. The museum, on the banks of the Brandywine River, is housed in a nine-

The N. C. Wyeth House, where the painter-patriarch raised a family of artists. PHOTO BY JIM GRAHAM, BRANDYWINE RIVER MUSEUM

The N. C. Wyeth Studio, which seems frozen in time, gives visitors a glimpse of the famous painter's workplace. PHOTOS BY MICHAEL KAHN, BRANDYWINE RIVER MUSEUM

Visiting Brandywine River Museum and N. C. Wyeth House and Studio

U.S. Route 1, Chadds Ford, PA 19317

PHONE: 610-388-2700
E-MAIL: inquiries@brandywinemuseum.org
WEBSITES: www.brandywinemuseum.org
www.brandywineconservancy.org
ADMINISTRATION: The Brandywine Conservancy, a nonprofit membership organization, administers the Brandywine River Museum and the Environmental Management Center.
HOURS: Open daily, 9:30–4:30, except Christmas.
ADMISSION FEES: $6 for adults; $3 for students, seniors, and children ages 6–12. Audio tours an additional $3. Studio tour $3 (April to mid-November).
TOURS: Guided tours for groups of 15 or more available with reservations.
TIME NEEDED: At least 1 hour for museum; 1 hour for house and studio tour.
SPECIAL EVENTS: "A Brandywine Christmas" from Thanksgiving through New Year's. Craft fairs, concerts, slide programs, lectures, and other events throughout year. Special theme programs available for all ages and school groups.
SPECIAL CONSIDERATIONS: Museum is handicapped-accessible through the riverside entrance; reserved handicapped parking available in riverside parking area; Wyeth house and studio tour includes shuttle bus ride and is handicapped-accessible.
PARKING: On-site parking.
SALES OUTLETS: Museum shop offers books, posters, reproductions, and gifts. A restaurant, open 10–3, offers sandwiches, soups, salads, desserts, and beverages. Box lunches may be ordered in advance.
DIRECTIONS: Located on U.S. Route 1 just south of PA Route 100 in Chadds Ford. The museum is 28 miles southwest of Philadelphia and 12 miles north of Wilmington, Delaware.

teenth-century gristmill that has been adaptively restored. Its three floors of galleries hold paintings that represent the artistic heritage of the Brandywine Valley, including one of the most comprehensive collections of the works of N. C., Andrew, and Jamie Wyeth. Many familiar works and others rarely on public view may be seen in the permanent collection and regularly changing exhibitions.

Outdoors, surrounding the museum, are the Brandywine Conservancy's Wildflower and Native Plant Gardens, with a nature trail and wildflower garden featuring plants native to the Brandywine Valley.

A short trip by shuttle bus takes the visitor to see N. C. Wyeth's house and studio, where the family patriarch set down roots that for nine decades have nourished this family of extraordinary creativity. The house remains filled with many of the original furnishings used by the painter and his family, including a long, narrow table around which the family gathered for meals. The studio appears as though N. C. just walked out, leaving behind a clutter of props, picture frames, jars, brushes, Indian artifacts, and a large mural depicting William Penn.

Also on the grounds, although not open to the public, is the Environmental Management Center of the Brandywine Conservancy, a nonprofit organization devoted to conserving the land and water resources of the Brandywine Valley. Techniques of integrating conservation with development are studied through three program areas: land stewardship, municipal assistance, and conservation design.

In Rockland, Maine, you may see other paintings by three generations of Wyeths at the Farnsworth Art Museum and the Wyeth Center.

Dwight D. Eisenhower

(1890-1969)

The organizational and persuasive ability that Dwight D. Eisenhower exhibited as a young man playing and coaching football hinted at the characteristics that later pushed him to the fore in becoming one of America's leading military commanders and political leaders.

When he learned that his high school in Abilene, Kansas, offered no competitive football league, Eisenhower organized one. He put together a schedule with other high school teams in the area, once even arranging for a freight train to carry him and his teammates to an away game. These and other skills proved invaluable in later years when he became supreme commander of all Allied Forces in Europe in World War II and when he was elected president of the United States.

Dwight David ("Ike") Eisenhower was born in 1890, the third of seven sons of David and Ida Eisenhower. He grew up in the small town of Abilene, where his father worked as a mechanic at the local creamery. Life in Abilene in those days emphasized hard work and self-sufficiency, and Ike and his brothers all had part-time jobs. Since sending him to college seemed impossible for his poor family, he and a friend took the examination for a service academy, hoping for a free education at the U.S. Naval Academy. Instead, he won an appointment to the U.S. Military Academy at West Point, where he was an above-average student and a promising running back on the football team until he badly injured a knee. Unable to play anymore, he became a cheerleader and coach of the junior varsity.

He graduated in 1915. On his first assignment as a "shavetail" lieutenant in the U.S. Army, he met eighteen-year-old Mamie Geneva Doud at Fort Sam Houston in San Antonio, Texas. Nine months later, the two were married at the home of Mamie's parents in Denver, and they embarked on a peripatetic army career, moving thirty-five times in as many years.

World War I was a frustration for Eisenhower. He ached to be sent overseas, but instead the army, recognizing his organizational ability, put the young officer in command of Camp Colt, located on the battlefield at Gettysburg. It was established as a camp for inductees who would become

177

Dwight D. Eisenhower, during his presidency. EISENHOWER NATIONAL HISTORIC SITE

members of the new Army Tank Corps. Eisenhower had ten thousand men and six hundred officers under his command, training them in the rudiments of military life and in tank warfare.

In the years after World War I, Eisenhower served on the staffs of Gen. Fox Conner in Panama and Gen. Douglas MacArthur in the Philippines, becoming a serious student of military warfare and an early advocate of the use of armored tanks, together with his colleague George Patton. At home, in 1917, Mamie gave birth to Doud Dwight, "Icky," who died when he was three and a half years old. A second son, John Sheldon Doud, was born in 1922. By 1941, Eisenhower was an experienced colonel and chief of staff of the Third Army, directing maneuvers in Louisiana and fully expecting to retire in a few years.

After the attack on Pearl Harbor brought the United States into World War II, he was abruptly ordered to Washington, D.C., by Gen. George Marshall and put in charge of U.S. Army strategy as a brigadier general. In June 1942, he was appointed commanding general of American forces in Europe and left Washington for London to coordinate plans for defeating Nazi Germany and liberating the European countries occupied by the invader. Later he was selected as commander in chief of Allied Forces, North Africa, and organized and led the North African invasion launched in November 1942.

Subsequently he commanded the troops that invaded Sicily in May 1943, followed by the invasion of Italy. In December 1943, even before the conclusion of the Italian campaign, he was transferred to command the forthcoming Normandy invasion. Operation Overlord was the code name for the prospective cross–English Channel invasion of Europe, and he was given the title of supreme commander, Allied Expeditionary Force.

When Eisenhower gave the order to launch the D-Day operation on the overcast day of June 6, 1944, he set in motion the greatest amphibious assault in history, supported by the largest air and sea armadas ever assembled. This combined operation involved 170,000 Allied soldiers, 5,000 ships, and 12,000 aircraft. Two months later another Allied force invaded southern France. The combined U.S., Canadian, British, and French forces battled their way across France, Belgium, and the Netherlands on a broad front, while Soviet troops tightened the vise from the eastern front. A strong wintertime German counterattack, the Battle of the Bulge, was repulsed in January 1945, and the offensive pushed ahead into the German homeland. Nazi Germany surrendered unconditionally to the Allies in May 1945, and the Red Army marched into

Berlin. The occupied German capital was later partitioned into four Allied sectors.

By the time of the surrender, Eisenhower had become the symbol of all the Allied forces that had defeated the Nazis. Victory celebrations followed, and he rode triumphantly in parades in London and back home in Washington, New York City, and Abilene. But much to his chagrin, Eisenhower was ordered to remain in Europe for seven more months as head of the American Occupation Zone.

When General Marshall resigned as army chief of staff, President Harry Truman appointed Eisenhower to replace him, capping his meteoric rise from colonel to five-star general in barely four years. It was a difficult time of transition, however: He had to deal with conflicting issues unique to the times, such as military demobilization, universal military training, unification of the armed services, nuclear weapons, and the containment of Soviet aggression.

This duty done, in 1948, he retired from active duty in the army after thirty-seven years and became a civilian for the first time since boyhood. He accepted the presidency of Columbia University, turning aside many appeals for him to run for the presidency of the United States because he did not desire political office, and because he was confident that the campaign would be won by Republican governor Thomas Dewey of New York. It was at this time that he set down on paper his account of the victorious campaign against the Nazi regime. His book *Crusade in Europe* was published in 1948 and was serialized and reprinted in many different editions. The book was also translated into twenty-two languages and sold millions of copies.

In 1951, however, the reelected President Truman called him back to active duty as commander, Allied Powers in Europe, with the task of organizing the armed forces of the North Atlantic Treaty Organization (NATO) to rearm the European nations and the United States against the growing threat of Soviet aggression. Experienced in dealing with Europe's leaders, Eisenhower threw himself wholeheartedly into strengthening NATO, which he hoped would lead toward greater European unity.

Back in the United States, many felt in 1952 that Eisenhower was the best-qualified person to become president. He was still reluctant but believed that "the presidency is something that should never be sought [but] could never be refused." Furthermore, he believed strongly that certain trends in the United States, such as deficit financing and isolationism, were wrong for the country. So in February 1952, he agreed to run on the Republican ticket, then left his NATO position and came home to campaign.

He won the Republican nomination on the first ballot over conservative Sen. Robert Taft, and then defeated Gov. Adlai Stevenson of Illinois in the general election. Following up on a key campaign promise, he went to Korea seeking a way to bring an end to the stalemated war between U.N. forces and communist North Korea and its Red Chinese ally.

Some of the hallmarks of his first term as president were his efforts to reach a balanced federal budget by reducing the armed forces and armaments while relying on nuclear missiles to protect the United States, negotiating a compromise that ended the fighting in Korea, helping Europe to unite militarily under NATO, organizing the Southeast Asia Treaty Organization (SEATO) to counteract aggressive actions by the Chinese communists, and sending U.S. troops as advisors to South Vietnam. To promote peace with the Soviet Union, he offered to share nuclear knowhow, limit the arms race, and open each country's airspace to the other. Each of these proposals was rejected by the Soviets. In a controversy over Egyptian control of the Suez Canal, he supported Egypt and repudiated Britain and France.

At home, his administration launched one of the greatest public-works projects in U.S. history, building a network of interstate highways. With Canada, he initiated construction of the St. Lawrence Seaway, which would link the Atlantic Ocean with Lake Ontario. Economically, the United States enjoyed a period of growing gross national product, low inflation, and low unemployment.

In spite of a heart attack he suffered in 1955, Eisenhower ran and was elected to a second term in 1956, defeating Stevenson a second time. In his second term, he supported a Supreme Court decision that mandated racial integration of public schools and reluctantly had to send federal troops to enforce the integration of Central High School in Little Rock, Arkansas. In 1957, after the Soviet Union surprised the United States by launching Sputnik, the world's first man-made satellite into earth orbit, Eisenhower reorganized the nation's space research program, establishing the National Aeronautic and Space Agency (NASA). In the final year of his presidency, he failed to achieve a nuclear test ban treaty with the Soviets, an effort that fell apart when a U.S. high-altitude spy plane was detected and shot down over the Soviet Union.

Upon retirement from the White House in 1961, the Eisenhowers were ready to move full-time to their home and farm in Gettysburg, a town they remembered from their earlier Camp Colt days. They had purchased the farm while he was president of Columbia University. In their married life, this was the only house the Eisenhowers ever owned. At the farm, Ike gloried in his pastoral pursuits, painted as a hobby, and entertained friends with Mamie. He maintained an office at nearby Gettysburg College and also wrote an ambitious two-volume memoir of his presidency, titled *The White House Years,* and another book, *At Ease: Stories I Tell to Friends.* He was often consulted as an elder statesman; John F. Kennedy sought his advice on Cuba, and Lyndon Johnson consulted him on the conflict in Vietnam.

Eisenhower suffered a second heart attack in 1965 and a third in 1968. He died at Walter Reed Hospital in Washington, D.C., in March 1969, and was buried at the Place of Meditation at the Eisenhower Center in Abilene, Kansas. "Everybody liked Ike," observed his vice president, Richard Nixon. And that, he concluded, was because "Ike loved everybody."

Eisenhower National Historic Site

When you pay a visit to Eisenhower National Historic Site, you see the culmination of the fondest desires of this remarkable couple. For Dwight Eisenhower, the farm was "a piece of land" he could leave to posterity "a little better than [he] found it." For Mamie Eisenhower, it represented the only home this military wife ever owned, designed, furnished, and decorated herself.

The Eisenhowers retired to this farm in Gettysburg after the president's second term. The two-hundred-year-old brick-and-timber house was converted into a modern home with eight bedrooms, eight baths, living room, dining room, and glassed-in porch, where the couple spent most of their hours together. EISENHOWER NATIONAL HISTORIC SITE

Visiting Eisenhower National Historic Site

250 Eisenhower Farm Rd., Gettysburg, PA 17325

PHONE: 717-338-9114

E-MAIL: EISE_site_manager@NPS-gov

WEBSITE: www.nps.gov/eise

ADMINISTRATION: Administered along with Gettysburg National Military Park by the National Park Service.

HOURS: Open daily, 9–4. Closed Thanksgiving, Christmas, and New Year's Day.

ADMISSION FEES: $5.75 for adults; $3.75 for children ages 13–16; $2.50 for children ages 6–12. Purchase tickets at the Gettysburg National Military Park visitors center.

TOURS: All visits are by shuttle bus from the Gettysburg National Military Park visitors center. Orientation tour conducted by staff; self-guided tour of house, grounds, and cattle barn. Ten-minute video shown in reception center where exhibits are displayed.

TIME NEEDED: At least 2 hours.

SPECIAL EVENTS: Fabulous Fifties Weekend in June; weeklong Eisenhower Academy for teachers each summer, covering Eisenhower foreign and domestic policies as well as 1950s' popular culture; World War II Week-end in September; Eisenhower Seminar in October; and an Eisenhower Christmas in December.

SPECIAL CONSIDERATIONS: Shuttle bus to site has wheelchair lift, and loaner wheelchairs are available. There is a photo album of the second floor of the Eisenhower home, as well as large-print guides. Eisenhower video is captioned.

PARKING: Park at the Gettysburg National Military Park visitors center and take the shuttle bus to site.

SALES OUTLETS: Bookstore in reception center offers books, videos, posters, and other items related to the Eisenhowers and World War II.

DIRECTIONS: Gettysburg is located at the junction of U.S. Routes 30 and 15. From Exit 17 of the Pennsylvania Turnpike, travel south 30 miles on Route 15 to Steinwehr Avenue Exit and follow signs to visitors center.

A shuttle bus takes visitors the mile from the Gettysburg National Military Park visitor center to the Eisenhower farm, which lies adjacent to the battlefield. A ranger gives a brief orientation to the site, and then leads visitors to the Eisenhower home, a contemporary Georgian-style farmhouse. The Eisenhowers had incorporated part of the two hundred-year-old brick-and-timber farmhouse into the new structure with eight bedrooms, eight baths, elegant living room, formal dining room, large kitchen, and a large glassed-in porch where the couple spent most of their hours together.

This was their retreat from the rigors of public life both during Eisenhower's presidency and during his retirement years. But the demands of state were met here as well. The home frequently served as a meeting place with heads of state and as a backdrop for decisions that shaped the world. Today it remains largely unchanged from those Cold War years, when Eisenhower hosted people like West German chancellor Konrad Adenauer or painted on the sunlit porch. After a short ranger talk in the formal living room, visitors tour the house on their own, with a folder that provides details of every room.

Outside the house are the big barn where Eisenhower stored hay, his automobiles, and a jeep; his rose garden; his golf putting green; and a guest house where Viscount Bernard Montgomery, a World War II colleague, once stayed. A small reception center shows a video of Eisenhower's life.

A short walk takes you to adjoining farms that Eisenhower leased. Besides producing corn, wheat, and hay, the farms were home first to dairy cattle and later to a prize-winning herd of Angus cattle. The show barn where the Angus were raised today holds some of the machinery used to run the farms. Another short walk takes you to Eisenhower's skeet range, where an interpretive sign describes his enthusiasm for the sport.

Pearl S. Buck
(1892–1973)

She was born Pearl Sydenstricker, in Hillsboro, West Virginia, at a time when her parents, Presbyterian missionaries to China, were on home leave after twelve years in the interior of China. She was the fourth of seven children, only three of whom survived to adulthood. Within months, her parents and their newborn baby girl returned to China, where Pearl grew up in the small city of Chinkiang in eastern China, a city near where the Grand Canal meets the Yangtze River.

She learned to speak Chinese before English as she listened to stories told by her Chinese nurse. Her missionary father went on frequent journeys to remote areas and brought back tales of his adventures, while her mother talked for hours about her own childhood in West Virginia.

Pearl's mother taught her at home, having her write a composition every week. Soon her mother began sending these short pieces to the *Shanghai Mercury*, an English-language newspaper that had a weekly edition for children. A number of these compositions were printed.

But these were troubled times in China, as trade concessions forced on the Chinese by European and American companies made the Chinese resentful of foreign interference. This resentment boiled over in 1901 with the Boxer Rebellion, and Pearl and her sister Grace fled with their mother to Shanghai for safety while their father remained behind.

In 1910, at age eighteen, Pearl returned to the United States and enrolled at Randolph Macon Women's College in Lynchburg, Virginia, where her older brother, Edgar, lived and was a newspaper editor. Developing into a campus leader, she was elected president of her class. She wrote for the college paper and in her senior year won two literary prizes, one for the best short story.

After graduation, Pearl wanted to stay in the United States and go into teaching, but her father asked her to return to China to help care for her mother, who was seriously ill. After her mother's health improved, Pearl met and married John Lossing Buck, an agricultural missionary, in 1917. The young couple moved to a rural village, where Lossing endeavored to teach Chinese farmers new agricultural methods. In the two and a half years she lived in Nanhsuchou, Pearl absorbed a deep understanding of the rural people, later putting her observations on paper in her landmark novel, *The Good Earth.*

In 1919, she and Lossing left their isolated village for the city of Nanking, where he accepted a position as a professor of agriculture at the university. The move brought great changes to Pearl's life as well. In March 1920, she gave birth to a baby girl, Carol, whom she later realized was afflicted with phenylketonuria (PKU), a rare genetic disease that left her profoundly mentally retarded. In 1921, after her mother's death, Pearl wrote a family remembrance that would be published fifteen years later as *The Exile,* a title reflecting her mother's life and longing for her U.S. home. It was the first prose she had written since college, and she was pleased with her accomplishment.

While teaching English literature at Nanking University, she decided to write an article about Chinese young people. Hesitantly, she mailed it to the *Atlantic Monthly* back in the United States, and the magazine published it under the title "In China, Too." The editor of another magazine wrote to the unknown author and asked her to write something for him. She sent a piece entitled "Beauty in China" and now began to think of herself as an accomplished writer.

Pearl S. Buck, c. 1964, by Freeman Elliott.
PEARL S. BUCK INTERNATIONAL

In 1925, Lossing was awarded a sabbatical leave at Cornell University in New York, where he and Pearl both earned master's degrees, he in agricultural economics, she in English. On the long voyage to the United States, she had written the story that grew into her first novel, *East Wind, West Wind,* which was published first as a magazine article in 1926 and later as a book. By the fall of 1926, she was back in Nanking, now writing in earnest and sending articles to a literary agent back in New York.

While in New York, she and Lossing had adopted a second daughter, Janice. In 1927, as the rural warlords fought over Nanking, killing the vice president of Nanking University, the family escaped harm when a servant hid them in her small house, then helped the so-called "white devils" to avoid the pillaging soldiers and find refuge in Japan. In the turmoil, Pearl lost an important manuscript of one of her novels.

The year 1930 was one of both heartache and triumph for Pearl Buck. On another trip to the United States, she placed her mentally retarded daughter, Carol, in an institution in New Jersey, and then sadly returned to Nanking. But this was also the year she completed *The Good Earth,* the heartfelt novel about rural life in China that suddenly transformed this unknown author into a literary luminary. Published the next year, it won praise from critics and for twenty-one months was on the U.S. best-seller list. Pearl Buck won the Pulitzer Prize that year for the best novel by an American author. The book was later translated into more than forty languages and inspired a popular motion picture.

Now a steady stream of books flowed from her pen. *Sons* (1932) and *A House Divided* (1935) were sequels to *The Good Earth* and formed a trilogy entitled *House of Earth,* which was published in one volume in 1935. Her novel *The Mother* (1934) portrayed the changing role of women in China. Biographies of her mother and father—*The Exile* and *Fighting Angel* (both 1936)—attracted considerable worldwide attention. In recognition primarily of *The Good Earth* and the two biographies, she was awarded the Nobel Prize in literature in 1938, which came as a complete surprise to her. She was the first American woman ever to win this honor.

Later, when she decided to write about American topics rather than Asian ones, she used a pseudonym. Between 1945 and 1953, she issued five volumes under the name John Sedges. The first of these works, *The Townsman,* won both popular and scholarly acclaim for its accurate depiction of Kansas in the 1850s.

Her marriage had been troubled for many years, and in 1933, the couple began proceedings for a divorce. In 1934, Pearl returned permanently to the United States because of deteriorating conditions in China and to be closer to Carol. She married Richard Walsh, her publisher and advisor, in 1935 and bought Green Hills Farm, a sixty-acre estate with an old farmhouse in Bucks County. Over the years, she and Richard filled their home with six more adopted children.

Although she continued to write prolifically, Pearl Buck turned more and more to humanitarian causes. In 1941, she and her husband founded the East and West Association, a nonprofit group designed to promote understanding between Americans and Asians. During World War II, she wrote scripts for broadcasts to China and worked for United China Relief. She spoke out against racism, whether related to Asians or blacks. She also became active in American civil rights and women's rights and gave numerous talks on the lecture circuit.

After the war, she founded Welcome House, the first international and interracial adoption agency designed to find adoptive homes for biracial children, many the offspring of U.S. servicemen overseas. Welcome House has assisted in the placement of over six thousand children in five decades. In 1964, she established the Pearl S. Buck Foundation to provide support for Amerasian children who are not eligible for adoption.

Richard Walsh died after a long illness in 1960. Pearl S. Buck died in Danby, Vermont, in March 1973 and is buried at Green Hills Farm. By the time of her death, this late-starting novelist had published more than eighty books—novels, collections of stories, biographies, and an autobiography—poetry, drama, children's literature, and translations from the Chinese.

The Pearl S. Buck House

The rambling 1835 stone farmhouse in Bucks County north of Philadelphia, part of which dates back to 1740, now a national historical landmark, was Pearl Buck's home in the United States for thirty-eight years and remains much as she left it. She filled it with a collection of Pennsylvania country furniture as well as many possessions from her homes in China. Among other objects, you will see oriental rugs, Chinese decorative screens, and a silk wall hanging presented to her by the Dalai Lama. A rice china tea set she owned is in the dining room, and a Chinese inkstone and scholar's screen are on display.

Pearl S. Buck House. PEARL S. BUCK INTERNATIONAL

Visiting the Pearl S. Buck House

520 Dublin Rd.; P.O. Box 181, Perkasie, PA 18944

PHONE: 215-249-0100 or 800-220-2825
E-MAIL: pearl-s-buck.org
WEBSITE: www.pearlsbuck.org
ADMINISTRATION: Pearl S. Buck International (PSBI).
HOURS: Tuesday–Saturday, 11–4; Sunday, 1–4. Closed January–February and major holidays.
ADMISSION FEES: $6 for adults; $5 for students and seniors; $5 for group tours of 10 or more; $15 for families (parents with children 10 and under).
TOURS: Guided tours Tuesday–Saturday at 11, 1, and 2, Sunday at 1 and 2.
TIME NEEDED: 2 hours.
SPECIAL EVENTS: PSBI Day in early June; Bucks County Spring Challenge Series, with seven races benefiting local nonprofit organizations; summer children's theater; Pearl S. Buck Golf Classic in September; Holiday Festival and Craft Show from mid-November to December 30.
SPECIAL CONSIDERATIONS: House has stairs and is not handicapped-accessible.
PARKING: Free on-site parking.
SALES OUTLETS: Gift shop offers Buck's books and unique Asian giftware.
DIRECTIONS: From Pennsylvania Turnpike Exit 27 (Willow Grove/Doylestown), follow PA Route 611 Bypass North to PA Route 313 West. Turn left and continue to fourth traffic light in center of town of Dublin. Turn left on Maple Avenue, and immediately bear right on Dublin Road. Look for PSBI sign about 1 mile on the right.

Atop the handcrafted hardwood desk on which Pearl Buck wrote *The Good Earth,* as well as other novels, is her leather portfolio with handwritten documents and drafts of several articles. In the library, nine thousand books reach from floor to ceiling. A table in the kitchen was the desk that her husband, Richard Walsh, used when he was the publisher of John Day Company, which published many of her books.

The verdant sixty-acre estate also offers scenic walking trails, a garden of perennial flowers, and Pearl S. Buck's gravesite. An 1827 red barn has been converted into facilities for business and social group functions. The offices of Pearl S. Buck International (PSBI), the humanitarian service organization created and endowed by the late author, are also on the site. The organization provides assistance in health, education, and work skills to children of other countries who have been abandoned or are orphans, refugees, or victims of HIV/AIDS. A separate adoption service is devoted to finding permanent homes for orphaned children.

Marian Anderson

(1897-1993)

The girl who was to become a world-renowned contralto grew up in the crowded streets of South Philadelphia. Her father, John, sold ice and coal at the Reading Terminal Market, while her mother, Anna, worked as a cleaning woman at the popular John Wanamaker department store. After working long hours, Anna also took in laundry.

Much of the family's social life revolved around the Union Baptist Church, which was located only a few blocks from their home. Marian, with her mother and father, and sisters Alyce and Ethel, attended regularly, and her father served as an usher.

From her earliest days, Marian loved music, and it was her church that first encouraged the talented girl. She grew up singing in the church choirs, performing duets and solos, and even singing a tenor or bass part if needed because of the extraordinary range of her voice.

After her father died when she was twelve, Marian and her mother and sisters moved in with her grandparents nearby. Marian began accepting fees for singing at benefits and church socials. She was popular, and soon her performance fees rose from $1.50 to $5. Out of each concert fee, she gave $2 to her mother and $1 to each of her sisters, keeping $1 for herself.

The girl with the mellow voice and broad range might never have progressed beyond church socials but for the timely help of others. Roland Hayes, a famous African-American tenor, recommended her to Mary Patterson, a locally known soprano, who gave her free voice lessons.

There were setbacks as well. A music school in Philadelphia turned her down as a student because she was black. Although the Yale School of Music did accept her, she could not afford to attend.

But she auditioned and was accepted as a student by Giuseppe Boghetti, a prominent Italian opera coach. The members of Union Baptist Church held a benefit to raise the $1,600 Marian needed to pay Boghetti for a year's lessons. After that year, however, Boghetti never charged the budding contralto again, even though he coached Marian during the rest of his life.

Prepared by her excellent voice training, she now selected an accompanist and began a series of concerts at churches, schools, and black colleges. Just before her twenty-fifth birthday, Marian was able to make a down payment on the row house open to visitors today, a three-bedroom house across the street from where she had lived with her grandparents. Later, her sister Ethel lived next door. Marian then purchased seven additional houses on the same street as rental properties, eventually owning eleven houses.

Winning musical competitions in Philadelphia and New York City earned her the opportunity to sing in an open-air concert with the New York Philharmonic Orchestra. Determined to increase her experience and improve her German, she went to Europe, financed by a foundation grant. She gave her first European concert in Berlin in 1930 and toured Scandinavia, where a warm reception by audiences bolstered her confidence.

Back in the United States in 1931, Anderson gave twenty-six concerts in fifteen states. Between 1933 and 1935, she toured Europe again. Her reputation as one of the finest singers on the concert stage continued to grow. "Yours is a voice such as one hears once in a hundred years," said the world-famous conductor Arturo Toscanini. She was honored to meet the Finnish composer Jean Sibelius, who offered a champagne toast to Anderson after hearing her sing, and later dedicated a composition to her.

Marian Anderson had come a long way from Union Baptist. Impresario Sol Hurok agreed to take her as a client and scheduled her appearances for the remainder of her long career. The Finnish pianist Kosti Vehanen now became her accompanist.

In 1935, she returned to the United States to give a concert at New York City's Town Hall, which helped restore her confidence after an appearance made eleven years earlier, when only a handful of people had come to hear the unknown black singer. But now a new obstacle arose. Anderson had broken her foot on the ship back to the United States. Gamely, she appeared on stage in a long gown that covered the floor-

Marian Anderson. MARIAN ANDERSON HISTORIC SITE

to-knee cast, supporting herself against the piano as she sang. The audience, including her mother, her sisters, and Boghetti, gave her a tumultuous ovation. Critics the next day agreed that a new American star had risen. Marian Anderson was finally recognized as a top-flight vocal artist in her own country.

But that country had its shortcomings. As a black performer, Anderson had long felt the effects of racial discrimination, and in 1939 the Daughters of the American Revolution, owners of Constitution Hall in Washington, D.C., refused to allow her to sing there. In protest, First Lady Eleanor Roosevelt resigned from the board of directors and from the DAR itself. Instead, on Easter Sunday, the date set for the concert, the famous contralto sang on the steps of the Lincoln Memorial to a crowd of seventy-five thousand appreciative music lovers that included Supreme Court justices and cabinet secretaries. "I am deeply touched that I can in any way be a symbol of democracy," she said after the concert. "When I sang that day I was singing for the entire nation." Four years later, the contralto was invited by the DAR to sing at Constitution Hall.

In the ensuing years, Marian Anderson continued to fill concert dates in the United States and abroad—in Europe, the Soviet Union, Africa, South America, the Caribbean, Central America, Israel, and Asia. During 1943, she made her eighth transcontinental tour of the United States. Once the tour was over, she married architect Orpheus "King" Fisher, who had admired her for years, and the couple bought a country home near Danbury, Connecticut.

In 1955, Marian Anderson attained another landmark in her career—she sang at the Metropolitan Opera in New York, the first time a black artist had sung at the famous opera house. The role was Ulrica, the sorceress in the opera *The Masked Ball*. She sang in Italian with outstanding Metropolitan stars Zinka Milanov and Richard Tucker. The cast was called back for eight curtain calls, then insisted that Anderson go back onstage to take a last bow by herself. She later said she felt "privileged to serve as a symbol." Now, she hoped, "doors everywhere may open increasingly to those who have prepared themselves well."

Honors flowed to the world-famous singer. Her hometown of Philadelphia gave her its Bok Award as Philadelphia's outstanding citizen, accompanied by a check for $10,000, which she used to establish a fund to help young singers gain professional training. She sang at the second inauguration of President Dwight D. Eisenhower, who later appointed her a member of the U.S. delegation to the United Nations. She also sang at the inauguration of President John F. Kennedy and enjoyed several visits to the White House as a performer and guest. In 1963, she became one of the few Americans to be awarded the Presidential Medal of Freedom for her lifetime achievements, presented to her by President Kennedy.

Anderson sang her final concert at Carnegie Hall in New York City on Easter Sunday in 1965, climaxing a tour she had begun at Constitution Hall the previous October. She returned to her 150-acre farm in Danbury, where she lived in retirement. Her husband, Orpheus Fisher, died in 1986 in Danbury. Marian Anderson died in April 1993 in Portland, Oregon, where she had gone to live with her talented nephew, Oregon Symphony music director James DePreist, the son of her sister Ethel.

"To say farewell to Marian Anderson will not be easy for the American people," wrote correspondent Vincent Sheean. "She has been . . . a living part of the national consciousness, the voice of the American soul."

Marian Anderson Residence Museum and Birthplace Museum

Visitors get a better understanding of Marian Anderson, the striving concert singer, at her South Philadelphia row house at 762 S. Marian Anderson Way (formerly S. Martin St.). This comfortable house was home base for the contralto for many years, the place to which she returned after her extensive concert tours. Its interior was designed by her architect husband.

A grand piano, although not hers, sets the scene in the living room while the recorded voice of this talented singer fills the room, just as it did when she lived here. Anderson often practiced her vocal exercises in a small back room on the second floor. In the Music Room are a large painting of the singer; photographs showing her at performances, greeting President Kennedy at his inau-

The house at 762 S. Marian Anderson Way was purchased and preserved as Marian Anderson Residence Museum by Blanche Burton-Lyles, protégé of Anderson and founder of the Marian Anderson Historical Society. PHOTO BY THE AUTHORS

Visiting Marian Anderson Residence Museum and Birthplace Museum

762 S. Marian Anderson Way, Philadelphia, PA 19146,
and 1833 Webster St., Philadelphia, PA 19146

PHONE: 856-966-1688
E-MAIL: mariandhstsoc@aol.com
WEBSITE: www.mariananderson.org
ADMINISTRATION: Museums are administered by the Marian Anderson Historical Society.
HOURS: By appointment.
ADMISSION FEES: $10 for each museum; $5 for students.
TOURS: By appointment.
TIME NEEDED: 30 to 45 minutes for each museum.
SPECIAL EVENTS: Birthday miniconcerts on weekend nearest February 27.
SPECIAL CONSIDERATIONS: Entrances to both museums have several steps.
PARKING: On-street parking.
SALES OUTLETS: Postcards, brochures, memorabilia, and a biography of Anderson are available.
DIRECTIONS: From Philadelphia City Hall, go south on Broad Street to Catharine Street. Turn right and follow Catharine Street five blocks, then turn right on Marian Anderson Way (formerly S. Martin Street), which is only one block long.

In the music room are a portrait of Anderson, pictures and memorabilia of her career, and personal artifacts. PHOTO BY THE AUTHORS

guration, and giving her famous concert at the Lincoln Memorial; and a selection of her concert programs.

A walking tour takes visitors through Marian Anderson Village, which includes the South Marian Anderson Way residence museum; the Union Baptist Church; the E. M. Stanton Elementary School, from which she graduated in 1910; the Anderson Recreation Center; and the Birthplace Museum at nearby 1833 Webster Street. Marian's parents, who had come from Lynchburg, Virginia, rented one room on the second floor of the Webster Street row house where Marian was born on February 27, 1897. The birthplace has been converted into a small museum with additional photographs of Anderson's career and a video that portrays the singer's life.

Both the residence and birthplace have been purchased, renovated, and preserved by their dedicated owner, Blanche Burton-Lyles, herself a concert pianist, for whom Marian Anderson was an inspiration and who recommended her as a student at the Curtis Institute of Music. Burton-Lyles went on to become the first African-American woman pianist to graduate from Curtis. The Marian Anderson Historical Society provides financial assistance, housing, and travel accommodations to young professional classical singers each year.

Rachel Carson, c. 1962, by Erich Hartmann. MAGNUM PHOTOS

Rachel Carson

(1907-64)

People were usually surprised at meeting Rachel Carson for the first time. Could this seemingly shy, serious woman, so conservative in her dress, be the literary genius and crusading environmentalist they had heard and read so much about?

Rachel Carson was born in 1907, the third child of Robert and Maria Carson, in a two-story frame farmhouse on sixty-five acres of open land in Springdale, a small town on the western bank of the Allegheny River fifteen miles north of Pittsburgh.

With her two older children in school, Rachel's mother, a former teacher, encouraged her daughter's love of nature. She later recalled that Rachel was always "happiest with the birds and creatures" she observed in the hours she spent roaming the woods and fields near her home.

Rachel also loved writing, and at an early age, she began submitting stories to *St. Nicholas,* a popular children's magazine. At age ten, she won the magazine's Silver Badge, a $10 prize, and was thrilled when she saw her story in print. Even at that early age, she later remembered, she was determined that she "would someday be a writer."

After high school, Carson attended the nearby Pennsylvania College for Women, now Chatham College, on a $100 scholarship, majoring in English. But money for tuition was scarce, and it took a loan from the college to allow her to continue, which she later repaid by selling a portion of her family's land.

A requirement that every student take two semesters of science put her in the class of an inspiring biology teacher, Mary Skinker, and led Carson to change her major to zoology. Her friends thought this switch to be a wrong choice because few women found jobs in science, then very much a man's field.

Nevertheless, she graduated *magna cum laude* from PCW in 1928 and got a plum assignment of a summer job at the Marine Biological Laboratory at Woods Hole, Massachusetts, where she saw the ocean for the first time. She followed this by entering Johns Hopkins University, this time with a full scholarship, where she earned a master's degree in marine zoology. She managed to supplement her stipend by working for two genetics professors and teaching zoology at the nearby University of Maryland.

At the suggestion of Mary Skinker, she applied for and was hired by the U.S. Bureau of Fisheries in Washington, D.C., to write scripts for a radio show on marine life. A year later, she qualified for a permanent civil-service position as a junior aquatic biologist, one of only two women then employed at the bureau at a professional level.

But Carson's career was handicapped by difficulties within her family, which would follow her throughout her life. Her father died in 1935, leaving Rachel to support her mother. Tragically, the following year, her older sister, Marion, died of pneumonia at age forty, leaving two young daughters and no husband. Assuming full responsibility for the family, Carson brought them to live with her at her home in suburban Washington, D.C.

But if her home life was troubled, Carson's professional life was moving swiftly. When she was assigned to write an introduction for a booklet on the sea, her boss rejected her piece for being too long and inappropriate, but suggested she submit the well-written piece instead to the *Atlantic Monthly*. The magazine published the article, "Undersea," in its September 1936 issue, her first publication in a national magazine. Her essay inspired praise from scientists, naturalists, and literary critics alike. "Undersea" also confirmed Carson's conviction that science and literature were compatible. Her passion for biology and her talent for writing could be pursued in harmony. Science gave her wondrous subjects to write about, and writing let her share these wonders with the world.

Impressed by the *Atlantic Monthly* article, the publisher Simon and Schuster contracted with Carson to write her first book, *Under the Sea Wind*, which came out in November 1941 to critical acclaim but poor sales—Pearl Harbor was bombed within weeks, and the public's attention shifted elsewhere.

For the next year, Ray Carson, as her friends called her, wrote four pamphlets promoting fish as a wartime alternative for foods in short supply, and wrote or edited twelve more booklets that illuminated the conservation of natural resources for the U.S. Fish and Wildlife Service, successor to the Bureau of Fisheries. On her own, at home, in between family responsibilities, she outlined a book she thought should be read by "anyone who has looked out upon the ocean with wonder." She obtained a literary agent in New York City who could help market her manuscript. For the next two years, she gathered material from many sources and from research voyages out of Woods Hole. Giving up the weekend nature hikes that she loved and other recreation with her friends, she worked late into the night as she patiently pieced together these facts into *The Sea around Us,* an ambitious effort to portray "the dominating role played by the ocean in the course of earth history."

At the suggestion of her agent and other professionals she consulted, she often reorganized whole sections and rewrote endlessly to perfect her prose. As the book neared completion, one chapter won a science writing award, and *The New Yorker* magazine enthusiastically serialized part of the forthcoming book. Finally, in 1951, Oxford University Press published *The Sea around Us* to immediate acclaim. One critic commended the author for "removing the mystery of the sea . . . while leaving us its poetry." It was chosen as a Book of the Month Club selection and remained on the *New York Times* best-seller list for an amazing eighty-six weeks.

Her financial success now assured, Rachel Carson felt free to leave the Fish and Wildlife Service to write full-time. She bought seashore property in Maine and built a cottage to which she retreated each summer with family members and several cats.

After four more years of tramping barefoot across ocean beaches and peering into tide pools in the rocks, she published her third book, *The Edge of the Sea,* a book that describes "the intricate fabric of life along the seashore by which one creature is linked with another, and each with its surroundings." *The New Yorker* once again excerpted portions of the book in advance of publication, and *Reader's Digest* offered a condensed version. The title remained on the *New York Times* best-seller list for twenty-six weeks.

A decade earlier, Carson had suggested to *Reader's Digest* an article based on research showing that certain chemicals were harmful to wildlife. The magazine had turned down the idea. Now a challenge arrived in a letter from Olga Huckins, a woman in Massachusetts who said that birds in her neighborhood were dying because vegetation was being sprayed with the pesticide DDT.

Over the next four years, Carson sifted through thousands of notes, articles, correspondence, and scientific research abstracts, all the while herself suffering what she called a "catalog of illnesses," including arthritis, iritis (inflammation of the eye), ulcers, viral infections, and a heart attack. She devoted whatever spare moments she could find to Roger, the grandnephew she had adopted when her niece Marjorie died.

Silent Spring would be a much different book—not unveiling the drama of the ocean depths or the seashore, but sounding the alarm for man to cease spreading dangerous chemicals that disrupted the normal processes of nature. Knowing she would meet strong opposition, she carefully documented all her findings, but courageously pulled no punches.

When published in September 1962, the book sparked a firestorm of public outrage. More than a quarter million copies were sold by the end of the year. Once again the author was on the best-seller list. U.S. Supreme Court Justice William O. Douglas called it "the most important chronicle of this century for the human race."

The volume and fervor of these favorable reviews were matched only by the intense attacks of the chemical industry and those the industry influenced. Despite poor health, Carson responded to these attacks by defending her position, giving speeches before various organizations, testifying at congressional hearings, appearing on televised segments of "CBS Reports," and conferring with President John F. Kennedy and his Science Advisory Committee. The Advisory Committee's report on pesticide use and control confirmed every point highlighted in *Silent Spring*. The next day, a subcommittee of the Senate started a two-year investigation of government and industry regulations regarding pesticides. As a consequence, DDT was finally banned nationwide in 1972.

Tragically, Rachel Carson never saw the success of her efforts. She died in 1964, at the peak of her influence, from breast cancer, which she had kept hidden from the public for four years. One of the many citations that lauded her work put it this way: "Miss Carson has successfully invaded a man's field and with a poet's eye, a scientific mind, and a woman's intuition, has taught the world to wonder."

"The lasting pleasures of contact with the natural world," she once wrote, "are not reserved for scientists but are available to anyone who will place himself under the influence of earth, sea, and sky, and their amazing life."

In 1995, Pennsylvania designated the new home of the state's Department of Conservation and Natural Resources as the Rachel Carson State Office Building in Harrisburg. Years later, a pair of peregrine falcons nested on a ledge of the fifteenth floor and hatched four young fledglings. Peregrine falcons that had vanished entirely from the eastern United States in the early 1960s because of DDT have now returned.

Rachel Carson Homestead

Visitors see firsthand the influences that led Rachel Carson to become a pioneer of the environmental movement at the home where she grew up, led by a guide around the rooms of the partially restored house. Rachel

Visiting Rachel Carson Homestead

613 Marion Ave.; Box 46, Springdale, PA 15144

PHONE: 724-274-5459
E-MAIL: rcarson@salsgiver.com
WEBSITE: www.rachelcarsonhomestead.org
ADMINISTRATION: The Rachel Carson Homestead Association, a private, nonprofit organization.
HOURS: March–November, Saturday, 10–4; Sunday, 1–5; December–February, by appointment.
ADMISSION FEES: $4 for adults; $2.50 for students.
TOURS: Tours include the two-story farmhouse where Carson grew up, exhibits on environmental issues, and a nature trail.
TIME NEEDED: 1 hour.
SPECIAL EVENTS: Rachel Carson Day is celebrated the third Saturday in May; a hands-on environmental learning program is held the third Saturday of each month. Educational programs include school field trips, in-school programs, and community outreach.
SPECIAL CONSIDERATIONS: First floor of house, exhibit area, and bookstore mostly handicapped-accessible; full flight of stairs to second floor.
PARKING: On-street parking.
SALES OUTLETS: Bookstore offers Carson's books and other books and products related to environmental issues and souvenirs.
DIRECTIONS: From Pennsylvania Turnpike, take Exit 5, Allegheny Valley. Following signs for Cheswick/Springdale, take Freeport Road for 2.5 miles through Cheswick into Springdale. Freeport Road becomes Pittsburgh Street. Turn left on Colfax Street, and follow it up the hill for six blocks. Turn right on Marion Avenue; homestead is 613 on the left.

and her family lived in this four-room farmhouse on sixty-five acres of land that sloped down to the Allegheny River. The farmhouse, now preserved by the Rachel Carson Homestead Association, was heated in those early days by fireplaces only. For lighting, it had oil lamps but no electricity. It had no running water and no indoor bathrooms. Outside were a barn, chicken coop, orchard, grape arbor, springhouse, and outhouse. The Carsons kept cows, a pig, chickens, rabbits, a horse and buggy that Rachel rode partway to school, plus numerous cats and dogs.

Although the farmhouse is now surrounded by modern suburban homes, it still captures the scene much the way it was when Rachel was a girl, with a chamber pot, treadle sewing machine, and square grand piano. Pictures on the wall portray her parents, siblings Marion and Robert, and

Carson grew up in this four-room farmhouse near the Allegheny River in Springdale. The site is now the home of the Rachel Carson Homestead Association and serves as a museum and environmental center. PHOTO BY THE AUTHORS

classmates at college. Copies of stories she wrote for children's magazines such as *St. Nicholas* are displayed. The association also serves as an international resource for information about her life and work.

Behind the house, the quarter-mile-long Wild Creatures Nature Trail winds through a small wooded area. Signs along the trail identify plants and trees and underscore environmental lessons. The homestead serves as the center for environmental activities for schools, Boy and Girl Scouts, and family groups.

James A. Michener

(1907-97)

Like many thousands of Americans, James A. Michener's life took a new direction as a result of his experiences in World War II. Enlisting in the U.S. Navy late in 1942, one step ahead of being drafted, the thirty-six-year-old Michener was soon awarded a commission. After stateside duty as a publications editor in Washington and Philadelphia, he was sent to the South Pacific, where he followed behind the advancing naval forces to survey navy airfields, replenish supplies, and reassure the natives of the conquered islands. During 1944 and 1945, he served on forty-nine islands and traveled some 150,000 miles, getting to know firsthand the local island history and lifestyles.

A close call in a belly-landing plane crash convinced Michener that he needed to put his impressions down on paper. So in a lantern-lit, mosquito-filled shack, he began writing *Tales of the South Pacific.* Though he did not realize it at the time, his life as a writer had just begun.

His was a troubled childhood. Although born of uncertain parentage to a Quaker widow, his mother raised him with love while she took in other children and ran a foster home in Doylestown. He loved to read and had a nearly photographic memory, but at Doylestown High School he had to overcome initial razzing about his shabby clothes to become a model student. In his senior year, he was elected class president, became editor of the school paper, and played as a forward on the school's championship basketball team.

Michener earned a scholarship to Swarthmore College, where his determination pushed him to graduate *summa cum laude* in 1929, just as the country went into economic depression. It seemed like he was destined for an academic career when he accepted a job teaching English at a private preparatory school, the Hill School in Pottstown. In 1931, he left the Hill School to tour Europe for two years on a fellowship awarded by Swarthmore, gaining insights into both Nazism in Germany and communism in the Soviet Union. Returning to the United States, he taught from 1934 to 1936 at the George School, a private preparatory school near his old hometown.

In 1935, he married Patti Koons, the athletic daughter of a Lutheran minister, and the next year, the couple went to the University of Northern Colorado, where Michener pursued a master's degree while teaching social studies in an experimental high school devoted to preparing its students for "responsible citizenship." Granted a leave of absence, he spent 1940 as a visiting professor at Harvard University.

Back at Northern Colorado, he was angered to learn that he had not been considered for an academic job because he did not have a Ph.D. So when an editor for MacMillan Publishing Company came to the campus seeking an editor of social studies textbooks, Michener accepted the job, against the advice of his academic friends.

He was working at MacMillan when he went into the navy; Patti, meanwhile, joined the Women's Army Corps. After his duties ended with naval aviation and the war came to a close, he was assigned as a naval historian to gather information about the navy's role in the Pacific in World War II. At the same time, he was writing *Tales of the South Pacific,* and by 1945, he had sent his manuscript to MacMillan under a pseudonym.

Completing his duties as a naval historian, he came home as a lieutenant commander to resume his old job and to revise and complete the manuscript for *Tales.* He and Patti had grown apart during the war and were divorced in 1946.

Before MacMillan published the entire book, Michener sold two of its stories to the *Saturday Evening Post,* which published them for its three million

readers in December 1946. MacMillan published the full book two months later, initiating for the author a heady series of events. *Tales of the South Pacific* sold well, and Michener then sold several other magazine articles. MacMillan offered him a top editor's job, which he turned down in favor of working part-time for the firm while pursuing a freelance writing career. In 1948, he was amazed when he won the Pulitzer Prize for fiction for *Tales of the South Pacific.* In 1949,

James A. Michener by C. P. Vaughn. The original graphite paper, 24.625 x 30.625, is in the Doylestown museum. JAMES A. MICHENER ART MUSEUM

he published his second novel, *Fires of Spring,* a strongly autobiographical story that became another best-seller. Also in 1949, the musical *South Pacific* opened as a play on Broadway to enthusiastic audiences—and Michener married for a second time, to Vange Nord, herself an aspiring writer.

The successes of the musical and the later motion picture were important to Michener because they gave him the financial foundation that every freelance writer dreams of. Richard Rodgers and Oscar Hammerstein generously invited the author to become a part owner of the show and even advanced him a $4,500 loan to do it. Michener later said the $10,000 each year he received as his return from the show covered his necessities and gave him the freedom to continue as a freelance writer.

With these successes under his belt, Michener turned his attention once more to Asia, this time as a journalist rather than as a novelist. He spent the next several years as a roving ambassador, introducing the Asian region to almost every American home through his magazine articles, books, and lectures. After returning from several trips to Asia, he gathered together much of what he had written into two books, *Return to Paradise* and *The Voice of Asia.* By the end of 1951, no American writer had contributed more to America's knowledge of Asia than Michener, except perhaps his friend and fellow Bucks County resident Pearl S. Buck.

At this time, he reached an agreement with the *Reader's Digest* that would make any freelancer green with envy. "You can go anywhere in the world you want to go," the *Digest* told him. "You can write anything you want to write. . . . We'll pay all your expenses. . . . All that is required is that you let us have first shot at what you've written." The offer, which he gladly accepted, made him one of the most financially secure writers in America and allowed him to take future risks that other writers could not afford.

Michener's focus on Asia coincided with U.S. participation in the Korean War. Now he made the war vivid to Americans with *The Bridges of Toko-Ri,* a bitter novel that defended the U.S. presence in Asia. Once again, a Michener book was turned into a motion picture.

The author underlined his optimistic belief that peoples of the world could live peacefully together with the novel *Sayonara,* the dramatic story of the love of an American serviceman and a Japanese woman. More than any other novel of its time, *Sayonara* brought the issue of interracial marriage into focus. His long absences from home had led to the breakup of his own marriage, but in 1955, he married for the third and last time. His wife was Mari Yoriko Sabusawa, a second-generation Japanese-American who had been among those unfairly interned at the beginning of World War II. She was now an assistant editor for the American Library Association and in the future would share fully in Michener's work and his love of art.

The writer now hit his stride with the historical novels for which he is best known. The trailblazer was *Hawaii*, a million-word novel that evoked divided opinions among Hawaiians when it was published in 1959. Then he wrote *Caravans*, about Afghanistan; *The Source*, about Israel; and *Iberia*, about Spain. In between, this world traveler published *The Bridge at Andau*, a searing nonfiction report on the refugees from the Soviet repression of Hungary.

Michener was always intensely interested in politics and in 1962 diverged from writing to run unsuccessfully as a Democrat for Congress. In 1968, he served as secretary of a commission that updated the Pennsylvania constitution.

Although slowed by a heart attack in 1965, this prolific, disciplined, and hard-working writer wrote *The Drifters*, about American youth abroad (1971); *Centennial*, about the settlement of the American West (1974); *Chesapeake* (1979); *The Covenant*, about South Africa (1980); *Space* (1982); *Poland* (1983); *Texas* (1985); *Legacy* (1987); *Alaska* (1988); *Journey* (1989); *Caribbean* (1989); *Mexico* (1992); and *Recessional* (1994). In all, Michener wrote forty-seven books that were translated into some fifty languages, with sales of approximately one hundred million copies.

Now world famous, the author was awarded honorary degrees from several universities and served on advisory committees for both the U.S. Information Agency and the National Aeronautics and Space Administration (NASA). "The prolific writings of this master storyteller have expanded the knowledge and enriched the lives of millions," President Gerald Ford said as he awarded James Michener the Presidential Medal of Freedom in 1977 in a ceremony at the White House. The one-time poor boy from Doylestown had left a remarkable literary legacy for his devoted readers.

Michener maintained his deep roots in Bucks County. He and Mari were proud of the fact that they lived, voted, and paid taxes in the county from 1948 until the mid-1980s. Mari died in 1994. James A. Michener died in 1997 at his home in Austin, Texas, where he had moved some years before, when he was researching his novel about the Lone Star State.

James A. Michener Art Museum

Visitors to the James A. Michener Art Museum in Doylestown learn that the noted author not only was interested in literature, but had a lively interest in art as well. As an enthusiastic supporter of all the arts, he had

Michener grew up in Doylestown, now the home of the James A. Michener Art Museum. Housed in what was the Bucks County Jail from 1884 to 1986, the museum preserves, interprets, and exhibits the art and cultural heritage of Bucks County. PHOTO BY JAMES A. MICHENER ART MUSEUM

The working office of Michener is exhibited to the left of the museum entrance, with his desk preserved as if still in use. PHOTO BY THE AUTHORS

dreamed of a regional art museum as early as 1960 and contributed $7 million and a number of paintings to the Doylestown museum.

The contemporary gallery, which was converted from the nineteenth-century Doylestown jail, displays what is said to be the finest collection of Pennsylvania Impressionist paintings in public or private hands. The Mari Sabusawa Michener Wing, endowed by and dedicated to Michener's wife,

Visiting James A. Michener Art Museum

138 S. Pine St., Doylestown, PA 18901

PHONE: 215-340-9800
E-MAIL: jamam1@michenerartmuseum.org
WEBSITE: www.michenerartmuseum.org
ADMINISTRATION: The museum is a private, nonprofit membership organization.
HOURS: Tuesday–Friday, 10–4:30; Wednesday evenings until 9; Saturday and Sunday, 10–5.
ADMISSION FEES: $6 for adults; $5.50 for seniors; free for children under 12.
TOURS: Group tours of 15 or more are admitted for $4 per person when registered two weeks in advance; free 45-minute tours Saturday and Sunday at 2. Access to the Art Research Library is by appointment.
TIME NEEDED: 1 to 3 hours.
SPECIAL EVENTS: Exhibition-related programs, lectures, and workshops for adults and children; traveling exhibitions throughout the year. Summer camp programs for children ages 3–18.
SPECIAL CONSIDERATIONS: Handicapped-accessible; wheelchairs available. Sign language tours for deaf visitors upon arrangement.
PARKING: On-street parking and nearby lot.
SALES OUTLETS: Shop offers books, videos, jewelry, arts and craft items, and gifts. Café offers homemade soups, salads, beverages, and pastries.
DIRECTIONS: From Philadelphia, take I-95 North to PA Route 132 West, Street Road. Follow to PA Route 611 North, and take to Doylestown Exit (Main Street) on right. Follow to first traffic light, and turn right on Ashland Street. From Ashland, turn right on Pine Street and follow to museum.

holds a multimedia exhibit that brings to life the works of many authors, playwrights, lyricists, and composers who lived and worked in Bucks County. Yet another room is devoted to the late George Nakashima, the world-renowned woodworker who lived and worked in the area.

Near the museum entrance is a re-creation of Michener's home office that gives visitors an up-close look at the author's desk, chair, typewriter, and the dictionary he used for fifteen years. A framed drawing of the author and photographs of his career grace the walls. In the typewriter is part of the original draft he wrote for his book *The Novel*. A video presentation summarizes Michener's life, including the awarding of the Medal of Freedom, which is on display.

Outside, a sculpture garden includes works by Bucks County artisans in its landscaped grounds.

James Stewart

(1908-97)

Unlikely as it may seem, it was Jimmy Stewart's adeptness at playing the accordion that set him on the path that led to his stardom as an actor in films, Broadway dramas, radio, and television.

When Alex Stewart, Jimmy's father, was given an accordion by a customer in payment for a debt at his hardware store in Indiana, Pennsylvania, he passed it along to Jimmy's younger sister, Ginny, but she was too small to play it. So Jimmy's mother, Bessie, herself an accomplished pianist, gave it instead to Jimmy so that the instrument would not "go to waste." Jimmy, who also played the piano, soon mastered it.

Jimmy's accordion playing later opened doors for him. At Mercersburg Academy, it secured him a spot in the school orchestra. His accordion playing also got him a summer job accompanying a traveling professional magician. When he went to Princeton University, his father's alma mater, his accordion earned him a place as a freshman in the Triangle Club, the college drama group. And when he graduated from Princeton in 1932 in the midst of the Depression years, his classmate and future director Josh Logan hired him to play his accordion in the tearoom next to a summer stock theater on Cape Cod. In addition, the job gave Stewart the opportunity to perform bit parts in several plays.

James Maitland Stewart was born at his parents' home in Indiana in western Pennsylvania in 1908. The Stewart family had deep roots in the county—one of their forebears had been captured by Indians and later served in the Revolutionary army.

Jimmy had a typical small-town boyhood. He and his two sisters presented magic shows and impromptu plays in the basement of their home for neighborhood children. Some of the plays were inspired by various artifacts their father had sent home from France when he served in the U.S. Army in World War I. Young Jimmy was also an active Boy Scout and built model airplanes and radios.

He attended Mercersburg Academy and Princeton University, where he majored in architecture and won a scholarship for graduate studies with a design for a new airport. But extracurricular activities intrigued him as well. In addition to acting in Triangle Club plays, he became head cheerleader and helped bring big-name jazz bands to the campus.

When he graduated, poor economic conditions made jobs in architecture scarce, so he joined Logan's University Players on Cape Cod, meeting a young actor named Henry Fonda. He played the accordion, worked as a stagehand, designed sets, and generally learned the theater business from the inside out. In 1932, when the group had the opportunity to stage *Carrie Nation* on Broadway, Stewart played a number of small roles that included a constable, a vigilante, an innocent bystander, and a gardener. While living in New York, he roomed with Fonda, continuing a friendship that would endure until Fonda's death in 1982.

Though *Carrie Nation* ran only seven weeks in New York, Stewart caught the attention of the critics. He also received favorable reviews for his roles in other Broadway plays, *Goodbye Again* (1932), *Spring in Autumn* (1933), and *All Good Americans* (1933). *Goodbye Again* had a nine-month Broadway run before moving to Boston, where he was then cast in *We Die Exquisitely*. He left to become stage manager for *Camille* (1933) and moved back to Broadway to play Sergeant O'Hara in *Yellow Jack* (1934). This performance earned him a screen test with Metro-Goldwyn-Mayer (MGM) but still left him unemployed, so he returned temporarily to his family's home in Indiana.

Several months later, MGM called him to Hollywood. After playing the role of a newspaperman in the film *Murder Man* in 1935, he appeared in nineteen motion pictures over the next four years. He played a doctor, lawyer, teacher, newspaperman, mechanic, executive, hayseed, soldier, skater, farmer, football star, speed driver, detective, and even a murderer. During this period, he appeared with most of the leading actresses of the time, including Joan Crawford, Katharine Hepburn, Marlene Dietrich, Margaret Sullavan, Jean Harlow, Carole Lombard, Ginger Rogers, Claudette Colbert, Jean Arthur, and Elinor Powell. In addition to film, Stewart also did voice work for the studios and

James Stewart, c. 1955. JIMMY STEWART MUSEUM

radio networks, including "The Lux Radio Theatre," "The Screen Guild Theatre," and MGM's promotional program, "Good News of 1938."

The year of 1939 was pivotal for Jimmy Stewart. He performed in his first western, *Destry Rides Again,* one of nineteen adult westerns he made in which he played frontiersmen, lawmen, and cowboys. His performance as Sen. Jefferson Smith in Frank Capra's *Mr. Smith Goes to Washington* earned him an Academy Award nomination for best actor and elevated him to star status. He made four more pictures before playing the role that would finally win him an Oscar, that of reporter Mike Connor in *The Philadelphia Story* (1940). He costarred in that film with Katharine Hepburn, Cary Grant, John Howard, and Ruth Hussey.

Now war clouds gathered, and Stewart, true to his family's military tradition, reported as a draftee for duty in the U.S. Army in February 1941. He was rejected, however, because of his low weight but was finally accepted a month later in March. He was already a licensed pilot who had flown home to Pennsylvania numerous times to visit his parents, so the army assigned its new private to the Army Air Corps. He then logged an additional hundred hours of flying time at his own expense so he could pass the stiff proficiency board examination and was commissioned a second lieutenant in the Air Corps at age thirty-three. After spending two years stateside as an instructor, he was assigned to fly B-24 Liberators for the 453rd Bomb Group at Old Buckenham, England.

Stewart's war record included twenty dangerous combat missions over Germany as a command pilot. He came home from the hostilities as a colonel with a Distinguished Flying Cross with two oak leaf clusters, the Air Medal with three oak leaf clusters, and the French Croix de Guerre with Palm. After the war, he remained with the Air Force Reserve and was promoted to brigadier general in 1959. He retired from the Air Force Reserve in 1968, receiving the Distinguished Service Medal.

Returning to civilian life, Stewart wondered whether he would still be able to act. The answer came with the role of George Bailey in *It's a Wonderful Life,* under his favorite director, Frank Capra. This motion picture about hometown values, although not a commercial success at the time, later became a classic seen annually around Christmas-time by millions on television. Maybe the warm family life of the film rubbed off, because three years later, the forty-one-year-old Stewart married Gloria Hatrick McLean, who had two sons by an earlier marriage, Ronald and Michael. The next year, the Stewarts added twin daughters, Kelly and Judy. Ronald, later a U.S. Marine officer, was killed in Vietnam in 1969.

With his acting career reignited, Stewart appeared in fifty-two more motion pictures after *It's a Wonderful Life*. He won Oscar nominations as best actor not only for *It's a Wonderful Life*, but also for *Harvey* (1950) and *Anatomy of a Murder* (1959). He worked with Hollywood's most notable directors, including Alfred Hitchcock (*Rear Window* and *Vertigo*), John Ford *(The Man Who Shot Liberty Valence)*, and Anthony Mann (*The Far Country* and *The Man From Laramie*). In other movies, he played popular heroes such as Charles Lindbergh, orchestra leader Glenn Miller, and baseball pitcher Monte Stratton. He returned to the Broadway stage as Elwood P. Dowd in *Harvey* in 1947, 1970, and 1972 and in London in 1975. He added another distinction when he wrote a book of poetry.

Stewart became a businessman and a rancher and was the recipient of many personal honors. He was honored at the Kennedy Center in 1983 and was awarded the Medal of Freedom, the nation's highest civilian award, in 1985. That same year, he received a Lifetime Achievement Award from the Academy of Motion Picture Arts and Sciences. The American Film Institute, in awarding him its Life Achievement Award, stated: "Stewart has captured the essence of American hopes, doubts and aspirations. His idealism, his determination, his vulnerability, and above all, his basic decency shine through every role he plays."

Jimmy Stewart died in 1997 at the age of eighty-nine. Once asked how he wanted to be remembered, he said: "As somebody who worked hard for what happened and who had certain values that he believed in: Love of family, love of community, love of country, love of God."

The Jimmy Stewart Museum

When the modest Jimmy Stewart agreed with citizens of his hometown of Indiana, Pennsylvania, to cooperate in fashioning a museum that would bring visitors to the town, he insisted that it be a homegrown effort. As a result, the Jimmy Stewart Museum is housed in converted space on the third floor of the Indiana Free Library Building at the corner of Philadelphia Street and Ninth Street in the heart of downtown. The museum is across the street from the site of his father's hardware store and just two blocks from where he was born.

The James M. Stewart Museum Foundation was formed. A local architect designed the museum pro bono; one hundred volunteers worked on fifteen committees; local banks provided construction loans; students from the local vocational-technical school helped build it. Curtains for its

Visiting The Jimmy Stewart Museum

Indiana Free Library Building, Third Floor,
845 Philadelphia St., Indiana, PA 15701

PHONE: 1-800-83JIMMY
E-MAIL: curator@jimmy.org
WEBSITE: www.jimmy.org
ADMINISTRATION: The James M. Stewart Museum Foundation is a nonprofit corporation and educational organization, funded through admissions, contributions, and membership society programs.
HOURS: Monday–Saturday, 10–5; Sunday, 12–5. Closed Monday and Tuesday, January–March, and major holidays.
ADMISSION FEES: $5 for adults; $4 for seniors, military, and college students; $3 for children ages 7–17; free for children under age 7.
TOURS: Individual tours self-guided; docents available for groups for additional fee.
TIME NEEDED: At least 2 hours.
SPECIAL EVENTS: Jimmy Stewart's birthday with the Harvey Award dinner in May; "It's a Wonderful Life" Festival the weekend before Thanksgiving; and "Light-Up Night" the night after Thanksgiving.
SPECIAL CONSIDERATIONS: Handicapped ramp in front of building to first floor, and elevator to museum on third floor; wheelchairs available.
PARKING: Limited parking behind building; metered street parking or parking garage two blocks away; free parking for tour buses one block away.
SALES OUTLETS: Store offers posters, videos, books, films, clothing, gifts, and collectibles.
DIRECTIONS: From Pittsburgh area, take U.S. Route 22 East to Indiana Exit (just beyond Blairsville). Take U.S. Route 119 North to Indiana, where it becomes Wayne Avenue. Turn left on Philadelphia Street, and go two blocks to Ninth Street. Museum is on right.

fifty-seat theater came from Indiana High School and the seats from another school.

Visitors enter the museum not through the library's main door, but through a separate entrance on the Ninth Street side. A dimly lit corridor called It's a Wonderful Life Gallery, its walls covered with movie posters and scenes, leads to the elevator, which is outlined with small, round lights like a movie marquee. The third-floor museum includes four galleries: The Hollywood Gallery depicts Stewart's extensive film and stage career; the Military Gallery describes his Air Corps flying days of World War II and afterward; the Awards Gallery displays his personal desk and chair, and

The Jimmy Stewart Museum is located on the third floor of the Indiana Free Library, less than two blocks from where Stewart was born and across the street from the location of his father's hardware store. PHOTO BY THE AUTHORS

recognizes his numerous awards and charitable interests; and the Indiana Gallery portrays the history of the region and the story of the Stewart family. A video portrays the parade through town and ceremonies that marked the opening of the museum in 1995, with Jimmy Stewart represented by his two daughters. One of Stewart's eighty feature films is shown in the theater at a matinee each Saturday, and other films and biographies are shown daily.

"Entering a building which houses a museum named after me is a privilege I could never have anticipated," Stewart wrote to its sponsors. "I hope that its visitors will enjoy their stay there. After all, they are the ones who really built it."

Mario Lanza

(1921-59)

Mario Lanza's life is a rags-to-riches story of a man possessed of a magnificent natural singing voice whose death at age thirty-eight cut short a promising musical future.

There was no mistaking the quality of his rich tenor voice, even in his early years. As a singer, he had one of the broadest and most powerful ranges ever recorded, and he was compared with the great tenors, including Enrico Caruso, his boyhood idol. Dorothy Kirsten, the Metropolitan Opera soprano who performed with many great singers, described Lanza's voice as truly unique, a great gift, and was convinced that he could have performed "in any opera house in the world."

Mario Lanza was born in 1921 as Alfredo Arnold Cocozza, the only child of a working-class, first-generation Italian-American family in South Philadelphia. He found his voice early in life. Stories abound of how he spent hours listening and vocalizing to the large collection of opera records collected by his father. He is reported to have listened to a Caruso recording twenty-seven times at a single sitting.

He grew into a stocky, barrel-chested teenager, spoiled at home, rebellious at school, uninterested in working, energized primarily by music. His first professional break came in 1942, when his voice coach arranged for him to audition before conductor Serge Koussevitsky after the conductor had completed a concert at Philadelphia's Academy of Music. Koussevitsky was immediately impressed with the young tenor and secured a scholarship for him to that summer's Berkshire Music Festival at Tanglewood, Massachusetts. The exposure brought the first national recognition to the twenty-one-year-old, and the music critic of the *New York Times* praised his "superb natural voice."

After a two-year stint in the Army Air Corps, where he remained stateside singing in armed-services musicals, he married Betty Hicks, whom he had met in California, and went to New York City to resume his musical career. When he was advised to get further voice training, a New York real-estate agent, Sam Weiler, himself a former voice student, financed his training and became his professional manager.

Adopting the name Mario Lanza, a masculine form of his mother's maiden name, he studied with Enrico Rosati, who had been the former voice coach of operatic tenor Benjamino Gigli. "I have waited for you for 34 years—ever since Gigli," Rosati is reported to have told Lanza when he heard his powerful voice.

Mario Lanza never learned to read music and had to memorize the notes and words of each aria or song, but despite his lack of technical musical training, within fifteen months he was able to draw seventy-six thousand people to hear him sing at a summer concert in Chicago's Grant Park. He also sang the lead role of Lieutenant Pinkerton in two perform-ances of *Madame Butterfly* in New Orleans, the only time in his career that Lanza performed in a live opera.

In 1947, Lanza, as a member of the Bel Canto trio, which also included soprano Frances Yeend and baritone George London, performed a concert at the Hollywood Bowl with Louis B. Mayer in the audience, and as a result, Metro-Goldwyn-Mayer signed Lanza to a seven-year film contract.

Placed in the hands of producer Joe Pasternak, who was largely respon-

sible for the splashy and polished tech-nical musicals for which MGM was then well known, Lanza spent his first year as a contract player for the studio, los-ing 100 of his 265 pounds. It was as a svelte romantic lead alongside Kathryn Grayson that Lanza made his film debut in 1949 in *That Midnight Kiss,* followed in 1950 by *The Toast of New Orleans,* also with Grayson. The latter film intro-duced the hit song "Be My Love," Lanza's first recording to sell over a mil-lion copies.

Now that Lanza's films and record-ings were so popular and making money, his MGM bosses decided to take the risk of openly identifying Lanza with his idol Caruso by casting Lanza as the lead in a film biography of the legendary

Mario Lanza. MARIO LANZA MUSEUM

singer. *The Great Caruso,* which was released in 1951, made musical and film history. *Time* magazine, which featured Mario Lanza on its cover, touted him as "the first operatic tenor in history to become a full-blown Hollywood star." He also was the first recording artist with RCA Victor's venerable Red Seal label, reserved for classical artists, to sell more than a million records. *The Great Caruso*'s premiere at the Radio City Music Hall in Manhattan broke a box office record by earning $1.5 million in its first ten weeks there. Enrico Caruso Jr., the late tenor's son, said, "I can think of no other tenor, before or since Mario Lanza, who could have risen with comparable success to the challenge of playing Caruso in a screen biography."

Despite these successes, however, Lanza displayed a persistent lack of discipline and on the set often used coarse language that displeased his fellow actors. To many, he seemed to use overeating as an excuse for his insecurities and as a way to escape the responsibilities that went with stardom. On one occasion, the studio discovered that the unpredictable Lanza was ordering meals for three people under different names from the commissary, consuming them all himself. During his career, his weight seesawed from 165 to nearly 300 pounds, creating problems for the wardrobe department and his directors.

The singer completed a twenty-two-city tour to promote *The Great Caruso* and attracted sold-out, enthusiastic audiences everywhere. The most nostalgic stop took place March 13, 1951, in Philadelphia when a sell-out crowd at the famed Academy of Music gave him a hero's welcome. It was at this site where, as an unknown singer, he had auditioned for Koussevitzky only nine years earlier. The academy stands only a few blocks from where Mario Lanza grew up.

The tenor also sang regularly on the popular Coca-Cola radio show, prerecording the songs that would be broadcast on the show. Two songs he recorded for this show sold more than a million records each: "The Loveliest Night of the Year" and "Because You're Mine."

As it turned out, these days marked the peak of Lanza's career. After a crash effort to lose weight for his next film, *The Student Prince,* Lanza failed to appear to begin shooting, provoking a dispute with MGM. The studio thereupon canceled his contract. A lawsuit was averted only when Lanza agreed to relinquish the lead to British actor Edmund Purdom, while allowing the studio to use his prerecordings of the music to be mouthed by Purdom. Ironically, the soundtrack of the picture, converted into a record, sold more than three million copies.

His career drifted. He fired his longtime manager and drank and smoked heavily. RCA terminated his recording contract, although the company later reinstated it.

Finally, after a year of inactivity, Lanza was to appear on a CBS television program, "Shower of Stars." But as a result of dieting to prepare for the show, the singer said he was too weak to sing, so earlier recordings of the songs were substituted while Lanza mouthed the words. When the public learned of the hoax, the network apologized, and Lanza was embarrassed. Only a short while later, the singer walked out on a Las Vegas nightclub appearance. In addition, the Internal Revenue Service sued him for taxes he had not paid.

When it seemed that everything was going wrong, Mario Lanza made a comeback, costarring in the film *Serenade* with actress Joan Fontaine for a different Hollywood studio. He also resumed recording, singing Broadway show tunes and Neapolitan favorites once again for RCA Victor.

To get a new lease on life and to fulfill a promise to act and sing in a motion picture, Lanza moved his wife, Betty, and their four young children to Rome, Italy. Here he made the 1958 film *The Seven Hills of Rome* and undertook a European tour that included a command performance at London's Royal Albert Hall. In the picture, he sang a nostalgic duet with an unknown young female street singer that he had insisted be in the movie. The scene, one writer said, "was one of the most touching in the film."

In April 1959, Mario Lanza went to a clinic suffering from high blood pressure and phlebitis in his right leg, an ailment caused by blood clots. He had been dieting again to lose weight for his next film. In September, he admitted himself again to the clinic, suffering from a fever, rapid pulse rate, and chest pains. On October 7, he fell unconscious and died despite a physician's attempt to save him.

Other singers acknowledge that Mario Lanza possessed a glorious and natural voice with one of the broadest and most powerful ranges ever recorded. He could easily vault to a high C, a feat difficult for many tenors, and his teachers were all amazed at his breath control.

But perhaps his greatest contribution to the appreciation of music was his ability to make classical music and opera appealing to those who would otherwise never have listened. The millions of records that his admirers flocked to buy attest to the popularity of his heartfelt renderings of operatic arias, romantic ballads, and Neapolitan songs. Later popular tenors such as Luciano Pavarotti, Placido Domingo, and Jose Carreras testified that Lanza's voice inspired them as young singers. Metropolitan Opera soprano Licia Albanese summed it up when she said, "He always sang with his heart on his lips."

Mario Lanza Institute and Museum

This small museum is housed in a former church rectory, now called Columbus House, on Montrose Street in South Philadelphia, scarcely two blocks from Lanza's birthplace.

The walls of the first-floor museum are covered with paintings, photographs, movie posters, album covers, and programs that trace the career of the South Philadelphia singer. Videos of Lanza's films are shown daily, and his voice on the sound system forms the background to the exhibits and displays. To one side sits a terra cotta bust of the singer that was smuggled out of communist Hungary. Several of his gold record awards are on display as are the costumes and jewelry he wore.

The museum maintains contacts with other Mario Lanza fan clubs that have been formed in Great Britain, Canada, Germany, Russia, Italy, the Netherlands, Ireland, Sweden, Australia, and the United States. Also worth

The Mario Lanza Museum is located in a former church rectory located two blocks from Lanza's birthplace. Here, two rooms display the singer's photographs, costumes, and memorabilia of a colorful career. PHOTO BY THE AUTHORS

Visiting Mario Lanza Institute and Museum
712 Montrose St., Philadelphia, PA 19147

PHONE: 215-468-3623
E-MAIL: mli@mario-lanza-institute.org
WEBSITE: www.mario-lanza-institute.org
ADMINISTRATION: Mario Lanza Institute.
HOURS: Monday–Saturday, 10–3. Closed Saturday, July–August.
ADMISSION FEES: Free.
TOURS: Self-guided.
TIME NEEDED: 1 to 2 hours.
SPECIAL EVENTS: Concert in the spring; anniversary ball in November to announce scholarship winners.
SPECIAL CONSIDERATIONS: Wheelchair-accessible with elevator service; four steps at entrance.
PARKING: On-street.
SALES OUTLETS: Sales of books, videos, films, CDs, audiotapes, photographs, apparel, and memorabilia to benefit the scholarship program. Catalog available.
DIRECTIONS: From Center City Philadelphia, head south on South Broad Street. Turn left on Christian Street, and follow to Eighth Street. Turn right, and go two blocks to Montrose Street. Turn left. Columbus House will be on the right.

---

visiting is the mural depicting Mario Lanza and his career that graces the side of a building on the northwest corner of the Avenue of the Arts (South Broad Street) and Reed Street.

The Mario Lanza Institute, of which the museum is a part, awards several scholarships each year to promising young singers from the Philadelphia metropolitan area and around the world. Scholarship judges are from the nearby Settlement Music School, which offers instruction in instrumental and vocal music and dance to those in the community without regard to ethnicity or ability to pay. The winners are announced at the gala Anniversary Ball held each November.

Andy Warhol

(1928-87)

Andy Warhol grew up as Andrew Warhola in a working-class family in Pittsburgh, the youngest of three brothers, whose parents had immigrated from what is now the Slovak Republic in Eastern Europe. Early on, the slight, shy boy displayed a natural artistic talent. His artistic ability increased when he enthusiastically attended the Saturday morning art classes that were offered free to Pittsburgh children by the Carnegie Museum of Art.

He enrolled in the printing and design department of the Carnegie Institute of Technology, today's Carnegie Mellon University, where he became art editor of the student journal. As a student, he also exhibited the "in-your-face" challenge to everyday convention that became his hallmark later in life. For a citywide art competition, he submitted a painting of a boy picking his nose. Not amused, the judges rejected his entry.

After graduation from Carnegie Tech, Warhol immediately set off for New York City, the mecca of commercial artists, where he shared an apartment with a Pittsburgh friend and several Broadway dancers. He made the rounds of the magazine publishers with his portfolio and quickly received his first assignment—to illustrate ladies' shoes for *Glamour* magazine. Other jobs soon followed. Like other illustrators, he sometimes traced from photographs, and he seemed to possess a natural ability for conceptualizing a pictorial solution that could sell a product. With one art director, he engineered an award-winning advertising campaign that revitalized the image of a women's shoe company. By 1954, he had become a sought-after commercial artist in the Manhattan art world.

He had also developed a bohemian lifestyle. He brought his mother from Pittsburgh, and they lived in a cluttered apartment filled with cats. He dressed shabbily, but in expensive clothes. He would often rise late, go for breakfast at a first-class hotel where he could be seen by prospective clients, make the rounds of publishers, spend the evening at an East Side tavern, then come home and work until early morning.

Despite his success in commercial art, Warhol craved recognition in the fine-arts world. His first solo exhibition at a gallery in New York featured drawings that illustrated the writings of Truman Capote, by then a successful novelist and a figure with whom Warhol was immensely fascinated. A homosexual himself, Warhol admired gay writers like Capote and other gay artists. For his private enjoyment, he drew thousands of pictures of male figures and consorted openly with male companions.

With his erotic art largely ignored by the galleries, Warhol decided to try something different. Using some of the same reproduction techniques he had practiced in his commercial artwork, he produced some large canvases of commercial icons such as a bottle of Coca-Cola, starkly displayed. When several critics praised his unconventional Coke bottle painting, Warhol launched himself on a course using mechanical techniques to produce noncommercial art that nonetheless had an obviously commercial cast—Campbell soup cans, money, Brillo boxes, coffee cans. He began to use a silk-screen technique that transferred a photographic image to canvas in a matter of minutes. When several of Warhol's creations were displayed at a show in 1960, they were labeled "pop art" and began to displace the abstract expressionist paintings that had been the popular style.

When these stylized paintings caught on with the public, this artist of the commonplace added silk-screened renditions of easily recognized social icons—Marilyn Monroe, Elvis Presley, Jacqueline Kennedy, and Mao Tse-tung—setting them off against splashily colored backgrounds. Next he produced death and disaster images of car crashes and suicides that were guaranteed to shock the observer. For a studio, he rented the fourth floor of an old industrial building, called it the Factory, and started turning out his fast-selling images.

Andy Warhol, 1986, self-portrait. ANDY WARHOL MUSEUM

In the midst of his popular and financial success with silk-screened images, Warhol suddenly decided to do something different. This time it was to make movies. These films were not only unorthodox in technique, but focused on the seamy side of life not generally viewed in movies. Many of these productions were made with a single, tripod-mounted camera that focused on one subject for an extended time, simply recording the unscripted action that followed no plot line, as though the camera were eavesdropping on the subject. He rarely paid his "actors," for they were willing to take part to become known.

The Factory attracted a steady stream of artists, musicians, curators, writers, collectors, and celebrities. "In the future," he once said, "everyone will be world famous for 15 minutes." Warhol cultivated the idea of glittering fame, creating around himself an environment of social happenings that not only helped him keep in touch with the latest trends in fashion, music, and art, but also attracted buyers for his art.

In 1965, he stepped into the pop music scene by sponsoring a rock band, the Velvet Underground, which provided music for a multimedia show at a Manhattan discotheque that Warhol had created called The Exploding Plastic Inevitable. Later, when the group returned from a West Coast engagement, its members decided to go their own way under a new manager.

The spirited competition that Warhol fostered in those who worked with him arose to haunt him in 1968, when an aspiring and mentally disturbed writer, Valerie Solanis, appeared at the Factory and shot him several times in the abdomen. She was angered that Warhol had neither filmed nor returned a movie script she had submitted. Critically wounded, he came close to death but recovered after several months.

A year later, Warhol inaugurated *Interview,* a monthly magazine that began as a film journal but later focused on glamour, personalities, and gossip of the motion picture and art worlds.

Although he had said he was finished with painting, Warhol appeared at major exhibitions of his work at the end of the sixties—in Paris, London, Stockholm, Kassel, Berlin, Rhode Island, and Houston. Celebrities and jet-setters commissioned him to do their portraits, which he made by taking a Polaroid photograph of his subject, then silk-screening it against a vivid color background. During this period, one of his earlier soup can paintings sold for $60,000.

Andy Warhol died in New York in 1987, at the age of fifty-eight, following gall bladder surgery. A memorial service on April 1 at St. Patrick's Cathedral drew more than two thousand mourners. At the time of his death, he was the emblematic figure of contemporary art that made the U.S. culture both the source and the subject. He had discovered a way to simultaneously express his personal desires and dreams by imagery chosen from the public domain of mass culture. His art titillated the avant-garde and outraged the conservative. But he seemed to realize that his images held no deeper meaning. "Just look at the surface of my paintings and films and me; and there I am," he once said. "There's nothing behind it."

The Andy Warhol Museum

From the outside, the former storage warehouse that houses the extensive collection of artist Andy Warhol looks like a typical seven-story, turn-of-the-twentieth-century industrial building. It stands in the developing North Side of Pittsburgh, across the Allegheny River from where Warhol

The Andy Warhol Museum, with a collection of approximately 900 paintings, 1,500 hundred drawings, 608 "time capsules," and an archives of videotapes, audiotapes, photographs, scripts, diaries, and correspondence, is housed in a renovated seven-story factory building. PHOTO BY PAUL ROCHELEAU, ANDY WARHOL MUSEUM

Visiting The Andy Warhol Museum

117 Sandusky St., Pittsburgh, PA 15212

PHONE: 412-237-8300

WEBSITE: www.warhol.org

ADMINISTRATION: The Andy Warhol Museum is one of the four Carnegie Museums of Pittsburgh and is a collaborative project of the Carnegie Institute, Dia Center for the Arts, and the Andy Warhol Foundation for the Visual Arts, Inc.

HOURS: Tuesday–Thursday, Saturday, Sunday, 10–5; Friday, 10–10. Closed Monday.

ADMISSION FEES: $8 for adults; $7 for seniors; $4 for students and children.

TOURS: Special tours available for groups of 10 or more with three weeks' notice. One-hour general tours available with focused discussions on specific works and/or themes customized to the group's interest. Tours free with museum admission. Ongoing educational programs and weekly hands-on art activities.

TIME NEEDED: Allow 2 hours.

SPECIAL EVENTS: "Good Fridays"—every Friday from 5–10, free gallery admission, cash bar, and special programs.

SPECIAL CONSIDERATIONS: The seven-story museum is equipped with elevators, and all facilities are handicapped-accessible.

PARKING: Museum parking one block north of museum on Sandusky Street. Additional public parking behind museum in General Robinson Street parking garage. Prices may vary during nearby stadium events.

SALES OUTLETS: Store offers books, posters, videos, postcards, and souvenir items.

DIRECTIONS: The museum is located on the North Shore of Pittsburgh. From I-376 East, follow the signs to downtown Pittsburgh. Take the Stanwix Street Exit. Go four blocks, veer right onto Liberty Avenue. Go three blocks, then turn left on Seventh Street. Go across the Seventh Street Bridge. The museum is at the first stoplight after the bridge, at the corner of General Robinson and Sandusky.

was born and grew up. It was chosen for the Andy Warhol Museum because it was reminiscent of the Factory in New York City, where Warhol produced his images and movies.

On the inside, it has been transformed into seven floors of roomy galleries that display a variety of works by this unconventional but versatile artist—more than five hundred of Warhol's four thousand pop paintings of consumer products; drawings; "sculptures," such as sets of boxes and polymer resin forms; sketchbooks; photographs; and posterizations. One

This acrylic-and-silkscreen-on-canvas self-portrait of Warhol from 1966 is among the countless holdings at the Andy Warhol Museum. ANDY WARHOL MUSEUM

gallery showcases examples of wallpaper and contains a roomful of air-blown helium balloons. A theater shows one of the 273 films Warhol produced; he also produced 2,500 videos. The museum is said to be the largest repository of the art of a single artist in the world.

In the third-floor Archive Study Center, visitors are invited to see working materials collected by Andy Warhol that gave him inspiration for his unorthodox artistic creations. Filling one wall are 130 of the 610 cardboard boxes Warhol called "time capsules." They are filled with photographs, newspaper clippings, magazines, even unpaid bills—all reflecting the everyday life, events, and memorabilia of a particular year. The archive also preserves audiotapes, scripts, diaries, and correspondence that mirror what was going on in the artist's life.

Famous Pennsylvanians without Sites

Not all of the well-known sons and daughters of the Commonwealth have sites where they are recognized and honored. Here are some other remarkable Pennsylvanians who have earned our admiration.

Louisa May Alcott (1832–88)

Born in Germantown in Philadelphia, she grew up in Boston and wrote about family life in New England. Her semiautographical books such as *Little Women* became classics of children's literature.

Richard Allen (1760–1831)

The son of a slave, he grew up in Philadelphia, became a Revolutionary-era preacher and founded the African Methodist Episcopal Church for blacks in New York, New Jersey, Delaware, and Maryland.

H. H. Arnold (1886–1950)

Nicknamed "Hap," he was an aviation pioneer from Gladwyne who, as general of the Air Force, was instrumental in building the largest and most powerful Air Force in the world during World War II.

John Barrymore (1882–1942)

Philadelphia-born, the handsome, romantic Barrymore became one of the most famous actors of the early 1900s, along with his brother Lionel and sister Ethel.

Chuck Bednarik (1925–)

Considered the last of the great two-way (offense and defense) football players, he was the outstanding college player of the year in 1948 at the University of Pennsylvania, and then played fourteen seasons with the professional Philadelphia Eagles.

Alexander Calder (1898–1976)

Born in Philadelphia, he represented the third generation of an American family of sculptors. He is best known for his mobiles, suspended abstract forms and animal shapes that grace dozens of public buildings and plazas in the United States and other countries.

Mary Cassatt (1844–1926)

A nineteenth-century Impressionist painter from Philadelphia's Main Line who spent most of her life in Paris, she depicted her subjects in informal, natural positions, painting them in soft colors.

George Catlin (1796–1872)

A self-taught painter born in Wilkes-Barre who gave up a practice of law for painting, Catlin is remembered for his many portraits and sketches depicting the vanishing customs of Native Americans of the West. A historical marker is located at River and South Streets in Wilkes-Barre.

Wilt Chamberlain (1936–99)

The seven-foot, one-inch Chamberlain, born in Philadelphia, was the scoring leader of the National Basketball Association for six consecutive seasons in the mid-1900s and was elected to the Basketball Hall of Fame.

Bill Cosby (1937–)

The Philadelphia-born comedian became the first black American to star in a prime-time television series, *I Spy.* He later produced and acted in *The Cosby Show,* a family comedy that ran from 1984 to 1992. The versatile actor has performed in the theater, acted in motion pictures, made recordings, and written several books.

John Dahlgren (1809–70)

Naval ordnance officer from Philadelphia who in 1850 introduced an innovative design for a type of large-caliber cannon, the Dahlgren gun, that was later adapted to shipboard use and played a critical role as an armament of the U.S. Navy.

John Dickinson (1732–1808)

Philadelphia lawyer and Revolutionary-era statesman who played a leading role in drafting the U.S. Constitution and at one point was elected president (governor) of both Delaware and Pennsylvania. He was one of the founders of Dickinson College.

Jimmy Dorsey (1904–57) and Tommy Dorsey (1905–56)

Born in Shenandoah near Hazleton, Jimmy and his younger brother, Tommy, sons of a coal miner and part-time music teacher, became leaders of popular bands during the swing era of the 1930s and 1940s. Both bands drew enthusiastic dance fans, were featured in movies, and produced recordings.

Thomas Eakins (1844–1916)

A Philadelphia-based painter whose realistic paintings of people sailing, rowing, and hunting had a strong influence on the course of American naturalistic painting of the early 1900s.

W. C. Fields (1879–1946)

A Philadelphia-born juggler who became a comedian, he gained fame in the Ziegfeld Follies of 1915 on the New York stage, and then continued his career in motion picture comedies, including the shorts *The Dentist* (1932), *The Fatal Glass of Beer* (1933), and *The Barbershop* (1933), and the features *It's a Gift* (1934), *My Little Chickadee* (1940), and *The Bank Dick* (1940).

Martha Graham (1893–1991)

Born in Pittsburgh, she was one of the most influential figures in American dance for more than fifty years, developing an expressive style and training hundreds of young dancers.

Red Grange (1903–91)

Born in Forksville, north of Williamsport, he was named three times as an all-American football player at the University of Illinois in the 1920s, and then led the Chicago Bears and helped popularize professional football.

Henry J. Heinz (1844–1919)

He became America's largest producer of pickles, ketchup, and vinegar in the mid-1800s, while emphasizing good working conditions for his employees in Pittsburgh. His grandson, Henry J. Heinz II, expanded the food business into an international corporation. A great-grandson, H. J. (John) Heinz, served as a U.S. senator from Pennsylvania.

Lee Iacocca (1924–)

A native of Allentown, Iacocca rose from a salesman to become president of the Ford Motor Company, where he introduced the popular Mustang. He then became president of Chrysler Corporation, developing the innovative minivan and returning the auto company to profitability.

Gene Kelly (1912–96)

Best-known for his tap and ballet dancing in numerous motion picture musicals, including *An American in Paris* (1951) and *Singin' in the Rain* (1952), Pittsburgh-born Kelly was also an accomplished choreographer, actor, and director of stage and screen.

Grace Kelly (1929–82)

After perfecting her acting skills in summer stock companies, this Philadelphia-born actress played roles in ten feature Hollywood films, including *High Noon* (1952), *Rear Window* (1954), and *High Society* (1956). Married in 1956 to Prince Rainier III of Monaco, she became active in charitable affairs in the principality and raised three children.

George C. Marshall (1880–1959)

Born in Uniontown, he became chairman of the Joint Chiefs of Staff and organized the U.S. Armed Forces during World War II as general of the Army. Later, as secretary of state, he was the author of the Marshall Plan, which restored the postwar economies of Europe. There is a historical marker in Uniontown, at 142 Main Street.

George McClellan (1826–85)

This Philadelphian, a West Point graduate, led the Army of the Potomac during part of the Civil War, and then was appointed commander in chief of the Union army as a major general in 1861, but failed to capture the Confederate capital, Richmond. Later defeated as the Democratic candidate for president of the United States, he became governor of New Jersey (1878–81).

Margaret Mead (1901–78)

Curator of ethnology (1926–78) at the American Museum of Natural History in New York City, she later studied patterns of child rearing and the cultures of New Guinea, Samoa, and Bali in the South Pacific. She was born in Philadelphia.

George G. Meade (1815–72)

A career army officer who started as an engineer, he became a battlefield commander and led Pennsylvania troops in several major battles of the Civil War, and then directed Union forces to victory in the pivotal Battle of Gettysburg in 1863.

Andrew Mellon (1866–1937)

His bank in Pittsburgh financed the growing coal, iron and steel, and oil industries of the time. He later became secretary of the Treasury under three presidents: Harding, Coolidge, and Hoover. He left an extensive art collection to establish the National Gallery of Art in Washington, D.C.

Lucretia Mott (1793–1880)

An organizer of the American Anti-Slavery Society in 1833, whose home near Philadelphia was once a stop on the Underground Railroad, she turned her attention to securing equal rights for women, temperance, and universal peace. There is a historical marker along PA Route 811, north of Cheltenham Avenue in Elkins Park.

Stan Musial (1920–)

As outfielder and first baseman for the St. Louis Cardinals, this Donora native established more records, including the most extra base hits, than any other major league baseball player and was elected to Baseball's Hall of Fame in 1969.

Arnold Palmer (1929–)

The first golfer to win the Masters Championship four times, as well as the U.S. and British Open tournaments, Palmer drew big crowds whenever he played in the late 1900s, thus popularizing professional golf. He lives in Latrobe.

Owen J. Roberts (1875–1955)

Born in Philadelphia, he served fifteen years on the U.S. Supreme Court (1930–45), after teaching law at the University of Pennsylvania and serving as a federal prosecutor.

John Roebling (1806–69)

A pioneer in the construction of suspension bridges such as the Brooklyn Bridge, this German immigrant established the first U.S. factory in 1842 in Saxonburg, near Pittsburgh, to manufacture the steel wire rope that made these bridges possible. A historical marker is located on PA Route 1010 near Saxonburg.

Fred Rogers (1928–2003)

Born in Latrobe, he earned degrees in music and divinity, and then developed *Mister Rogers Neighborhood,* a program for public television that "encouraged children to grow" and attracted thousands of young viewers for more than thirty years.

Jonas Salk (1914–95)

While he was a research professor of bacteriology at the University of Pittsburgh, Salk and his colleagues developed an inactivated vaccine against polio in 1952, which greatly reduced the incidence of this crippling disease.

B. F. Skinner (1904–90)

Well-known psychologist, born in Susquehanna, who was the foremost exponent in the United States of the behaviorist school of psychology, in which human behavior is explained in terms of physiological response to external stimuli.

Carl Spaatz (1891–1974)

Born in Boyertown, he served as the U.S. Air Force combat commander during World War II and as the first chief of staff of the newly independent U.S. Air Force. There is a historical marker on PA Route 562 at West Second Street in Boyertown.

Gertrude Stein (1874–1946)

Born in Allegheny, she lived most of her life in Paris where she wrote nonfiction, fiction, operas, and poetry and provided a meeting place and artistic encouragement to writers and artists who later gained fame.

John Stevens (1792–1838)

A pioneer inventor who, in the early 1800s, built one of the first steamboats to operate on the Delaware River, as well as steam ferries, and steam locomotives, he influenced the establishment of the U.S. patent system.

Thaddeus Stevens (1792–1868)

Longtime Republican member of Congress from Pennsylvania at the time of the Civil War, he was a strong advocate for civil rights for black Americans. A historical marker in Lancaster recognizes his accomplisments.

Leopold Stokowski (1882–1977)

Born in London, he was the longtime conductor of the Philadelphia Orchestra, directing premieres of more than two thousand works by twentieth-century composers.

William Strickland (1787–1854)

An architect and engineer, he combined Greek Neoclassical design with practical, efficient floor plans to produce elegant buildings of the colonial era in Philadelphia and elsewhere.

Jim Thorpe (1887–1953)

Star running back and kicker on the Carlisle Indians football team from 1908 to 1912, he won the pentathlon and decathlon events at the 1912 Olympic Games.

Johnny Unitas (1933–2002)

Professional football quarterback of the late 1900s who led the Baltimore Colts to three National Football League championships and was three times voted most valuable player in the league.

John Updike (1932–)

Pulitzer Prize–winning author whose characters in novels such as *Rabbit Run* (1960) navigate through middle-class life in the changing America of the late twentieth century. He was born in Shillington, near Reading.

Honus Wagner (1874–1955)

Born in Carnegie and nicknamed "The Flying Dutchman" when he played for the Pittsburgh Pirates in the mid-1900s, he is considered one of the greatest shortstops in the history of baseball.

John Wanamaker (1838–1922)

Pioneer of the department store with its "one-stop shopping," this successful businessman of Philadelphia and New York later served as postmaster general of the United States from 1889 to 1893.

Fred Waring (1900–84)

Beginning with a four-piece band when he was a student at Penn State, he developed one of the most popular orchestras and choruses in the country, a group regularly featured on radio, on television, and in the movies from the 1930s to the 1980s. He also developed and marketed the Waring Blender and owned the Shawnee Inn in the Poconos.

Index

Also by the Millers

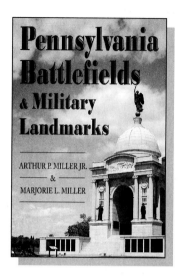

PENNSYLVANIA BATTLEFIELDS & MILITARY LANDMARKS

Arthur P. Miller Jr. and Marjorie L. Miller

A comprehensive guide to 35 battlefield sites and memorials.

$19.95 • PB • 224 pages • 46 photos • 15 maps
0-8117-2876-5

WWW.STACKPOLEBOOKS.COM
1-800-732-3669